THE BEST TV TRIVIA
AND
QUIZ BOOK EVER

THE BEST TV TRIVIA
AND
QUIZ BOOK EVER

Malcolm Vance

Bonanza Books
New York

Designed and packaged by Tribeca Communications, Inc.

Copyright © 1982 by Tribeca Communications, Inc.

This 1982 edition is published by Bonanza Books,
distributed by Crown Publishers, Inc.

Manufactured in the United States of America

Library of Congress Cataloging in Publication Data

Vance, Malcolm.
  The best TV trivia and quiz book ever.

  1. Television programs—United States—
Miscellanea.   I. Title.
PN1992.3.U5V34   791.45'0973   82-4153
ISBN 0–517–364123   AACR2

h g f e d c b a

Dedicated to Hal

Acknowledgments

The Best TV Trivia and Quiz Book Ever, like its companion, *The Best Movie Trivia and Quiz Book Ever*, was designed primarily for enjoyment. The author and his editors had fun planning the quizzes and reminiscing throughout the trivia section. If a particular favorite film, TV series, or star is missing, blame it on the author. *His* favorites are here and, in the words of that TV series, it's "Diff'rent Strokes" for diff'rent folks.

Grateful acknowledgment for their help goes to: Judie Annino; Bob Armour; David Cohn; Judith Feinstein; Hal Haskell; Noreen Kremer; Jim Mann; my editors, Rowena McDade and Chuck Adams; and of course, my agent, Lewis Chambers.

Contents

PHOTO QUIZ   *11*

KEEP IT IN THE FAMILY   *17*

MALE CALL (1)   *18*

MALE CALL (2)   *19*

MALE CALL (3)   *20*

MALE CALL (4)   *21*

MALE CALL (5)   *22*

MALE CALL (6)   *24*

A STAR IS BORN   *26*

CALL ME MISTER   *27*

WHO WAS THAT LADY? (1)   *28*

WHO WAS THAT LADY? (2)   *30*

WHO WAS THAT LADY? (3)   *31*

WHO WAS THAT LADY? (4)   *33*

WHO WAS THAT LADY? (5)   *34*

WHO WAS THAT LADY? (6)   *35*

BORN AGAIN   *36*

AFFIRMATIVE ACTION (1)   *37*

AFFIRMATIVE ACTION (2)   *38*

CONNECTIONS (1)   *40*

CONNECTIONS (2)   *40*

SECOND BANANAS (1)   *41*

SECOND BANANAS (2)   *42*

WHAT'S IN A NAME? (1)   *43*

WHAT'S IN A NAME? (2)   *44*

EVERYTHING IS RELATIVE (1)   *45*

EVERYTHING IS RELATIVE (2)   *46*

LOVE AND MARRIAGE (1)   *48*

LOVE AND MARRIAGE (2)   *48*
. . . BOB, BOB, BOBBING ALONG . . .   *49*
REINCARNATION   *49*
STREET WISE   *50*
IDENTITY CRISIS (1)   *51*
IDENTITY CRISIS (2)   *52*
WHERE IN THE WORLD? (1)   *53*
WHERE IN THE WORLD? (2)   *54*
WHERE IN THE WORLD? (3)   *55*
WHERE IN THE WORLD? (4)   *56*
HISTORY LESSON   *56*
THOSE WONDERFUL WOMEN . . .   *60*
FAIR GAME (1)   *74*
FAIR GAME (2)   *75*
ALTER EGOS   *77*
SIDESADDLE   *78*
TALL IN THE SADDLE (1)   *79*
TALL IN THE SADDLE (2)   *80*
TALL IN THE SADDLE (3)   *81*
TALL IN THE SADDLE (4)   *82*
THE ANIMAL KINGDOM   *83*
CHILD'S PLAY   *84*
SO YOU WANT TO LEAD A BAND . . .   *86*
HORSING AROUND   *87*
WHEN IRISH EYES ARE SMILING . . .   *88*
THEY'RE PLAYING THEIR SONGS (1)   *89*
THEY'RE PLAYING THEIR SONGS (2)   *90*
BEDSIDE MANORS   *91*
READING, 'RITING, 'RITHMETIC   *92*
MIXED DOUBLES   *93*
A CHORUS LINE   *94*
WITH ENEMIES LIKE THESE . . .   *96*
SMALL FRY (1)   *98*
SMALL FRY (2)   *100*
FRONT MONEY   *101*
SOBRIQUETS   *102*
SPORTIN' LIFE   *103*
LATHER UP (1)   *104*
LATHER UP (2)   *106*

HOME SWEET HOME   107
DON'T I KNOW YOU?   107
IFS, ANDS, AND MUTTS (1)   109
IFS, ANDS, AND MUTTS (2)   110
SCHIZOPHRENIA   111
VOX POPULI   112
VERBATIM (1)   113
VERBATIM (2)   114
MOUTHPIECES   114
THE PEN IS MIGHTIER . . .   115
TO BE CONTINUED . . .   116
SCANDALS IN VIDEOLAND   126
JUST FOLLOW THE SIMPLE DIRECTIONS . . .   127
WOULD YOU BELIEVE . . .?   128
ONLY THE NAMES HAVE BEEN CHANGED . . .   129
    . . .AND YOU WERE THERE!   131
BITS AND PIECES   131
THE BRITISH ARE COMING . . . AND COMING . . .
    AND COMING . . .   134
NUMERO UNO   134
IT'S A LIVING   136
GET THE SCOOP (1)   137
GET THE SCOOP (2)   138
WOMEN IN WHITE   139
FLYING HIGH   140
PLEASE BE BRIEF (1)   141
PLEASE BE BRIEF (2)   142
IS THERE A DOCTOR IN THE HOUSE? (1)   144
IS THERE A DOCTOR IN THE HOUSE? (2)   145
CLOAKS AND DAGGERS   146
SCHOOLDAYS, SCHOOLDAYS . . .   147
LAW AND ORDER (1)   148
LAW AND ORDER (2)   149
LAW AND ORDER (3)   150
LAW AND ORDER (4)   151
IN A NUTSHELL (1)   152
IN A NUTSHELL (2)   152
IN A NUTSHELL (3)   153
IN A NUTSHELL (4)   154

¿QUIÉNES?   *155*

IT'S GREEK TO ME (1)   *156*

IT'S GREEK TO ME (2)   *156*

IT'S GREEK TO ME (3)   *157*

IT'S GREEK TO ME (4)   *157*

BIG SCREEN, LITTLE SCREEN   *158*

REGARDS TO BROADWAY   *160*

WHEN IN ROME . . .   *162*

MISSING LINKS (1)   *163*

MISSING LINKS (2)   *164*

AND THE WINNER WAS . . . DRAMA (1)   *166*

AND THE WINNER WAS . . . DRAMA (2)   *167*

AND THE WINNER WAS . . . DRAMA (3)   *168*

AND THE WINNER WAS . . . DRAMA (4)   *169*

AND THE WINNER WAS . . . DIRECTORS (1)   *170*

AND THE WINNER WAS . . . DIRECTORS (2)   *171*

AND THE WINNER WAS . . . COMEDY OR MUSICAL
   VARIETY (1)   *172*

AND THE WINNER WAS . . . COMEDY OR MUSICAL
   VARIETY (2)   *175*

MAJOR EMMY AWARD NOMINEES AND WINNERS
   FROM 1948-1981   *187*

THE TROPHY CASE   *228*

ANSWER SECTION   *231*

Photo Quiz

There are 90 photos scattered throughout this book. Here you'll find many popular television stars in addition to some less well-known actors and actresses. Test your knowledge of the medium by identifying the performers and answering the questions listed below. Answers to this photo quiz will be found at the back of the book at the beginning of the answer section. Enjoy this quiz and the 111 others you'll find in this book.

1. Name the show.
2. Name the show and the episode.
3. Name five series this actor has appeared in as a regular.
4. What was this actor's occupation on *The Name of the Game?*
5. What was this actor's occupation on TV's longest running western?
6. Who played this actor's daughter on occasional episodes of *The Streets of San Francisco?*
7. What year did *Bonanza* premiere?
8. On what show was this actress a regular in 1961/62 playing a character named Stella Barnes?
9. Who plays this actress's boyfriend, Carmine, on her series?
10. Name the show.
11. What was this actress's TV relationship to Paul Sand on his show *Friends and Lovers?*
12. What was the name of this star's short-lived 1978 comedy-variety series?
13. Name the show.
14. What was this actress's occupation on the series in which she co-starred?
15. What was the 1974 pilot series in which the TV character played by this actor originated?

11

16. Name this actor's series and his character.
17. Name the show.
18. Name the show.
19. On what short-lived 1961 series did this actor play a retired criminal lawyer?
20. Who played this actor's wife on the situation comedy in which he co-starred?
21. What was this actor's 1964 situation comedy?
22. Who are these men?
23. Name the show.
24. Name the show. What was the character's name of the youngest cast member?
25. When this actor was a child, what show did he co-host with Jack Lescoulie?
26. On what famous movie actor did this comedienne drop a tray of desserts at the Brown Derby in episode #114 of *I Love Lucy*?
27. What was this star's nickname?
28. On which network did this actress have a show from 1953 to 1961?
29. What is this actress's occupation on her latest series?
30. What was the name of the character this actress portrayed on her series?
31. Who was this singer's pianist on her 1951/57 live 15 minute show?
32. On what 1964/65 variety series was this performer a co-star?
33. On what series did this performer play a character named Peter Newkirk?
34. What was the name of the married couple this star and Imogene Coca created on *Your Show of Shows*?
35. What was this performer's role on *Howdy Doody*?
36. For what police force was this actor employed on *Hawaii Five-O*?
37. For what company was Archie Bunker employed as a dock foreman?
38. With what big band did this singer perform on a 1951 series?
39. Name the show.
40. With what big band did this singer come to prominence?
41. On what series did this actor play a character named Steve Nelson?
42. Name the show. On what popular series did this actress guest star as one of the co-star's "earth" mother?
43. Name the three series this actor has appeared in as a regular.
44. Name the show and its creator.

45. Name the show.
46. Name the show.
47. Name the show and identify the father's occupation.
48. Name the show.
49. Name the five series this actor has appeared in as a regular.
50. Name the show.
51. Name the show.
52. Name the show.
53. Name the show.
54. Name the show.
55. Name the show.
56. Name the show.
57. Name the show.
58. Name the show.
59. Name the show.
60. On what network is this daytime drama seen?
61. What was the name of the show of the performer on the right; name his two back-up singers on the show?
62. On which network was this performer a major star in the 1950s?
63. Name the show.
64. Who played this star's sister-in-law on two of his series; what was the name of the character?
65. What was this actor's 1964/65 situation comedy?
66. What was this actress's job on *Emergency*?
67. In what field of entertainment was this actor employed before he gained popularity on TV?
68. What was the full name and rank of the character this actor played from 1966 to 1969?
69. What actor, who turned down the role, was the producer's first choice to play Lieutenant Columbo?
70. What Western marshal did this actor provide the radio voice for before the popular TV series came into being?
71. Who replaced this actress on *Charlie's Angels*? In what role?
72. What was the name of the character this actress portrayed on *The New Dick Van Dyke Show*?
73. On what two situation comedies was this actress featured?
74. Name the show.
75. Name the show.

13

76. On which network did this actress appear in a situation comedy as a woman with extraordinary powers?

77. Who was Sergeant Bilko's immediate superior?

78. What was this actress's 1973 situation comedy?

79. What is the name of these performers' daughter?

80. On what show is this porcine glamour girl featured? Who is its host and its creator?

81. What famous comedy team made its TV debut on the premiere of this star's *Toast of the Town*?

82. Name the show.

83. What was this actress's occupation on the two situation comedies in which she has starred?

84. Name the show.

85. On what short-lived 1949 musical variety series was this performer a regular?

86. What was the name of the journalist this actor portrayed in his 1962/63 drama anthology series?

87. Name the series in which these performers starred together. Name his later series.

88. What is the full name of the character portrayed by this actress on her hit series?

89. What was the title of this actor's 1978 series? What was the name of his character?

90. What were the names of the characters this actor portrayed in the two series in which he was featured?

THE BEST TV TRIVIA
AND
QUIZ BOOK EVER

KEEP IT IN THE FAMILY

The family names which are listed on the left have been featured in the programs which are listed on the right. Match the names with the programs.

1. Day	A. *Father Knows Best*
2. Bunker	B. *Little House on the Prairie*
3. Petrie	C. *The Patty Duke Show*
4. Williams	D. *Family*
5. Anderson	E. *My Friend Flicka*
6. Hansen	F. *Please Don't Eat the Daisies*
7. Douglas	G. *Petticoat Junction*
8. Ingalls	H. *Hazel*
9. McLaughlin	I. *Leave It to Beaver*
10. Clayton	J. *The Dick Van Dyke Show*
11. Cunningham	K. *That Girl*
12. Lawrence	L. *Mama*
13. Lane	M. *How the West Was Won*
14. Bradley	N. *Life With Father*
15. Marie	O. *The Jimmy Stewart Show*
16. Cleaver	P. *Margie*
17. Howard	Q. *Make Room For Daddy*
18. Nash	R. *My Three Sons*
19. Macahan	S. *Happy Days*
20. Baxter	T. *All in the Family*

Photo 1

MALE CALL (1)

Listed below on the left are the names of characters in series and on the right are the actors who portrayed these roles. Match the actors with the characters and identify the shows.

1. Howard Adams	A. Gavin MacLeod
2. Fred Mertz	B. William Demarest
3. Flint McCullough	C. John Cassavetes
4. Heath Barkley	D. Charles Farrell
5. Wilhelm Klink	E. Steve Harmon
6. Maxwell Smart	F. Alan Young
7. Jerry North	G. Carl Betz
8. Jonas Grumby	H. Richard Long
9. James K. Howard	I. Howard Duff
10. Wilbur Post	J. Patrick McVey
11. Johnny Staccato	K. Robert Horton
12. Ensign Charles Parker	L. William Frawley
13. Ensign Frank Pulver	M. Werner Klemperer
14. Vernon Albright	N. Richard Denning
15. Harold Everett	O. James Stewart
16. Steve Wilson (50/54)	P. Don Adams
17. Steve Wilson (54/56)	Q. Alan Hale, Jr.
18. Murray Slaughter	R. Lee Majors
19. Clinton Judd	S. Tim Conway
20. Charley O'Casey	T. Mark Stevens

Photo 2

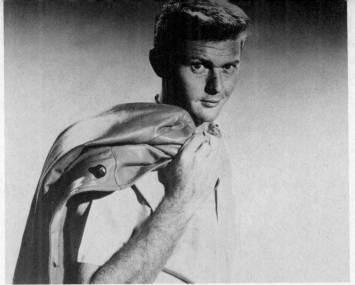

Photo 3

MALE CALL (2)

Listed below on the left are the names of characters in series and on the right are the actors who portrayed these roles. Match the actors with the characters and identify the shows.

1. Frank Savage	A. Eddie Albert
2. Gregg Miles	B. Milburn Stone
3. Adam Troy	C. Tony Randall
4. Francis Muldoon	D. James Brolin
5. Clarence Day	E. Don DeFore
6. Dan August	F. Conrad Bain
7. Pete Malloy	G. Gardner McKay
8. Oliver Wendell Douglas	H. Ward Bond
9. Robinson Peepers	I. Fred MacMurray
10. Uncle Fester	J. Robert Lansing
11. Festus Haggen	K. Peter Graves
12. Kato	L. Wally Cox
13. Thorny Thornberg	M. James Coburn
14. Felix Unger	N. Leon Ames
15. James Phelps	O. Fred Gwynne
16. Steve Douglas	P. Martin Milner
17. Steven Kiley	Q. Burt Reynolds
18. Seth Adams	R. Jackie Coogan
19. Arthur Harmon	S. Bruce Lee
20. Galen Adams	T. Ken Curtis

Photo 4

MALE CALL (3)

Listed below on the left are the names of characters in series and on the right are the actors who portrayed these roles. Match the actors with the characters and identify the shows.

1.	Robert Hogan	A.	Burt Reynolds
2.	Murray	B.	Robert Stack
3.	Frank DeFazio	C.	Marvin Miller
4.	Tom Lopaka	D.	Jack Klugman
5.	Gerald Lloyd Kookson III	E.	Bob Crane
6.	Ben Frazer	F.	Edd Byrnes
7.	Nick Belker	G.	Chuck Connors
8.	Matt Holbrook	H.	David Birney
9.	Lucas McCain	I.	Norman Fell
10.	Elliot Ness	J.	Ted Knight
11.	Frank Hardy	K.	Al Molinaro
12.	Frank Serpico	L.	Bruce Weitz
13.	Michael Anthony	M.	Clint Walker
14.	Kodiak	N.	Alan Alda
15.	Ted Baxter	O.	Phil Foster
16.	Richard Cunningham	P.	Robert Taylor
17.	Opie Taylor	Q.	Ron Howard
18.	Dr. Quincy	R.	Parker Stevenson
19.	Benjamin Franklin Pierce	S.	Ron Howard
20.	Stanley Roper	T.	Bob Conrad

MALE CALL (4)

Listed below on the left are the names of characters in series and on the right are the actors who portrayed these roles. Match the actors with the characters and identify the shows.

1. Alfred Delvecchio	A. Larry Hagman
2. Barney Fife	B. Abe Vigoda
3. Carmine Ragusa	C. Jack Kelly
4. Radar O'Reilly	D. Al Molinaro
5. Joseph Rockford	E. Michael Landon
6. Charlie Ingalls	F. Henry Jones
7. Owen Marshall	G. Billy Crystal
8. J. R. Ewing	H. Eddie Mekka
9. John Walton	I. Arthur Hill
10. Jack Tripper	J. Don Knotts
11. Jonathan Dexter	K. Sherman Hemsley
12. Lou Grant	L. Tommy Rettig
13. Mike Brady	M. Robert Reed
14. John Hawk	N. Ralph Waite
15. Phil Fish	O. Gary Burghoff
16. Jeff Miller	P. John Ritter
17. Jodie Dallas	Q. Ed Asner
18. Bernie Davis	R. Burt Reynolds
19. George Jefferson	S. Marty Brill
20. Bart Maverick	T. Noah Beery

Photo 5

MALE CALL (5)

Listed below on the left are the names of characters in series and on the right are the actors who portrayed these roles. Match the actors with the characters and identify the shows.

1. Potsie Weber	A. Ty Hardin
2. Capt. David Scott	B. Richard Greene
3. Mike Stivic	C. Karl Malden
4. Major Frank Burns	D. Anson Williams
5. Chico Rodriguez	E. Demond Wilson
6. Lamont Sanford	F. Lorne Green
7. Rudy Jordache	G. Ryan O'Neal
8. David Brewster Banner	H. Ben Alexander
9. Frank Smith	I. Barry Sullivan
10. Stan Wojohowicz	J. Peter Strauss
11. Bronco Layne	K. Michael Ansara
12. Cochise	L. Philip Carey
13. Ben Cartwright	M. Rob Reiner
14. Davy Crockett	N. Michael Douglas
15. Robin Hood	O. Larry Linville
16. Rob Petrie	P. Maxwell Gail
17. Steve Keller	Q. Fess Parker
18. Philip Marlowe	R. Dick Van Dyke
19. Rodney Harrington	S. Freddie Prinze
20. Mike Stone	T. Bill Bixby

23   Photo 6

MALE CALL (6)

Listed below on the left are the names of characters in series and on the right are the actors who portrayed these roles. Match the actors with the characters and identify the shows.

1. Joe Cartwright	A. Don Rickles
2. Philip Boynton	B. Phil Silvers
3. Seaman Pruitt	C. Jeff Richards
4. Danny Williams	D. Dan Blocker
5. Jules Bedford	E. Mike Evans
6. Don Hollinger	F. Lew Parker
7. Peter Gunn	G. John Travolta
8. Dick Tracy	H. Jim Nabors
9. Joe Bogert	I. Robert Rockwell
10. Ernie Bilko	J. Don Porter
11. Vinnie Barbarino	K. Ron Palillo
12. Lionel Jefferson	L. Jackie Cooper
13. Jefferson Drum	M. Michael Landon
14. Otto Sharkey	N. Craig Stevens
15. Gomer Pyle	O. James MacArthur
16. Lou Marie	P. Peter Isacksen
17. Sock Miller	Q. Ted Bessell
18. Peter Sands	R. Ralph Byrd
19. Arnold Horshack	S. Barnard Hughes
20. "Hoss" Cartwright	T. Danny Thomas

24

25   Photo 7

A STAR IS BORN

The stars listed below on the left all got their early TV starts in the shows which are listed on the right. Match the stars with the programs.

1. Warren Beatty
2. Ryan O'Neal
3. Carol Burnett
4. Mary Tyler Moore
5. Eydie Gorme
6. Barbara Eden
7. Marion Ross
8. Martin Milner
9. George Nader
10. Goldie Hawn
11. Patty Duke
12. Marlo Thomas
13. Farrah Fawcett

14. Burt Reynolds
15. Sally Field
16. Dick Van Patten
17. Jack Lemmon
18. Marilyn Monroe
19. Elvis Presley
20. Eva Marie Saint

A. *Richard Diamond, Private Detective*
B. *The Loretta Young Show*
C. *Harry-O*
D. *Mama*
E. *One Man's Family*
F. *The Joey Bishop Show*
G. *Many Loves of Dobie Gillis*
H. *The Garry Moore Show*
I. *Life with Father*
J. *Kitty Foyle*
K. *Gidget*
L. *Jack Benny Show*
M. *The Frances Langford-Don Ameche Show*
N. *Peyton Place*
O. *How to Marry a Millionaire*
P. *Tonight(Steve Allen—host)*
Q. *Stage Show*
R. *The Life of Riley*
S. *Gunsmoke*
T. *Laugh-In*

Photo 8

CALL ME MISTER

Listed below on the left are shows that featured the performers on the right. Match the programs with the stars.

1. *Mr. Adams and Eve*	A. Richard Denning
2. *Mr. and Mrs. Carroll*	B. Charles Quinlivan
3. *Mr. and Mrs. North*	C. Craig Stevens
4. *Mr. Arsenic*	D. Jim Backus
5. *Mr. Black*	E. Don Herbert
6. *Mr. Broadway*	F. Stephen Strimpell
7. *Mr. Citizen*	G. Burton Turkus
8. *Mr. Deeds Goes to Town*	H. Pat Morita
9. *Mr. District Attorney*	I. Paul Tripp
10. *Mr. Garlund*	J. Howard Duff
11. *Mr. I. Magination*	K. Fess Parker
12. *Mr. Lucky*	L. Andy Christopher
13. *Mr. Magoo, The Famous Adventures of*	M. Roger Smith
14. *Mr. Novak*	N. David Brian
15. *Mr. Peepers*	P. Jimmy Carroll
16. *Mr. Roberts*	P. Wally Cox
17. *Mr. Smith Goes to Washington*	Q. Allyn Edwards
18. *Mr. T and Tina*	R. James Franciscus
19. *Mr. Terrific*	S. John Vivyan
20. *Mr. Wizard*	T. Monte Markham

WHO WAS THAT LADY? (1)

Listed below on the left are the names of characters in series and on the right are the actresses who portrayed these roles. Match the actresses with the characters and identify the shows.

1.	Rosie Greenbaum	A.	Elizabeth Patterson
2.	Joanie Cunningham	B.	Vivian Vance
3.	Aunt Bea Taylor	C.	Michael Learned
4.	Sylvia Caldwell	D.	Judith Lowry
5.	Carol Brady	E.	Audra Lindley
6.	Lily Ruskin	F.	Carole Ita White
7.	Mrs. Trumble	G.	Cindy Williams
8.	Sister Bertrille	H.	Sada Thompson
9.	Mother Harper	I.	Gail Fisher
10.	Ida Morgenstern	J.	Erin Moran
11.	Mother Dexter	K.	Spring Byington
12.	Peggy Fair	L.	Sally Field
13.	Connie Brooks	M.	Linda Lavin
14.	Ethel Mertz	N.	Frances Bavier
15.	Olivia Walton	O.	Eleanor Parker
16.	Della Rogers	P.	Florence Henderson
17.	Helen Roper	Q.	Eve Arden
18.	Det. Janice Wentworth	R.	Nancy Walker
19.	Shirley Feeney	S.	Della Reese
20.	Kate Lawrence	T.	Vicki Lawrence

29   Photo 9

WHO WAS THAT LADY? (2)

Listed below on the left are the names of characters in series and on the right are the actresses who portrayed these roles. Match the actresses with the characters and identify the shows.

1. Nancy Kitteridge	A. Sally Struthers
2. Charlotte (Charley) Drake	B. Katherine Helmond
3. Donna Stone	C. Geraldine Brooks
4. Bridget Fitzgerald Steinberg	D. Roz Kelly
5. Chrissy Snow	E. Isabel Sanford
6. Alice Hyatt	F. Loretta Swit
7. Georgette Franklin Baxter	G. Betty Garrett
8. Elizabeth Miller	H. Elinor Donahue
9. "Buddy" Lawrence	I. Nancy Walker
10. Jessica Tate	J. Meredith Baxter
11. Audrey Dexter	K. Esther Rolle
12. Louise Jefferson	L. Georgia Engel
13. Florida Evans	M. Ellen Corby
14. Pinky Tuscadero	N. Donna Reed
15. Grandma Walton	O. Jane Rose
16. Betty Anderson	P. Suzanne Somers
17. Angela Dumpling	Q. Kristy McNichol
18. Gloria Bunker Stivic	R. Linda Lavin
19. Margaret Houlihan	S. Barbara Barrie
20. Irene Lorenzo	T. Bernadette Peters

Photo 10

WHO WAS THAT LADY? (3)

Listed below on the left are the names of characters in series and on the right are the actresses who portrayed these roles. Match the actresses with the characters and identify the shows.

1. Cinnamon Carter	A. Pamela Sue Martin
2. Victoria Barkley	B. Betty Garrett
3. Blanche Morton	C. Marion Ross
4. Martha Howard	D. Brett Somers
5. Sue Ann Nivens	E. Connie Stevens
6. Eve Drake	F. Barbara Bain
7. Agent 99	G. Ida Lupino
8. Nancy Drew	H. Dorothy Provine
9. Myrna Turner	I. Barbara Britton
10. Pamela North	J. Barbara Stanwyck
11. Mrs. Lovey Howell	K. Cynthia Pepper
12. Edna Babish	L. Marion Lorne
13. Mrs. Gurney	M. Gale Storm
14. Cricket Blake	N. Bea Benadaret
15. Phoebe Figalilly	O. Penny Marshall
16. Marion Cunningham	P. Julie Adams
17. Margie Albright	Q. Juliet Mills
18. Margie Clayton	R. Natalie Schafer
19. Pinkie Pinkham	S. Barbara Feldon
20. Blanche Madison	T. Betty White

Photo 11

31

Photo 12

WHO WAS THAT LADY? (4)

Listed below on the left are the names of characters and on the right are the actresses who portrayed these roles. Match the actresses with the characters and identify the shows.

1. Diana Prince		A.	Anne Francis
2. Miss Reubner		B.	Ann Sheridan
3. Mrs. Bonnie McClellan		C.	Bev Sanders
4. Aunt Esther		D.	Mary Wicks
5. Pepper Anderson		E.	Rachel Roberts
6. Nell McLaughlin		F.	Audrey Meadows
7. Karen Angelo		G.	Lynda Carter
8. Honey West		H.	Marlo Thomas
9. Alice Kramden		I.	Dorothy Malone
10. Emma Peel		J.	Karen Valentine
11. Margaret Williams		K.	Allyn Ann McLerie
12. Laura Petrie		L.	Dena Dietrich
13. Henrietta Hawks		M.	Diana Rigg
14. Constance Mackenzie		N.	Mildred Natwick
15. Alison Mackenzie		O.	LaWanda Page
16. Gwen Snoop		P.	Anita Louise
17. Gypsy Koch		Q.	Jean Hagen
18. Molly Gibbons		R.	Mia Farrow
19. Ann Marie		S.	Mary Tyler Moore
20. Miss Tully		T.	Angie Dickinson

WHO WAS THAT LADY? (5)

Listed below on the left are the names of characters in series and on the right are the actresses who portrayed these roles. Match the actresses with the characters and identify the shows.

1. Annie Bogert	A. Noreen Corcoran
2. Betty Ramsey	B. Cara Williams
3. Dee Thomas	C. Hope Lange
4. Gidget Lawrence	D. Marcia Strassman
5. Carolyn Muir	E. Elinor Donahue
6. Alice Gobel	F. Marie Wilson
7. Edie Hart	G. Pat Breslin
8. Kelly Gregg	H. Roxie Roker
9. Gladys Porter	I. Connie Stevens
10. Kate Bradley	J. Elizabeth Wilson
11. Julie Kotter	K. Joan Caulfield
12. Helen Willis	L. Aneta Corsaut
13. Mother Jefferson	M. Ann Sothern
14. Ellie Walker	N. Sally Field
15. Helen Crump	O. Zara Cully
16. Katie O'Connor	P. Bea Benadaret
17. Irma Peterson	Q. Mary Jane Croft
18. Liz Cooper	R. Lola Albright
19. Mandy People	S. Jeff Donnell
20. Savannah Brown	T. Danielle Spencer

Photo 13

Photo 14

WHO WAS THAT LADY? (6)

Listed below on the left are the names of characters in series and on the right are the actresses who portrayed these roles. Match the actresses with the characters and identify the shows.

1.	Susie McNamara	A.	Joyce DeWitt
2.	Sabrina Duncan	B.	Nancy Walker
3.	Nora Charles	C.	Rosemary DeCamp
4.	Audra Barkley	D.	Marcia Wallace
5.	Jaime Sommers	E.	Zina Bethune
6.	Margaret MacDonald	F.	Zohra Lampert
7.	Emily Hartley	G.	Ann Sothern
8.	Kelly Garrett	H.	Gertrude Berg
9.	Amy Fitzgerald	I.	Tina Louise
10.	Janet Wood	J.	Ann B. Davis
11.	Nancy Blansky	K.	Julie Sommars
12.	Gail Lucas	L.	Amanda Blake
13.	Norah Purcell	M.	Kate Jackson
14.	Ginger Grant	N.	Eva Gabor
15.	Molly Goldberg	O.	Linda Evans
16.	Lisa Douglas	P.	Phyllis Kirk
17.	Charmaine Shultz	Q.	Audra Lindley
18.	Kitty Russell	R.	Suzanne Pleshette
19.	J. J. Drinkwater	S.	Jaclyn Smith
20.	Carol Kester	T.	Lindsay Wagner

Photo 15

BORN AGAIN

Listed below on the left are TV programs and on the right are spin-offs from those original shows. Match the original and the spin-off.

1.	The Mary Tyler Moore Show	A.	Benson
2.	Happy Days	B.	Shirley
3.	All in the Family	C.	Fish
4.	Maude	D.	Gomer Pyle, U.S.M.C.
5.	Three's Company	E.	Pete and Gladys
6.	Soap	F.	The Bionic Woman
7.	The Andy Griffith Show	G.	Good Times
8.	Cheyenne	H.	Flo
9.	Bewitched	I.	Knots Landing
10.	What's Happening	J.	B.J. and the Bear
11.	Sanford and Son	K.	Lou Grant
12.	The Six Million Dollar Man	L.	Enos
13.	Police Story	M.	Tabitha
14.	Barney Miller	N.	Facts of Life
15.	Dallas	O.	Mork and Mindy
16.	December Bride	P.	Grady
17.	Alice	Q.	Police Woman
18.	Lobo	R.	The Jeffersons
19.	Dukes of Hazzard	S.	Bronco
20.	Diff'rent Strokes	T.	The Ropers

AFFIRMATIVE ACTION (1)

Listed below on the left are performers who have portrayed the characters listed on the right. Match the stars with the roles and identify the programs.

1.	Esther Rolle	A.	Boom Boom Washington
2.	Ron Glass	B.	Benson
3.	Denise Nicholas	C.	James Evans, Jr.
4.	Ernest Thomas	D.	Peggy Fair
5.	Diahann Carroll	E.	Paul Bratter
6.	Lawrence-Hilton Jacobs	F.	Alexander Scott
7.	Roxie Roker	G.	Della Rogers
8.	Lloyd Haynes	H.	Arnold Jackson
9.	LaWanda Page	I.	Christie Love
10.	Robert Guillaume	J.	Julia Baker
11.	Della Reese	K.	Jeff Ward
12.	Jimmie Walker	L.	Florida Evans
13.	Theresa Merritt	M.	Aunt Esther
14.	Scoey Mitchell	N.	Joe Broadhurst
15.	Robert Hooks	O.	Olivia Ellis
16.	Bill Cosby	P.	Eloise Curtis
17.	Teresa Graves	Q.	Pete Dixon
18.	Gary Coleman	R.	Ron Harris
19.	Gail Fisher	S.	Helen Willis
20.	Terry Carter	T.	Roger Thomas

Photo 16

AFFIRMATIVE ACTION (2)

Listed below on the left are performers who have portrayed the characters listed on the right. Match the stars with the roles and identify the programs.

1. Marla Gibbs	A. Rerun
2. Danielle Spencer	B. Beulah
3. Demond Wilson	C. James Evans
4. Scatman Crothers	D. Huggy Bear
5. Nipsey Russell	E. Kingfish Stevens
6. Louise Beavers	F. Isak Poole
7. Fred Berry	G. Raymond
8. Butterfly McQueen	H. Lt. Uhura
9. Tim Moore	I. Barney Collier
10. Paul Winfield	J. Jane Foster
11. John Amos	K. Louie
12. Clifton Davis	L. Jason Hart
13. Cicely Tyson	M. Florence
14. Ralph Wilcox	N. Terry Webster
15. Nichelle Nichols	O. Paul Carter
16. Lou Gossett	P. Dee Thomas
17. Antonio Fargas	Q. Clifton Curtis
18. Greg Morris	R. Lamont Sanford
19. Percy Rodriguez	S. Oriole
20. Georg Stanford Brown	T. Honey Robinson

Photo 17

CONNECTIONS (1)

Listed below are TV performers who have something in common—identify this common characteristic.

1. Robert Stack, Telly Savalas, Peter Falk, Craig Stevens.
2. Imogene Coca, Nanette Fabray, Janet Blair, Giselle Mackenzie.
3. E. G. Marshall, Richard Crenna, Peter Falk, Raymond Burr.
4. Imogene Coca, Shirley Booth, Louise Beavers, Nancy Walker.
5. Julius LaRosa, Frank Parker, Janette Davis, LuAnn Sims.
6. Bud Collyer, Peter Donald, Robert Q. Lewis, Eddie Bracken.
7. Linda Lavin, Angie Dickinson, Jessica Walter.
8. Eve Arden, Gabriel Kaplan, Karen Valentine.
9. Lynn Anderson, Lennon Sisters, Alice Lon, Norma Zimmer.
10. Rosemary DeCamp and Marjorie Reynolds.
11. Joyce Randolph and Jane Kean.
12. Steve Allen, Ernie Kovacs, Jack Lescoulie, Joey Bishop.
13. Marie Wilson, Penny Marshall, Ann Sothern, Carol Burnett.
14. Pert Kelton, Audrey Meadows, Sheila MacRae.
15. Esther Rolle and Hermione Baddeley.
16. William Gargan, Lloyd Nolan, Lee Tracy, Mark Stevens.
17. Elena Verdugo, Zina Bethune, Loretta Swit, Shirl Conway.
18. Warren Stevens, Ann Sothern, Paul Frees.
19. Robert Young, Richard Chamberlain, Alan Alda, Vince Edwards.
20. Giselle Mackenzie, Snookie Lanson, Russell Arms, Dorothy Collins.

CONNECTIONS (2)

Listed below are TV performers who have something in common—identify this common characteristic.

1. Preston Foster, Gardiner McKay, Paul Ford.
2. Bill Cosby, Robert Vaughn, Diana Rigg, Don Adams.
3. *Gone With the Wind, Airport, Love Story.*
4. Ronald Reagan, Stanley Andrews, Robert Taylor, Dale Robertson.
5. Kitty Carlisle, Peggy Cass, Orson Bean, Bill Cullen.
6. Ralph Bellamy and Frank Lovejoy.
7. Charles McGraw, Hope Emerson, Phil Gordon.
8. Edward Mulhare, Anne Jeffreys, Robert Sterling.
9. Irene Ryan, Ellen Corby, Beatrice Arthur.
10. Jan Clayton, Cloris Leachman, June Lockhart.

11.   Lee Bergere, Hal Holbrook, Billy Crystal, Ken Olfson.
12.   Hugh Marlowe, George Nader, Jim Hutton, Lee Bowman.
13.   James Slattery, Walter Denton, Richard Barrington III.
14.   Annette Crosbie, Dorothy Tutim, Anne Stallybrass, Elvi Hale, Angela
          Pleasance, Rosalie Crutchley.
15.   David Niven, Charles Boyer, Gig Young.
16.   Richard Green and Dick Gautier.
17.   Al Molinaro and Pat Morita.
18.   Audra Lindley, Betty Garrett, Mary Wickes.
19.   Dick Powell, Charles Boyer, Rosalind Russell, Joel McCrea.
20.   Ida Lupino and David Niven.

SECOND BANANAS (1)

Match the characters listed on the left with the performers listed on the
right and identify the shows on which they appeared.

1. Fred Mertz	A. Hermione Baddeley
2. Edna Babish	B. Elena Verdugo
3. Cricket Blake	C. Morey Amsterdam
4. Helen Willis	D. Julie Kavner
5. Ralph Malph	E. Lee Majors
6. Arnold Horshack	F. Leonard Nimoy
7. Miss Reubner	G. Gail Fisher
8. Ted Baxter	H. Dennis Weaver
9. Mrs. Naugatuck	I. Noah Beery
10. Buddy Sorrell	J. Roxie Roker
11. Chester Goode	K. Loretta Swit
12. Peggy Fair	L. Joan Hotchkiss
13. Mr. Spock	M. Connie Stevens
14. Brenda Morgenstern	N. Mary Wickes
15. Heath Barkley	O. Ron Palillo
16. Dr. Nancy Cunningham	P. William Frawley
17. Consuelo Lopez	Q. Allyn Ann McLerie
18. Joseph Rockford	R. Ted Knight
19. Margaret Houlihan	S. Donny Most
20. Miss Tully	T. Betty Garrett

SECOND BANANAS (2)

Match the characters listed on the left with the performers listed on the right and identify the shows on which they appeared.

1.	Carmine Ragusa	A.	Zara Cully
2.	Stan Wojohowicz	B.	Betty White
3.	Ethel Mertz	C.	Al Molinaro
4.	Blanche Morton	D.	Conrad Bain
5.	Florence	E.	Judith Lowry
6.	Squiggy Squiggman	F.	Greg Morris
7.	Murray Slaughter	G.	Barbara Hale
8.	Helen Roper	H.	Lorenzo Music
9.	Gov. Philip Grey	I.	Marla Gibbs
10.	Al Delvecchio	J.	Marion Lorne
11.	Sue Ann Nivens	K.	Vivian Vance
12.	Della Street	L.	Rose Marie
13.	Mrs. Gurney	M.	Eddie Mekka
14.	Dr. Arthur Harmon	N.	Audra Lindley
15.	Carlton, the Doorman	O.	Anson Williams
16.	Mother Dexter	P.	Richard Denning
17.	Mother Jefferson	Q.	Max Gail
18.	Barney Collier	R.	Gavin McLeod
19.	Sally Rogers	S.	Bea Benadaret
20.	Potsie Weber	T.	David L. Landau

Photo 18

WHAT'S IN A NAME? (1)

Listed below on the left are the title roles from TV shows and on the right are the stars who played the roles. Match the performers and their roles.

1. Hazel
2. Rhoda
3. Phyllis
4. Quincy, M.E.
5. Margie
6. Serpico
7. Columbo
8. Kojak
9. Beulah
10. Barney Miller
11. Mr. Peepers
12. Mannix
13. Julia
14. Philip Marlowe
15. Mama
16. Joe Forrester
17. Maude
18. Peter Gunn
19. Marcus Welby, M.D.
20. Mr. Roberts

A. Peggy Wood
B. Peter Falk
C. Mike Connors
D. Hal Linden
E. Craig Stevens
F. Diahann Carroll
G. Roger Smith
H. David Birney
I. Philip Carey
J. Valerie Harper
K. Robert Young
L. Jack Klugman
M. Beatrice Arthur
N. Louise Beavers
O. Cloris Leachman
P. Wally Cox
Q. Shirley Booth
R. Cynthia Pepper
S. Telly Savalas
T. Lloyd Bridges

Photo 19

WHAT'S IN A NAME? (2)

Listed below on the left are the title roles from TV shows and on the right are the stars who played the roles. Match the performers and their roles.

1.	Grindl	A.	Juliet Prowse
2.	Tabitha	B.	Tim Conway
3.	Rango	C.	James Franciscus
4.	Lou Grant	D.	Karen Valentine
5.	Kodiak	E.	Jack Warden
6.	Brenner	F.	Dennis Weaver
7.	Sally	G.	Imogene Coca
8.	Johnny Staccato	H.	Burt Reynolds
9.	Petrocelli	I.	David Janssen
10.	Kentucky Jones	J.	Ron Liebman
11.	Hennesey	K.	Ed Asner
12.	Mona McClusky	L.	Sally Field
13.	Harry-O	M.	Jackie Cooper
14.	Karen	N.	Tim Conway
15.	Mark Saber	O.	Lisa Hartman
16.	Gidget	P.	Edward Binns
17.	Jigsaw John	Q.	John Cassavetes
18.	Hawk	R.	Barry Newman
19.	Kaz	S.	Clint Walker
20.	Longstreet	T.	Joan Caulfield

Photo 20

EVERYTHING IS RELATIVE (1)

Listed below on the left are TV stars who are related to the stars listed on the right in various TV shows. Match the performers and identify the relationships and programs.

1. Leon Ames	A. Richard Keith
2. Michael Landon	B. Lisa Gerritsen
3. Kathleen Freeman	C. Frances Bavier
4. Valerie Harper	D. Johnny Washbrook
5. Desi Arnaz	E. Jack Kelly
6. Peggy Wood	F. Fred MacMurray
7. Dick Van Patten	G. Deborah Wally
8. Gower Champion	H. Burl Ives
9. Cloris Leachman	I. Tim Rooney
10. James Garner	J. Al Lewis
11. Adrienne Barbeau	K. Shirley Bonne
12. Andy Griffith	L. Lurene Tuttle
13. Mickey Rooney	M. Connie Newton
14. Eve Arden	N. Jack Klugman
15. Fred Gwynne	O. Dom DeLuise
16. Anita Louise	P. Beatrice Arthur
17. Elaine Stritch	Q. Julie Kavner
18. William Frawley	R. Dick Van Patten
19. Brooke Adams	S. Jack Whiting
20. Brett Somers	T. Melissa Gilbert

Photo 21

45

EVERYTHING IS RELATIVE (2)

Listed below on the left are TV stars who are related to the stars listed on the right in various TV shows. Match the performers and identify the relationships and programs.

1.	Fred Astaire	A.	Scott Baio
2.	Michael Learned	B.	Esther Rolle
3.	Florence Henderson	C.	Eileen Heckart
4.	Robert Young	D.	Ernest Truex
5.	Marlo Thomas	E.	Valerie Harper
6.	Ron Howard	F.	Jean Stapleton
7.	Henry Winkler	G.	Phil Foster
8.	Gale Storm	H.	James Stewart
9.	Jimmie Walker	I.	Lew Parker
10.	Nancy Walker	J.	Roxie Roker
11.	Mary Tyler Moore	K.	Robert Wagner
12.	Art Carney	L.	George Cleveland
13.	Brandon DeWilde	M.	Hugh Beaumont
14.	Franklin Cover	N.	Elinor Donahue
15.	Beatrice Arthur	O.	Cathryn Damon
16.	Jonathan Daly	P.	Joyce Randolph
17.	Tommy Rettig	Q.	Charles Farrell
18.	Penny Marshall	R.	Richard Thomas
19.	Jerry Mathers	S.	Andy Griffith
20.	Billy Crystal	T.	Robert Reed

47   Photo 22

LOVE AND MARRIAGE (1)

Listed below are the names of TV lovers and/or mates. Identify the performers and the programs.

1. Nick and Nora Charles
2. Matt Dillon and Kitty Russell
3. Don Hollinger and Ann Marie
4. Clarence and Vinnie Day
5. Clark Kent and Lois Lane
6. Jim and Margaret Anderson
7. Ted and Georgette Baxter
8. George and Louise Jefferson
9. Bert Beasley and Mrs. Naugatuck
10. Oscar and Blanche Madison
11. Richard C. Barrington and Charley Drake
12. Lionel Jefferson and Jenny Willis
13. Mike and Gloria Stivic
14. Chester and Jessica Tate
15. Andy Taylor and Helen Crump
16. Doug and Kate Lawrence
17. Richie Cunningham and Laurie Beth
18. Fred and Ethel Mertz
19. Ed and Trixie Norton
20. Arthur and Vivian Harmon

LOVE AND MARRIAGE (2)

Listed below are the names of TV lovers and/or mates. Identify the performers and the programs.

1. Arthur Fonzarelli and Pinky Tuscadero
2. Bernie Steinberg and Bridget Fitzgerald
3. Stanley and Helen Roper
4. Tom and Helen Willis
5. Joe Gerard and Rhoda Morgenstern
6. Howard Adams and Eve Drake
7. Bob and Emily Hartley
8. Frank DeFazio and Edna Babish
9. George and Dorothy Baxter
10. Murray and Marie Slaughter
11. Ralph and Alice Kramden
12. Archie and Edith Bunker
13. Burt and Mary Campbell
14. Alexander and Donna Stone
15. Danny and Margaret Williams
16. Ricky and Lucy Ricardo
17. John and Olivia Walton
18. Walt and Amy Fitzgerald
19. Howard and Marion Cunningham
20. Walter and Maude Findlay

... BOB, BOB, BOBBING ALONG ...

Name the actors who played the following roles and identify the shows.

1. Robert Hartley
2. David March
3. Tony Baretta
4. Elliott Ness
5. Bob Sanders
6. Bob Collins
7. Bob Carson
8. Marcus Welby
9. Jim Anderson
10. Miles C. Banyon
11. Robert Hogan
12. Bob Wilcox
13. Michael Stivic
14. Napoleon Solo
15. Corporal Louis LeBeau
16. Robert Dickson
17. Kelly Brackett
18. Pete Ryan
19. Jonathan Hart
20. Alexander Mundy

REINCARNATION

Name the stars described below.

1. Two real-life former baseball players to two TV Western heroes.
2. Two real-life brothers to TV Western hero and TV adventure hero.
3. Broadway child star of *A Member of the Wedding* to TV child star.
4. Former Hollywood child star to TV hero of Navy comedy.
5. Former Hollywood child star to TV uncle in "nutty" family series.
6. Former Hollywood matinee idol to father of TV heroine.
7. Former child actress to *Hollywood Squares* regular.
8. Former Hollywood child actress to TV hostess of children's stories.
9. Former Hollywood leading man to TV's *General Electric Theater* host.
10. Former Hollywood leading man to 1930s TV crime fighter.
11. Minor Hollywood comic to "Mr. Television."
12. Former newspaper columnist to TV host of *Toast of the Town.*
13. Oscar-winning actress to TV's *Peyton Place* heroine.
14. Latin lover in films to star of TV series with island setting.
15. Hollywood's Flash Gordon to TV's Capt. Michael Gallant.
16. Two real-life brothers to TV's Rob Petrie and Dave Crabtree.
17. Hollywood actor's daughter to TV's Samantha Stevens.
18. Goldwyn chorus girl to TV's favorite "redhead."
19. Hollywood's Tarzan to TV's Jungle Jim.
20. Stage and screen actress to TV's favorite maid.

49

STREET WISE

The addresses listed on the left are from TV programs listed on the right. Match the addresses with the shows.

1. 000 Cemetery Lane
2. 14 Maple Street
3. 49 W. 10th St., Greenwich Village, N.Y.C.
4. 12th Police Precinct, New York City
5. 518 Crestview Drive
6. 53rd Police Precinct, Bronx
7. 627 Elm Street
8. 485 Bonnie Meadow Road
9. 1164 Morning Glory Road
10. 211 Pine Street
11. 27th Police Precinct, New York City
12. 137 Amsterdam Avenue, Manhattan
13. 24 Maple Drive
14. 312 Maple Avenue
15. 328 Chauncey Street
16. 345 Stone Cave Road
17. 336 N. Camden Drive
18. 200 Ridgeway Avenue
19. 505 E. 50th Street, Manhattan
20. 332 W. 64th Street, Manhattan

A. *Bewitched*
B. *The Corner Bar*
C. *The George Burns and Gracie Allen Show*
D. *Rhoda*

E. *The Dick Van Dyke Show*
F. *Father of the Bride*
G. *Starsky and Hutch*
H. *The Beverly Hillbillies*
I. *Make Room for Daddy*
J. *The Honeymooners*
K. *The Addams Family*

L. *The Flintstones*

M. *Car 54, Where Are You?*
N. *Barefoot in the Park*
O. *The Jack Benny Show*
P. *N.Y.P.D.*
Q. *The Andy Griffith Show*
R. *Dennis the Menace*
S. *Leave It to Beaver*
T. *Barney Miller*

Photo 23

IDENTITY CRISIS (1)

Listed below are various roles played by the same actor on TV. Identify the stars and the shows.

1. Beau Maverick, Simon Templar, Brett Sinclair
2. Phoebe Goodheart, Dr. Peter Lawrence, Nick Charles
3. Lt. Chick Hennesey, Pete Campbell, Socrates Miller
4. Pappy Boyington, Tom Lopaka, Paul Ryan, Jake Webster, James T. West
5. Frank Savage, Steve Carella, Peter Brooks
6. Lew Archer, Matt Anders, Bill Davis, Dr. Sean Jamison
7. Alexander Mundy, Pete Ryan, Jonathan Hart
8. Raymond Rambridge, Napoleon Solo
9. Sam Adams, Andy Taylor, Andy Thompson, Andy Sawyer
10. John Quincy Adams, Bernie Steinberg, Mark Elliott, Frank Serpico
11. Opie Taylor, Richard Cunningham, Bob Smith
12. Howard Cunningham, Bob Landers, Bert Quinn, Louis Hedler, Himself
13. Walter Fitzgerald, John Bosley, Ted Atwater, Professor McCutcheon
14. Barney Fife, The Nervous Chap
15. Stoney Burke, Steve McGarrett
16. Captain Arthur P. Ryan, Bart Maverick, Dr. Parris Mitchell
17. Brett Maverick, Jim Rockford
18. Barnaby Jones, Jed Clampett, George Russell, Sgt. Hank Mariner
19. Dr. Kelly Brackett, Jess Harper, Cooper Smith
20. Danny Williams, Jules Bedford

IDENTITY CRISIS (2)

Listed below are various roles played by the same actress on TV. Identify the stars and the shows.

1. Amy Fitzgerald, Janet Scott, Laura Thompson, Helen Roper
2. Bridget Fitzgerald, Nancy Lawrence Maitland
3. Ida Morgenstern, Nancy Kitteridge, Nancy Blansky, Mildred, Emily
4. Sam, Laura Petrie, Mary Richards
5. Lynn Hall, Millie Bronson, Consuela Lopez
6. Joan Randall, Betty Anderson, Jane Mulligan, Ellie Walker, Miriam Welby
7. Margaret MacDonald, Peggy Riley, Amanda Renfrew, Aunt Helen, Helen Marie
8. Maureen Robinson, Ruth Martin, Dr. Janet Craig
9. Kate Bradley, Blanche Morton, Wilma the Housekeeper
10. Myrna Gibbons, Sally Rogers, Maggie the Housekeeper
11. Sue Ann Nivens, Joyce Whitman, Vicki Angel, Elizabeth White
12. April Dancer, Feather Danton, Jennifer Hart
13. Eunice, the Charlady, the Old Lady, Carol the Housewife, Marion the Housewife
14. Mary Backstage, Effie Perrine, Ruth Martin, Phyllis Lindstrom
15. Mitzi Maloney, Georgette Baxter
16. Sandy Stockton, Missy Anne
17. Kay Fox, Myra Bradley
18. Mrs. Belmont, Kate the Maid, Katie Harwell, Gertrude Linkmier
19. Charmaine Schultz, Alice, Miss Wilson
20. Jill Danko, Sabrina Duncan, Daphne Harridge

WHERE IN THE WORLD? (1)

Listed below on the left are TV shows and on the right are the locations of these shows. Match the settings with the shows.

1. *Adventures in Paradise*	A. New York City
2. *Peyton Place*	B. Philadelphia
3. *Phyllis*	C. Brooklyn
4. *The Mary Tyler Moore Show*	D. Los Angeles
5. *The Bob Newhart Show*	E. Corona, Queens
6. *Happy Days*	F. Pasadena
7. *Rhoda*	G. Washington, D.C.
8. *The Tony Randall Show*	H. Minneapolis
9. *Three's Company*	I. Phoenix
10. *Sanford and Son*	J. North Fork, New Mexico
11. *Family*	K. The South Pacific
12. *Welcome Back, Kotter*	L. New York City and Connecticut
13. *All's Fair*	M. Miss., Mo. and Ohio Rivers
14. *Alice*	N. New England
15. *The Rifleman*	O. Hollywood
16. *The Andy Griffith Show*	P. Mayberry, North Carolina
17. *All in the Family*	Q. San Francisco
18. *The Nancy Walker Show*	R. Santa Monica
19. *Riverboat*	S. Chicago
20. *I Love Lucy*	T. Milwaukee

Photo 24

WHERE IN THE WORLD? (2)

Listed below on the left are TV shows and on the right are the locations of these shows. Match the settings with the shows.

1.	*Little House on the Prairie*	A.	Milwaukee
2.	*Mannix*	B.	Alamesa Prison
3.	*The Waltons*	C.	Honolulu
4.	*The Odd Couple*	D.	Gull's Cottage, New England
5.	*Laverne & Shirley*	E.	Korea
6.	*One Day at a Time*	F.	Kansas City
7.	*C.P.O. Sharkey*	G.	Fort Baxter, Kansas
8.	*Have Gun, Will Travel*	H.	Bronx
9.	*I Dream of Jeannie*	I.	San Remo
10.	*M*A*S*H*	J.	Jefferson County, Virginia
11.	*The Untouchables*	K.	Hooterville
12.	*On The Rocks*	L.	Plum Creek, Minnesota
13.	*Car 54, Where Are You?*	M.	Sherwood Forest
14.	*Hawaii Five-O*	N.	Chicago
15.	*Pete Kelly's Blues*	O.	San Francisco
16.	*You'll Never Get Rich*	P.	Los Angeles
17.	*Petrocelli*	Q.	Cocoa Beach, Florida
18.	*Petticoat Junction*	R.	Indianapolis
19.	*The Adventures of Robin Hood*	S.	San Diego
20.	*The Ghost and Mrs. Muir*	T.	Manhattan

Photo 25

WHERE IN THE WORLD? (3)

Listed below on the left are TV shows and on the right are the locations of these shows. Match the settings with the shows.

1.	The Thin Man	A.	Jellystone National Park
2.	The Tall Man	B.	Australia
3.	Tallahassee 7000	C.	Denver
4.	Sea Hunt	D.	Sherwood Forest
5.	Soap	E.	Medicine Bow, Wyoming
6.	77 Sunset Strip	F.	London
7.	Steve Canyon	G.	Boston
8.	Sara	H.	Greenwich Village, N. Y. C.
9.	Whispering Smith	I.	Washington, D. C.
10.	Sky King	J.	Miami Beach
11.	Sergeant Preston of the Yukon	K.	Lincoln Territory (New Mexico)
12.	U.S. Marshal	L.	Malibu Beach, California
13.	Whiplash	M.	Big Thunder Air Force Base
14.	U.F.O.	N.	Dun's River, Connecticut
15.	That's My Mama	O.	Flying Crown Ranch
16.	The Tab Hunter Show	P.	Cochise, Arizona
17.	Yogi Bear	Q.	Hollywood, California
18.	21 Beacon Street	R.	Alaska
19.	The Virginian	S.	The Pacific Ocean
20.	When Things Were Rotten	T.	Independence, Colorado

WHERE IN THE WORLD? (4)

Listed below on the left are TV shows and on the right are the locations of these shows. Match the settings with the shows.

1. *Mickey*	A.	Alaska and Woodland Oaks, CA
2. *Rango*	B.	Los Angeles
3. *The Real McCoys*	C.	Royal Weatherly Hotel
4. *The Rogues*	D.	Newport Arms Hotel
5. *Mama*	E.	Mayfield
6. *The Partridge Family*	F.	Double R Bar Ranch
7. *Pistols 'n' Petticoats*	G.	London
8. *The Jimmy Stewart Show*	H.	New Orleans
9. *The Sandy Duncan Show*	I.	San Francisco
10. *Judd, For the Defense*	J.	Gopher Gulch, Texas
11. *The People's Choice*	K.	San Fernando Valley
12. *The Second Hundred Years*	L.	Ridgemont, New York
13. *The Patty Duke Show*	M.	Bartley House Hotel
14. *The Paul Lynde Show*	N.	Wretched, Colorado
15. *The Ann Sothern Show*	O.	Houston
16. *Please Don't Eat the Daisies*	P.	New City, California
17. *Leave it to Beaver*	Q.	San Pueblo, California
18. *The Rockford Files*	R.	Easy Valley, California
19. *Longstreet*	S.	Brooklyn Heights, New York
20. *The Roy Rogers Show*	T.	Ocean Grove, California

HISTORY LESSON

Television, like radio and motion pictures, owes a debt to Thomas Alva Edison who, in the early 1900s, discovered a method of allowing electricity to pass through space via burning filament wire.

Also, about 1905, the French inventors Rignoux and Fouriner invented a method of transmitting a crude moving image over communications wiring.

But the "Doctor of TV" title goes to Dr. Vladimir Zworykin. It was his invention in 1923 of the iconoscope, a total-electric viewing process, that became the basic "eye" of the TV camera.

NOTABLE DATES

May 1928—General Electric began experimenting with telecasts from its laboratories in Schenectady, New York.

1929–RCA, headed by David Sarnoff, developed an all-electronic TV receiver which utilized a screen tube.

1930–ATC (American Television Corporation) in Chicago, Illinois, produced a closed-circuit variety show which featured Milton Berle, Trixie Friganza, and others.

July 30, 1930–NBC opened its first TV station W2XBS in New York City, with its video antenna on top of the Empire State Building.

July 20, 1931–CBS opened its first TV station in New York City, operating out of Grand Central Terminal Building, with its antenna on the roof of the Chrysler Building.

1931–Allen Dumont and Lee De Forest created TV station W2XWT, calling themselves the Dumont Television Network and operating from Passaic, New Jersey.

December 23, 1931–Harry Lubke developed his own television set and created TV station W6XAO in Los Angeles, California.

July 20, 1931–CBS premiere telecast, Mayor Jimmy Walker of New York City was emcee. Songs and skits were performed by Kate Smith (singing "When the Moon Comes Over the Mountain"), the Boswell Sisters, George and Ira Gershwin, Helen Gilligan, and others.

1932–The Roosevelt–Hoover presidential contest received wide TV coverage.

March 10, 1933–The Los Angeles station, W6XAO (later to become KTLA) was the first to broadcast a full-length commercial movie. It was *The Crooked Circle*, which starred ZaSu Pitts. At that time there were only four sets in the Los Angeles area; at the Brown Derby restaurant and the three hotels, the Hollywood Roosevelt, the Ambassador, and The Beverly Wilshire.

The 1930s–Since the major studios were located in New York City, many visiting celebrities were interviewed on TV, such as the Duke and Duchess of Windsor, Admiral Richard E. Byrd, and others.

July 8, 1938–NBC presented "live" excerpts from the Broadway play, "Susan and God," with Gertrude Lawrence and Paul McGrath.

April 30, 1939–President Franklin D. Roosevelt was the first "live" president to be seen on TV when he delivered the opening address of the New York World's Fair at Flushing Meadow, Queens, New York.

1939/1940–Also at the World's Fair, the Bell Telephone Company demonstrated "television telephones," where one could see on a tiny screen the person you were calling (all done on the Fairgrounds, of course).

December 19, 1939–The New York premiere of *Gone With the Wind* at the Capitol Theater was televised.

March 24, 1940–Station KHJ-TV (formerly W6XAO) televised the Easter Sunrise Service from the Hollywood Bowl, followed by the Easter Parade on Wilshire Boulevard.

August 27, 1940–CBS conducted a test run of color TV for the FFC.

January 9, 1941–CBS conducted the first public demonstration of color TV.

1942–1945–Development of TV was curtailed due to World War II.

1945–NBC televised its first annual Macy's Thanksgiving Day Parade in New York City.

1946–The National Academy of Television Arts and Sciences was established, with Harry Lubke, TV pioneer, as its first president.

January 25, 1949–the first annual Emmy Awards were presented for the year 1948. The name Emmy was derived from TV jargon "immy," which stood for an image orthicon camera tube. Designer Louis McManus was given a special award that year for his concept of the Emmy statuette. There were only *five* other awards given out!

In 1938, there were 7,500 operating TV sets in the U. S., mostly in the New York and Los Angeles areas. By 1947, there were approximately 17,000 sets. Today, 98% of American homes have one or more sets.

PIONEERS

Milton Berle–known as "Mr. Television," made his debut in 1930 in Chicago.

Kate Smith–radio singing star made her debut for the CBS premiere telecast in 1930 singing her theme song, "When the Moon Comes Over the Mountain."

Gertrude Lawrence–appeared "live" in 1938 in excerpts from her Broadway hit, *Susan and God*.

Eleanor Holm–swimming star of Billy Rose's Aquacade, which was telecast in 1939–40 from the New York World's Fair.

Dinah Shore–debuted in 1939 on local New York shows as a singer/dancer.

Imogene Coca–debuted in 1939, doing comedy skits with then-partner Hiram Shumlin.

Tallulah Bankhead–helped sell war bonds via TV in 1942.

Tamara–singer/dancer starred in *CBS Music Workshop* in 1942.

Luise Rainer–appeared in variety shows for DuPont in 1944. Other notables appearing also were Dick Haymes, Henry Morgan, Fred Waring and his Glee Club.

Eddie Cantor–appeared in NBC variety shows in 1944.

Don McNeill–his *Breakfast Club* was first aired in 1945 (but not as a regular series until 1950).

Ethel Waters–appeared on *The Borden Show* in 1947.

Yul Brynner–with then-wife, Virginia Gilmore, appeared in the series *Mr. and Mrs.* in 1947–48.

First World Series baseball game was televised on September 29, 1947.

Fran Allison–debuted her *Kukla, Fran and Ollie* show in Chicago on October 13, 1947.

Buffalo Bob Smith, with Howdy Doody and Clarabell, debuted on December 27, 1947.

Ed Sullivan–his *Toast of the Town* debuted on May 20, 1948.

Shirley Dinsdale–female ventriloquist with her puppet Judy Splinters was the first female recipient of an Emmy for the 1948 season.

Patricia Morison–lost the first Emmy award as Outstanding Personality to Shirley Dinsdale.

Mike Stokey–his show *Pantomime Quiz Time* won first Emmy for Most Popular TV Program of 1948.

Ed Wynn–*The Ed Wynn Show*, a 30-minute variety show, debuted October 6, 1949. He was the first male recipient of an Emmy for Most Outstanding Personality of 1949. The show also won an Emmy.

Jackie Gleason–debuted as Chester Riley in *Life of Riley* on October 4, 1949.

Rosemary DeCamp–debuted as Peggy Riley opposite Gleason.

Eva Marie Saint–debuted as Claudia, the daughter, in TV's first soap opera, *One Man's Family,* on November 4, 1949.

Arthur Godfrey–his *Talent Scouts* program debuted on December 6, 1948. His *Arthur Godfrey and Friends* debuted on January 30, 1949.

Peggy Wood–debuted on *Mama* on July 1, 1949 with Dick Van Patten playing her son Nels.

Gertrude Berg–guested on *The Texaco Star Theater* with Milton Berle in 1948; went on to star as Molly in *The Goldbergs* and won the Best Actress Emmy for 1950.

Groucho Marx–won the 1950 Emmy as Most Outstanding Personality for his show, *You Bet Your Life.*

Alan Young–won the 1950 Best Actor Emmy for his *The Alan Young Show*.

Faye Emerson–known as the First Lady of Television, lost the 1950 Most Outstanding Personality award to Groucho Marx.

Helen Hayes–debuted in 1950 on the *Pulitzer Prize Playhouse* in *The Late Christopher Bean.*

Sid Caesar–another loser for the 1950 Most Outstanding Personality award; he won the 1951 award for Best Actor.

Imogene Coca–having debuted in 1939, she won the 1951 award for Best Actress.

Carl Reiner and **Howard Morris**–second bananas on *Your Show of Shows*.

Lucille Ball–her *I Love Lucy* show debuted on October 15, 1951.

THOSE WONDERFUL WOMEN . . .

LUCILLE BALL

Lucille Ball started in Hollywood as a Goldwyn chorine in 1933. She was signed by RKO and worked her way up from extra to secondary roles and finally became known as the Queen of the RKO B movies. One of the brighter spots during this period was her portrayal of a wise-cracking Broadway hopeful in *Stage Door*, which starred Katharine Hepburn and Ginger Rogers, RKO's two top female stars. Along with many other starlets Lucille did a screen-test for the role of Scarlett O'Hara in *Gone With the Wind*, losing out to Vivian Leigh. When Hepburn left RKO, Lucille was groomed to take leads and acquitted herself well enough for MGM to lure her away. She had finally become a star, but she never achieved the rank of superstar in the movies.

In 1948 Lucille starred in a radio series called *My Favorite Husband*. She was Liz, a zany housewife and the forerunner to Lucy Ricardo. She had married Cuban bandleader Desi Arnaz in 1943, and together they decided to enter television in 1956. They made a pilot film for *I Love Lucy*, producing and financing it themselves in an attempt to sell their idea for a series to the executives in a position to get it on the air. Of course, the rest is television history. Desi and Lucille were fortunate to have a sure-fire plotline and, with two superb second bananas, William Frawley and Vivian Vance, their show, *I Love Lucy*, skyrocketed to the number one spot and remained in the top ten for years.

Lucille herself won four Emmy awards as Best Comedienne. The birth of their son, Desi IV, coincided with the script and the birth of Ricky, Jr. in 1953, as all America watched. Lucy and Desi expanded their show to an hour for the 1957/58 season. When Howard Hughes relinquished hold of RKO Studios, Lucy and Desi bought it and renamed it Desilu, the ownership of which Lucy retained after she and Desi were divorced, thus fulfilling the typical Horatio Alger tale, female style. Lucy now owned the studio where she had once been a bit player.

After the divorce Lucy went on alone with *The Lucy Show*, which ran from 1961 through 1968. In this format, she portrayed Lucy Carmichael, a widow with two children. Her boarder, Vivian Bagley, was a divorcee who had one son. Naturally Mrs. Bagley was portrayed by Lucy's pal, Vivian Vance. In 1965, Vivian Vance retired and Lucy's new format found her the secretary to Gale Gordon, a bank vice-president. This version of the show ran until 1968.

From 1968 through 1974, Lucille Ball appeared in *Here's Lucy*, in which she portrayed Lucille Carter, a widow with two children, played by

Photo 26

her own children, Lucie and Desi, Jr., and still with Gale Gordon, this time playing her brother-in-law and employer at an employment agency. Lucille, always loyal to her friends, saw to it that her friend, Mary Jan Croft, was written into all three plots. One of her pals in the old RKO starlet days, Barbara Pepper, often cropped up on Lucy's shows.

Since her series have been over, Lucy has made several specials and has guested on innumerable shows. After her success with television, she has made a few films. She and Desi starred in two MGM movies and she made one with Bob Hope, *The Facts of Life*, and one with Henry Fonda, *Yours, Mine and Ours*. She starred in a Broadway musical and in 1974, bought the rights to and starred in the film version of *Mame* with Robert Preston. She married Gary Morton in 1961 and is now in semi-retirement. The character of Lucy Ricardo paved the way for the screwball antics of such TV comediennes as Debbie Reynolds on her show and Joan Davis on *I Married Joan* and Penny Marshall and Cindy Williams on *Laverne & Shirley*. *I Love Lucy* made a considerable contribution to the growth of the medium. Its success led to the widespread use of film instead of kinescopes so that programs could be rerun. At one time it was said that reruns of *I Love Lucy* were played daily in every country of the world where television was available.

FAYE EMERSON

Once the fledgling television industry got its feet off the ground, it seemed only natural for Hollywood stars to make the transition from films to TV. One of the first Hollywood actresses to make it big on TV was Faye Emerson. Faye had never been a superstar as such; she was relegated to playing leads in Warner's B films, or had secondary leads (usually someone's sister) in bigger films. Her minor career was somewhat eclipsed by the fact that she married Elliott Roosevelt, son of then President, Franklin D. Theirs was a war-time marriage (he was a Colonel) and did not last. She was ready for TV stardom and the TV cameras and audiences of the late '40s and early '50s were ready for her. A very striking woman with marvelous facial bone structure, a throaty, appealing voice, and excellent figure, she also possessed a sharp, penetrating mind and a glib, facile wit. She was also fond of wearing low-cut gowns, displaying ample cleavage, which caused quite a bit of controversy at the time. *The Faye Emerson Show* ran from 1949 to 1952, during which time she was nominated for an Emmy (in 1950) for Most Outstanding Personality. She subsequently married TV orchestra leader, Skitch Henderson, and together they did several variety and talk shows, including *Wonderful Town* (1951) and *Faye and Skitch* (1952/54). She was also a panelist for five years on *I've Got a Secret*.

63   Photo 27

LORETTA YOUNG

Having won an Oscar in 1947 for *The Farmer's Daughter*, Loretta Young swirled into television and captured three Emmy Awards for the *Loretta Young Show*. Always noted as a Hollywood fashion plate, she became TV's best-dressed actress and her trademark was her grand entrance at the opening of each show. Those were the days of bouffant skirts, with many crinoline petticoats, and no one wore them with more flair than Loretta. When she was thirteen years old, a call came from a studio for one of her two sisters who were in films. Neither was around at the time so Loretta went and was promptly hired. That was in 1926 and she made the transition from silents to talkies successfully. Her venture into TV began in 1953 with *Letter to Loretta*, which ran that season and then became *The Loretta Young Theater* until 1961. These were anthology-style shows, with a different plot each week. In 1962, she returned with *The Loretta Young Show*, which was a continuing series about a widow with seven children. She won her Emmy awards in 1954, 1956, and 1958/59, and was nominated four other times: in 1953, 1959/60, 1960/61, and in 1955 for Best Single Performance. Loretta's early marriage to actor Grant Withers in 1930 was annulled and she later married Tom Lewis in 1940. Her daughter, Judy Lewis, enjoyed a TV career also, appearing in the soap operas *Kitty Foyle*, *General Hospital*, *The Guiding Light*, and *The Secret Storm*. She also played the female lead in the series *The Outlaws*, opposite Don Collier. Loretta's brother-in-law is Ricardo Montalban of TV's *Fantasy Island*. Montalban was a frequent performer on *The Loretta Young Show*.

Photo 28

JANE WYMAN

Had Jane Wyman remained married to her second husband, she would today be the First Lady of the land. But, according to Ronald Reagan, her career came first, so they were divorced in 1948, after eight years of marriage. Having won an Oscar for *Johnny Belinda* and being nominated three other times, she tackled TV in 1956 as a hostess of *Fireside Theater*. The program became *The Jane Wyman Theater* then *The Jane Wyman Show* with new theme music and Ms. Wyman starring in most of the dramas. She is currently starring in TV's *Falcon Crest*.

In the 1962/63 season, she hosted rebroadcasts of the series in afternoon showings. She was nominated once for an Emmy in 1956. Her son, Michael Reagan, is an advertising executive in California. Her daughter, Maureen Reagan, is an active feminist with political aspirations who is often at loggerheads with her father, the President.

JANE WYATT

· The high point of Jane Wyatt's Hollywood career was playing the lead in *Lost Horizon*, opposite Ronald Colman in 1937. She had married Edgar Ward in 1935, they had two children and she never actively sought Hollywood stardom, being content to take what came along. However, with her children grown, she ventured into TV and, after an appearance on *Studio One*, she was given the lead opposite Robert Young in *Father Knows Best*, and a new career and lasting fame came to her. The program first aired on October 3, 1954, and the trials and tribulations of Jim and Margaret Anderson and their three offspring, Betty, Bud, and Kathy, became a "must" in every TV household. The show ran until 1962 and Jane won three Emmy awards: in 1957, 1958/59, and 1959/60. On May 15, 1977, NBC presented a 90-minute special, *The Father Knows Best Reunion*, which reunited the family on the 35th wedding anniversary of Jim and Margaret. In 1966, Jane was hostess for a series called, *Confidential For Women*. Ms. Wyatt made her television debut on *Robert Montgomery Presents*.

IDA LUPINO

The multi-talented Ida Lupino (actress, director, writer, producer) had a full and rewarding career in Hollywood before bringing her skills to television. Though never nominated for an Oscar, she did receive the New York Film Critic's award for other work in *The Hard Way* in 1942. Her foray into television began in 1953 on the *Four Star Playhouse*. When that anthology series started in 1952, the four alternating stars were Dick Powell, Charles Boyer, Joel McCrea, and Rosalind Russell. The latter two dropped out after the first season and were replaced by David Niven and Miss Lupino. She departed in 1955 and the series ended in 1956. Ida was hostess-star of the *Ida Lupino Theater* in 1956 and made appearances on *Batman* (as Dr. Cassandra) and on *Dick Powell's Zane Grey Theater*. From 1956 through 1958, she co-starred with her then-husband, Howard Duff, in *Mr. Adams and Eve*, a sitcom involving a married couple working in show business. Her TV directorial work includes various episodes in the following: *Alfred Hitchcock Presents, Gilligan's Island, Thriller, The Twilight Zone, The Untouchables,* and *The Ghost and Mrs. Muir*. She was nominated for an Emmy three times; in 1956 for *Four Star Playhouse*, in 1957 and 1958/59 for *Mr. Adams and Eve*.

DONNA REED

The Donna Reed Show ran eight years, from 1958 through 1966, and was a personal triumph for Donna. A Hollywood star and leading lady for years, she never reached the pinnacle of superstar status, although she won an Oscar (albeit as a Supporting Actress) for her role as Alma, the prostitute, in

Photo 30

From Here to Eternity. The Donna Reed Show was a family sitcom, depicting the lives of Donna and Alex Stone (a pediatrician), and their children, Mary and Jeff, and later, an unofficially adopted daughter, Trisha. Alex Stone was portrayed by Carl Betz. Daughter Mary was played by Shelley Fabares, the niece of actress Nanette Fabray. Son Jeff was played by Paul Petersen whose sister Patty played Trisha from 1963–1966. Miss Reed never captured an Emmy, but she was nominated four times: in 1958/59, 1959/60, 1960/61, and 1961/62. She married Tony Owens in 1945 and he was the producer of her TV series; they had two sons and two daughters.

BARBARA STANWYCK

That "grande dame" of Hollywood, "Missy" (as she is known to her friends) must have felt a great glow of pride as she strode across the stage on May 6, 1961 to pick up her Emmy for *The Barbara Stanwyck Show*. She was to repeat this same stride (Missy always strides—never walks or glides) on May 22, 1966, five years later for her role of Victoria Barkley in *The Big Valley*. Barbara had long been a Hollywood superstar and had been nominated four times for an Oscar but had never won. Her nominations were for *Stella Dallas* (1937), *Ball of Fire* (1941), *Double Indemnity* (1944) and *Sorry, Wrong Number* (1948). Additional TV appearances by Barbara were on *Dick Powell's Zane Grey Theater*, the *Ford Theater*, and as a semi-regular on *Wagon Train*, in which she played Kate Crowley, the girlfriend of John McIntyre, who had taken over the lead when Ward Bond died. She also made three TV movies: *The House That Wouldn't Die* (1970) with Richard Egan; *A Taste of Evil* (1971) with Barbara Parkins and Roddy McDowall; and *The Letters* (1973), an episodic tale, with Leslie Nielsen and Dina Merrill appearing in her vignette. Because of her television stature, Barbara was voted the Most Popular Female Star by Photoplay Readers in 1967 and 1968. She was also awarded the Screen Actor's Guild award in 1966 for "Outstanding Achievement in Fostering the Finest Ideals of the Acting Profession." This award was presented to her by then-Governor Ronald Reagan of California.

ELIZABETH MONTGOMERY

Refuting the theory that children in acting families seldom achieve the stardom of their parents, Elizabeth more than lived up to the fame of her father, Robert Montgomery. Appearing first on his *Montgomery's Summer Stock* show in 1953, she quickly became an established TV actress in many of the early "live" TV dramas. In 1964, however, she won permanent stardom with her series, *Bewitched*. This show, which featured her as a modern-day witch, ran until 1972. She was nominated for an Emmy four times for *Bewitched*, in 1965/66, 1966/67, 1967/68, and 1968/69, and once for Outstanding Single Performance in 1960/61 for *The Rusty Heller Story*. Another outstanding performance was her portrayal of Judith Traherne in *Dark Victory*, following in the footsteps of Tallulah Bankhead (stage) and Bette Davis (film). Ms. Montgomery was married to *Bewitched*'s producer/director, William Asher.

JUNE ALLYSON

Throughout her Hollywood career, June Allyson was known as "the girl next door." As she matured, she became everybody's "favorite wife" in such films as *The Glenn Miller Story, The Stratton Story, The McConnell Story,* etc. From 1959 through 1961, she was hostess-actress on *The Dupont Show with June Allyson* on television. In 1961, she joined husband Dick Powell as hostess on *The Dick Powell Show,* which ran until 1963. One of the hilarious highlights of her TV career occurred when she guested on *The Judy Garland Show* and she and Judy got "squiffed" during Judy's "tea segment." The women were not drinking tea in those teacups and they got quite hysterical recalling their mutual days at MGM. Recently, she and Van Johnson, her frequent Hollywood co-star, hosted a nostalgia show for cable TV.

JUNE LOCKHART

Another show-biz "brat," June Lockhart has surpassed the laurels of her acting parents, Kathleen and Gene Lockhart. Starting in Hollywood as a child actress, she entered the TV scene early in her adulthood, after moderate success on Broadway. In addition to appearing as a panelist or as quiz game participant (she has an extraordinary mind and always plays to win—her male counterpart being Tony Randall—they both argue with the answers even if *they* are wrong!), she started early in live dramas on the *Ford Theater* which ran from 1948 through 1957. But in 1958 she hit her stride as the mother in the *Lassie* series, replacing Jan Clayton. She later co-starred in the sci-fi series, *Lost in Space* (1965/68). She also made frequent appearances on *Petticoat Junction* as Dr. Janet Craig (1963 to 1970). From 1974 to 1976, she was the voice of Martha Day on the animated cartoon series, *These Are the Days.*

DORIS DAY

Dodo (as she is nicknamed) is a multi-talented performer—singer, dancer, comedienne, dramatic actress, recording star. She started her career as a band singer and had her first big recording hit with Les Brown's orchestra singing "Sentimental Journey," back in 1945. That was the year a lot of G.I.'s were returning home from World War II and the song had a very special meaning. Doris starred in her first film, *Romance on the High Seas* in 1948 and has remained a superstar ever since. She was nominated for an Oscar for her comedy, *Pillow Talk* in 1959, and a dramatic high spot was portraying Ruth Etting in *Love Me or Leave Me* (1955). She introduced two Academy Award songs: "Secret Love" in *Calamity Jane* and "Que Sera Sera" in *The Man Who Knew Too Much.* Small wonder, then, that when she entered the TV scene, her shows were sumptuously mounted. Always known as *The Doris Day Show,* it went through four different formats and ran from 1968 through 1973. She always played "Doris Martin" and was groomed to the teeth in whatever fashion prevailed at the time.

MARY TYLER MOORE

A TV "baby," Mary Tyler Moore worked her way slowly but steadily through the ranks to finally achieve stardom on the "idiot box." Starting innocuously as Happy Hotpoint, the dancing elf in the commercials on *The Adventures of Ozzie and Harriet* in 1955, she then graduated to the role of "Sam," in the *Richard Diamond, Private Detective* series in 1957 which starred David Janssen. In this role of Diamond's telephone service operator, only her legs were shown! During this same period, she made frequent appearances on *Bachelor Father,* starring John Forsythe, and *Thriller,* with host Boris Karloff. Finally in 1961, she landed the role of Laura Petrie on *The Dick Van Dyke Show,* and future fame beckoned. This series ended in 1966 and in 1970, she began her own series, *The Mary Tyler Moore Show,* in which she portrayed Mary Richards, a producer at a radio station in Minneapolis. Recently she starred on Broadway in the play, *Whose Life Is It Anyway?,* and received an Oscar nomination for the film, *Ordinary People.* Her Emmy record is a testament to her talent. Ms. Moore won two Emmies for *The Dick Van Dyke Show* and four for *The Mary Tyler Moore Show.*

DINAH SHORE

A "legend" in her own time, Dinah seems to defy the laws of longevity. At the age of 64 (at this writing), Dinah is still going strong. Like Doris Day, she started her career as a band singer, graduated to soloist, became a well-known recording and radio singer. One of her early hit records was "Blues in the Night." She made a few quite forgettable movies, one of which had the ridiculous title of *Aaron Slick from Pumkin' Crick.* Alan Young and opera star, Robert Merrill, were also involved in that disaster. Dinah's TV debut was on the *Ed Sullivan Show* and she found her niche on TV in 1951, alternating with Perry Como in early evening song fests. In 1956, she began her own hour-long series and she has remained a "top dog" ever since. Her famous blown kiss (Mmwah!) to the audience at the end of her show became her trademark. She was once married to George Montgomery and they had two chilren. In recent years she had a romance with Burt Reynolds which received a considerable amount of publicity. Her Emmy record rivals no one's. It includes:

1953–Best Female Star in Regular Series (nominated)
1954–Best Female Singer (winner)
1955–Best Variety Series (nominated)
1955–Best Female Singer (winner)
1956–Best Female Personality (winner)
1957–Best Female Continuing Personality (winner)
1958/59–Best Female Continuing Personality (winner)
1959/60–Outstanding Variety Program (nominated)
1960/61–Outstanding Variety Program (nominated)

Photo 31

Photo 32   72

CAROL BURNETT

Another TV fledgling, Carol Burnett ran the gamut of all facets of performing before achieving super-stardom. From 1949 through 1959, she was a frequent participant in Mike Stokey's *Pantomime Quiz* show. In 1956, she portrayed the girlfriend of Buddy Hackett in the short-lived series, *Stanley*. From 1958 through 1967 she was a regular on *The Garry Moore Show*, where her musical number, "I'm in Love with John Foster Dulles," was a tremendous hit. During this period (1964/65) she also appeared as hostess on *The Entertainers*. At last, in 1967, she launched her own series, *The Carol Burnett Show*, with regulars Harvey Korman, Vicki Lawrence, and Lyle Waggoner, and was an instant success. When Lyle left the show, Tim Conway became a regular. Throughout the years, she has appeared in specials with Julie Andrews, Martha Raye, and Beverly Sills, all of which were recorded and became hit records. Her innumerable characterizations have become legend: the Charlady with bucket; Eunice; Marion of "As the Stomach Turns," Carol of the domestic skit; Mrs. Whiggins, the secretary; the take-off on Charo; the distaff side of the Old Couple (get my rocker started!). Eventually, everyone knew that when she tugged at her ear in her closing song, "I'm So Glad We Had This Time Together," she was signalling goodnight to her grandmother. She has appeared in several films and had a Broadway hit in *Once Upon a Mattress*. She has won three Emmies.

* * *

The list of "made on TV" ladies is immeasurable. Linda Lavin served an apprenticeship on Broadway and was a semi-regular on the *Barney Miller* series before her hit program, *Alice*. And from *Alice*, we got Polly Holliday (*Flo*), who has been in show business for many years. From the *Mary Tyler Moore Show*, came both Valerie Harper and Cloris Leachman (*Rhoda* and *Phyllis*), two stars who had struggled for years on Broadway and in Hollywood without much recognition. Two others who deserve mention here are "Laverne and Shirley," a/k/a Penny Marshall and Cindy Williams. When they led the Macy's Thanksgiving Day Parade a few years back, they waved at me and I thought what a thrill it must have been after all those years of struggling to become top bananas. Remember Penny as Myrna Turner in *The Odd Couple*? And Cindy Williams in the film, *American Graffiti*? This film also had as one of its performers, Suzanne Somers, one-time star of *Three's Company*.

FAIR GAME (1)

Listed below on the left are personalities who hosted the shows listed on the right. Match the hosts with the programs.

1.	Peter Marshall	A.	*You Bet Your Life*
2.	Gene Rayburn	B.	*Tattletales*
3.	Alex Trebek	C.	*The Price Is Right*
4.	John Daly	D.	*$64,000 Question*
5.	Garry Moore	E.	*Celebrity Sweepstakes*
6.	Chuck Woolery	F.	*The Fun Factory*
7.	Jim Lange	G.	*Gambit*
8.	Bob Barker	H.	*Hollywood Squares*
9.	Dick Clark	I.	*Information Please*
10.	Bobby Van	J.	*Family Feud*
11.	Hal March	K.	*Password*
12.	Clifton Fadiman	L.	*High Rollers*
13.	Groucho Marx	M.	*The Match Game*
14.	Wink Martindale	N.	*Stop the Music*
15.	Bert Convy	O.	*The Dating Game*
16.	Chuck Barris	P.	*$20,000 Pyramid*
17.	Jim McKrell	Q.	*Wheel of Fortune*
18.	Allen Ludden	R.	*I've Got A Secret*
19.	Tom Kennedy	S.	*The Gong Show*
20.	Richard Dawson	T.	*What's My Line?*

Photo 33

FAIR GAME (2)

Listed below on the left are personalities who hosted the shows listed on the right. Match the hosts with the programs.

1. Bud Collyer	A.	*Dough Re Mi*
2. Bill Cullen	B.	*The G.E. College Bowl*
3. Art James	C.	*The Memory Game*
4. Jack Clark	D.	*Pantomime Quiz*
5. Rip Taylor	E.	*Make the Connection*
6. Gene Rayburn	F.	*The Showoffs*
7. Bob Barker	G.	*On the Go*
8. Art Fleming	H.	*Let's Make a Deal*
9. Allen Ludden	I.	*The Cross Wits*
10. Jim McKrell	J.	*Name That Tune*
11. Jack Barry	K.	*Beat the Clock*
12. Mike Stokey	L.	*Masquerade Party*
13. Jack Linkletter	M.	*Jeopardy*
14. Bobby Van	N.	*The Newlywed Game*
15. Monty Hall	O.	*Blockbusters*
16. Bert Parks	P.	*The Joker's Wild*
17. Joe Garagiola	Q.	*The $1.98 Beauty Show*
18. Tom Kennedy	R.	*The Honeymoon Game*
19. Jim McKay	S.	*The Family Game*
20. Bob Eubanks	T.	*Concentration*

Photo 34

ALTER EGOS

Listed below on the left are TV comic characters and on the left are the performers who created them. Match the stars with the characters.

1.	Art Fern	A.	Ernie Kovacs
2.	Fenwick Babbitt	B.	Louis Nye
3.	Crazy Guggenheim	C.	Bob Elliott
4.	Cool Cees	D.	Mel Brooks
5.	Maude Frickett	E.	Johnny Carson
6.	Ernestine	F.	Sid Caesar
7.	Percy Dovetonsils	G.	Cliff Arguette
8.	Charlie Weaver	H.	Cher
9.	Clem Kaddiddlehopper	I.	Red Buttons
10.	Jose Jimenez	J.	Frank Fontaine
11.	Laverne	K.	Jackie Gleason
12.	Maxie, the Taxi	L.	Lily Tomlin
13.	Wally Ballew	M.	Red Skelton
14.	Gordon Hathaway	N.	Eddie Cantor
15.	Kupke Kid	O.	Don Novello
16.	Father Guido Sarducci	P.	Flip Wilson
17.	The 2000 Year Old Man	Q.	Carol Burnett
18.	Eunice	R.	Bill Dana
19.	German Soldier	S.	Jonathan Winters
20.	Geraldine Jones	T.	Arte Johnson

SIDESADDLE

Listed below on the left are performers and on the right are the characters they played. Match the stars with their roles and identify the programs.

1.	Amanda Blake	A.	Annie Oakley
2.	Melody Patterson	B.	Anita Cabrillo
3.	Barbara Stanwyck	C.	Laura Thomas
4.	Linda Cristal	D.	Connie Garrett
5.	Gail Davis	E.	Candy Pruitt
6.	Linda Evans	F.	Kitty Russell
7.	Anna Lisa	G.	Audra Barkley
8.	Gloria Winters	H.	Samantha Crawford
9.	Annette Funicello	I.	Monique Devereaux
10.	Diane Brewster	J.	Carolyn Ingalls
11.	Audrey Totter	K.	Elizabeth Stoddard Cartwright
12.	Karen Sharpe	L.	Wrangler Jane
13.	Judi Meredith	M.	Nora Travers
14.	Jill Ireland	N.	Beth Purcell
15.	Terry Moore	O.	Marian Starett
16.	Karen Grassle	P.	Nell McLaughlin
17.	Anita Louise	Q.	Victoria Barkley
18.	Ann Robinson	R.	Helen Watkin
19.	Bridget Hanley	S.	Victoria Sebastian Cannon
20.	Geraldine Brooks	T.	Penny

TALL IN THE SADDLE (1)

Listed below on the left are the names of TV Western heroes and on the right are the stars who portrayed the roles. Match the actors with their roles and identify the shows.

1. Rowdy Yates	A. Kent Taylor
2. Capt. Zachary Wingate	B. Scott Forbes
3. Matt Dillon	C. Barry Sullivan
4. Paladin	D. Doug McClure
5. Howdy Lewis	E. Ty Hardin
6. Lucas McCain	F. Clint Walker
7. Ben Cartwright	G. Keith Larsen
8. Jarrod Barkley	H. George Montgomery
9. Jim Bowie	I. Clint Eastwood
10. Cash Connover	J. James Brown
11. Bat Masterson	K. Richard Boone
12. Brave Eagle	L. Lorne Greene
13. Tom Jeffords	M. Adam Kennedy
14. Capt. Jim Flagg	N. Preston Foster
15. Lt. Rip Masters	O. Chuck Connors
16. Bronco Layne	P. John Lupton
17. Dion Patrick	Q. Patrick Wayne
18. Cheyenne Bodie	R. Richard Long
19. Matthew Rockford	S. Gene Barry
20. Benjamin Pride	T. James Arness

TALL IN THE SADDLE (2)

Listed below on the left are the names of TV Western heroes and on the right are the stars who portrayed the roles. Match the actors with their roles and identify the shows.

1. Quint Aspen	A. Fess Parker
2. Joe Cartwright	B. John Gavin
3. Jason McCord	C. Leif Erickson
4. Marshal Jim Crown	D. James Arness
5. Simon Fry	E. Hugh O'Brian
6. Chester Goode	F. John Russell
7. Hopalong Cassidy	G. Don Durant
8. Zeb Macahan	H. Ward Bond
9. Daniel Boone	I. Peter Brown
10. Christopher Colt	J. Michael Landon
11. Ben Calhoun	K. William Boyd
12. Harrison Destry	L. Dan Haggerty
13. Jefferson Drum	M. Dennis Weaver
14. Big John Cannon	N. Henry Fonda
15. Johnny Ringo	O. Dale Robertson
16. Wyatt Earp	P. Chuck Connors
17. James Adams	Q. Jeff Richards
18. Chad Cooper	R. Stuart Whitman
19. Dan Troop	S. Wayde Preston
20. Seth Adams	T. Burt Reynolds

TALL IN THE SADDLE (3)

Listed below on the left are the names of TV Western heroes and on the right are the actors who played the roles. Match the actors with their roles and identify the shows.

1.	John Slaughter	A.	Robert Fuller
2.	Don Diego de La Vega	B.	Rory Calhoun
3.	Yancy Derringer	C.	Dan O'Herlihy
4.	Artemus Gordon	D.	Dale Robertson
5.	Jingles	E.	David Carradine
6.	Josh Randall	F.	Barry Sullivan
7.	Cooper Smith	G.	John Payne
8.	Judge Henry Garth	H.	Rocky Lane
9.	Doc Sardius McPheeters	I.	Scott Brady
10.	Bill Longley	J.	Steve McQueen
11.	Sheriff Pat Garrett	K.	John Bromfield
12.	Ranger Jace Pearson	L.	Guy Williams
13.	Jim Hardy	M.	Richard Egan
14.	Steve Gordon	N.	Jock Mahoney
15.	Shotgun Slade	O.	Lee J. Cobb
16.	Marshal Frank Morgan	P.	Tom Tryon
17.	Shane	Q.	Douglas Kennedy
18.	Vint Bonner	R.	Andy Devine
19.	Red Ryder	S.	Willard Parker
20.	Jim Redigo	T.	Ross Martin

TALL IN THE SADDLE (4)

Listed below on the left are the names of TV Western heroes and on the right are the actors who played the roles. Match the actors with their roles and identify the programs.

1. William Colton	A.	Chris Jones
2. Buffalo Baker	B.	John Smith
3. Buck Cannon	C.	Chad Everett
4. Joshua Bolt	D.	Peter Palmer
5. John Reid	E.	Jim Davis
6. The Cisco Kid	F.	James Stacy
7. Mr. Callahan	G.	Clu Gulager
8. Deputy Del Stark	H.	Paul Fix
9. Jesse James	I.	Charles Bickford
10. Kit Carson	J.	David Soul
11. Johnny Madrid Lancer	K.	John McIntire
12. Ranger Ben Jenkins	L.	Joel Higgins
13. Sgt. James Bustard	M.	Lloyd Bridges
14. Emmett Ryker	N.	Noah Beery
15. John Grainger	O.	Bill Williams
16. Micah Torrance	P.	Forrest Tucker
17. Chris Hale	Q.	Clayton Moore
18. Sam Best	R.	Duncan Reynoldo
19. Marshal Bill Winter	S.	Harry Carey, Jr.
20. Slim Sherman	T.	Cameron Mitchell

THE ANIMAL KINGDOM

The animals listed on the left were featured in the programs listed on the right. Match the animals with the programs and identify the species.

1. Boo-boo Kitty
2. Ruth
3. Sam
4. Fred
5. Tamba
6. Arnold
7. Ben
8. Dino
9. Bullwinkle
10. Enoch
11. Dolores
12. Bimbo
13. Webster Webfoot
14. SoSo
15. Kermit
16. Elsa
17. Scooby
18. Clarence
19. Sebastian
20. Batmite

A. Rocky and His Friends
B. Nanny and the Professor
C. The Pete Potamus Show
D. Circus Boy
E. Kukla, Fran and Ollie
F. Funny Bones
G. The Muppets
H. The Hathaways
I. New Adventures of Batman
J. Daktari
K. Born Free
L. Laverne & Shirley
M. Baretta
N. Gunsmoke
O. Gentle Ben
P. The Little People
Q. Green Acres
R. The Flintstones
S. Jungle Jim
T. Moby Dick & the Mighty Mentor

CHILD'S PLAY

Match the names listed on the left with the programs listed on the right.

1. Jack Barry
2. Jim Henson
3. George Reeves
4. Barney Rubble

5. Fran Allison
6. Clarabell
7. Annette Funicello
8. Buzz Corey
9. Bob Keeshan
10. Al Hodge
11. Don Herbert
12. Miss Frances
13. Clifton Fadiman
14. Marlin Perkins
15. Tommy Rettig
16. Peppermint Patty
17. Spanky McFarland
18. Wile E. Coyote
19. Snagglepuss
20. Jim Backus

A. *Kukla, Fran and Ollie*
B. *Space Patrol*
C. *Peanuts*
D. *Captain Video and his Video Rangers*
E. *The Road Runner*
F. *Ding Dong School*
G. *The Flintstones*
H. *Zoo Parade*
I. *The Quiz Kids*
J. *Juvenile Jury*
K. *Lassie*
L. *The Little Rascals*
M. *The Mickey Mouse Club*
N. *Superman*
O. *Yogi Bear*
P. *Mr. Magoo*
Q. *Captain Kangaroo*
R. *Mr. Wizard*
S. *Sesame Street*
T. *Howdy Doody*

85   Photo 35

SO YOU WANT TO LEAD A BAND . . .

Listed below on the left are band leaders and on the right are the TV shows with which they were associated. Match the musicians with the programs.

1.	Jose Melis	A.	*The Jack Paar Show* (afternoon)
2.	Milton DeLugg	B.	*$100,000 Name That Tune*
3.	Sammy Spear	C.	*Your Hit Parade*
4.	Skitch Henderson	D.	*The Joey Bishop Show*
5.	Frank DeVol	E.	*The Jack Paar Show* (evening)
6.	Pupi Campo	F.	*Tonight* (Steve Allen)
7.	Archie Bleyer	G.	*Garroway at Large*
8.	Doc Severinson	H.	*The Bob Hope Show*
9.	Joseph Gallichio	I.	*The Jim Nabors Show*
10.	Nelson Riddle	J.	*The Merv Griffin Show*
11.	Bob Rosengarden	K.	*What's My Line?*
12.	Joe Harnell	L.	*The Lux Show* (Rosemary Clooney)
13.	Joe Massimino	M.	*Arthur Godfrey's Talent Scouts*
14.	Les Brown	N.	*The Julie Andrews Hour*
15.	Raymond Scott	O.	*The King Family Show*
16.	Mort Lindsey	P.	*The Mike Douglas Show*
17.	Mahlon Merrick	Q.	*The Dick Cavett Show*
18.	Alvino Rey	R.	*The Jackie Gleason Show*
19.	Paul Weston	S.	*Jack Benny Program*
20.	Johnny Mann	T.	*Tonight* (Johnny Carson)

HORSING AROUND

The horses listed on the left were owned by the performers listed on the right. Match the horses with the players and identify the programs.

1.	Midnight	A.	Dan Blocker
2.	Cochise	B.	Clayton Moore
3.	Misty Girl	C.	Rocky Lane
4.	Marshal	D.	Johnny Washburn
5.	Buck	E.	Leo Carillo
6.	Diablo	F.	Chuck Connors
7.	Mr. Ed	G.	James Arness
8.	Thunder	H.	John Payne
9.	Chub	I.	Jay Silverheels
10.	Loco	J.	Lorne Greene
11.	Rafter	K.	Richard Simmons
12.	Silver	L.	Judi Bowker
13.	Razor	M.	Clint Eastwood
14.	Rex	N.	Michael Ansara
15.	Scar	O.	Barry Curtis
16.	Shiek	P.	Richard Boone
17.	Scout	Q.	Alan Young
18.	Flicka	R.	Duncan Renaldo
19.	Black Beauty	S.	Barbara Stanwyck
20.	Champion	T.	Michael Landon

WHEN IRISH EYES ARE SMILING . . .

Listed below on the left are characters from TV programs and on the right
are the stars who have played these roles. Match the performers with their
roles and identify the programs.

1. Susie McNamara	A. Robert Horton
2. Chester A. Riley	B. Pat O'Brien
3. Francis Muldoon	C. Linda Lavin
4. Kate McShane	D. James Brolin
5. First Mate Gilligan	E. Richard Crenna
6. Randy Monaghan	F. Cindy Williams
7. Flint McCullough	G. Ann Sothern
8. James Slattery	H. Art Carney
9. Steve McGarrett	I. Wayne Rogers
10. James Harrigan, Sr.	J. Anne Meara
11. Kitty Russell	K. William Demarest
12. Steven Kiley	L. Ernest Borgnine
13. Alice Hyatt	M. Fred Gwynne
14. John McIntyre	N. Robert Reed
15. Charley O'Casey	O. Loretta Swit
16. Shirley Feeney	P. Nan Leslie
17. Ed Norton	Q. Amanda Blake
18. Quinton McHale	R. William Bendix
19. Mike Brady	S. Jack Lord
20. Margaret Houlihan	T. Bob Denver

Photo 36

THEY'RE PLAYING THEIR SONGS (1)

The songs listed on the left were the themes of the programs listed on the right. Match the songs with the shows.

1. "There's a New Girl in Town"
2. "Love Nest"
3. "Those Were the Days"
4. "Love Is All Around"
5. "Let Me Be Your Friend"

6. "I'm So Glad"
7. "Love In Bloom"
8. "William Tell Overture"
9. "Ta-Ra-Ra-Boom-De-A"
10. "Lucky Day"
11. "Blue Star"
12. "Once in Love with Amy"
13. "I Believe in Music"
14. "Ballad of Paladin"
15. Overture to "The Flying Dutchman"
16. "Making Our Dreams Come True"
17. "Seattle"
18. "I Will Come Back"
19. "Keep Your Eye on the Sparrow"
20. "Thanks for the Memory"

A. The Mary Tyler Moore Show
B. The Jack Benny Show
C. Howdy Doody
D. The Ray Bolger Show
E. Captain Video and His Video Rangers
F. Your Hit Parade
G. Here Come the Brides
H. Have Gun, Will Travel
I. The Judy Garland Show
J. Alice
K. The Bob Hope Show
L. Laverne & Shirley
M. Baretta
N. The Carol Burnett Show
O. The Mac Davis Show

P. All in the Family

Q. Doc
R. Medic
S. The Lone Ranger

T. The George Burns and Gracie Allen Show

Photo 37

89

THEY'RE PLAYING THEIR SONGS (2)

The songs listed on the left were the themes of the programs listed on the right. Match the songs with the shows.

1. "Twelve O'Clock Rock"
2. "Ballad of Jed Clampett"
3. "Everybody Loves Somebody"
4. "Gentle on My Mind"
5. "Funeral March of the Marionettes"
6. "We're Movin' On Up"
7. "Here's Johnny"
8. "Horray for Captain Spaulding"
9. "The Ballad of Johnny Yuma"
10. "I Am Woman"
11. "Melancholy Serenade"
12. "Near You"
13. "I've Got a Lovely Bunch of Coconuts"
14. "It's Not Unusual"
15. "Que Sera Sera"
16. "Suicide Is Painless"
17. "Three Stars (Will Shine Tonight)"
18. "The Beat Goes On"
19. "Bubbles in the Wine"
20. "Danny Boy"

A. *Alfred Hitchcock Presents*
B. *The Tonight Show*
C. *The Rebel*
D. *The Jackie Gleason Show*
E. *The Merv Griffin Show*

F. *M*A*S*H*
G. *This Is Tom Jones*
H. *Happy Days*

I. *The Milton Berle Show*
J. *The Sonny and Cher Comedy Show*
K. *The Doris Day Show*
L. *The Lawrence Welk Show*
M. *The Glen Campbell Goodtime Hour*
N. *Dr. Kildare*
O. *Make Room for Daddy*
P. *The Beverly Hillbillies*
Q. *The Helen Reddy Show*

R. *You Bet Your Life*
S. *The Jeffersons*
T. *The Dean Martin Show*

Photo 38

Photo 39

BEDSIDE MANORS

Listed below on the left are medical facilities featured on the programs listed on the right. Match the programs with the facilities.

1. York Hospital
2. County General Hospital
3. Lowell Memorial Hospital
4. Blair General Hospital
5. Westside Clinic
6. Alden General Hospital
7. New North Hospital
8. L.A. Medical Center
9. L.A. County Medical Assn.
10. L.A. County Coroner's Office
11. David Craig Institute of New Medicine
12. Astrospace Industries Medical Office
13. City General Hospital
14. Valley Hospital
15. Capitol General Hospital
16. Hope Memorial Hospital
17. General Hospital
18. Lake General Hospital
19. City Hospital
20. Adult Emergency Services Hosp.

A. *Doc*
B. *Medic*
C. *Julia*
D. *Rafferty*
E. *The New Doctors*
F. *General Hospital*
G. *Young Dr. Malone*
H. *Julie Farr, M.D.*
I. *City Hospital*
J. *Breaking Point*
K. *Temperatures Rising*
L. *The Interns*
M. *Marcus Welby, M.D.*
N. *Ben Casey*
O. *A.E.S. Hudson Street*
P. *Dr. Kildare*
Q. *Medical Center*
R. *Doctor's Hospital*
S. *Quincy, M.E.*
T. *The Nurses*

READING, 'RITING, 'RITHMETIC

Listed below on the left are schools and colleges featured on the programs listed on the right. Match the schools with the shows.

1. James Buchanan High School
2. Madison High School
3. Walt Whitman High School
4. Jefferson Junior High School
5. Josiah Kessel College
6. Jefferson High, Milwaukee
7. Waverly High School
8. Ivy College
9. Kollege of Musical Knowledge
10. Concord Private High School
11. Bunker Hill High School
12. Foster School for Girls
13. Mrs. Nestor's Private Elementary School
14. Clinton College
15. Harry S. Truman Memorial High School
16. Western State University
17. U.C.L.A.
18. Austin School for the Handicapped
19. Comstock Co-Educational College
20. Carver High School

A. *Mr. Peepers*
B. *The Halls of Ivy*
C. *The Ray Milland Show*
D. *Hank*
E. *Funny Face*
F. *The White Shadow*
G. *Welcome Back, Kotter*
H. *Police Woman*
I. *Lucas Tanner*
J. *Room 222*
K. *The Jimmy Stewart Show*
L. *Our Miss Brooks*
M. *Happy Days*

N. *Kay Kyser's Show*
O. *The Headmaster*

P. *Our Miss Brooks*
Q. *James at 15*
R. *Nanny and the Professor*

S. *The Waverly Wonders*

T. *The John Forsythe Show*

MIXED DOUBLES

The women listed below on the left have been professionally—and personally—associated with the men on the right. Match the couples and identify their TV shows.

1. Paula Prentiss	A.	Hume Cronyn
2. Meredith Baxter	B.	Spike Jones
3. Brett Somers	C.	Sam Jaffe
4. Julie London	D.	Tex McCrary
5. Abbe Lane	E.	Stu Erwin
6. Anne Jeffreys	F.	Alvino Rey
7. Benita Hume	G.	Martin Landau
8. Cynthia Stone	H.	Jim Backus
9. Anne Meara	I.	Richard Benjamin
10. Barbara Bain	J.	Jack Klugman
11. Ida Lupino	K.	David Birney
12. Ursula Thiess	L.	Robert Taylor
13. Jessica Tandy	M.	Howard Duff
14. Bettye Ackerman	N.	Bobby Troup
15. June Collyer	O.	Xavier Cugat
16. Henny Backus	P.	Ronald Colman
17. Luise King	Q.	Robert Sterling
18. Dorothy Collins	R.	Jack Lemmon
19. Jinx Falkenberg	S.	Jerry Stiller
20. Helen Grayco	T.	Raymond Scott

A CHORUS LINE

Listed below on the left are TV variety performers and on the right are films in which they have appeared. Match the stars with the films.

1. Dinah Shore	A.	*The Jazz Singer*
2. Perry Como	B.	*Pete 'n' Tillie*
3. Nanette Fabray	C.	*Babes in Arms*
4. Kate Smith	D.	*Bells Are Ringing*
5. Danny Thomas	E.	*April in Paris*
6. Fred Astaire	F.	*Broadway Melody of 1938*
7. Carol Burnett	G.	*Damsel in Distress*
8. Dick Powell	H.	*Tonight and Every Night*
9. Dean Martin	I.	*Two Girls and a Sailor*
10. Doris Day	J.	*The Band Wagon*
11. Mickey Rooney	K.	*Hello, Frisco, Hello*
12. Betty Garrett	L.	*Mother Wore Tights*
13. Janet Blair	M.	*Aaron Slick from Pumkin' Creek*
14. Buddy Ebsen	N.	*It All Came True*
15. June Allyson	O.	*Neptune's Daughter*
16. June Havoc	P.	*Calamity Jane*
17. Gracie Allen	Q.	*This Is The Army*
18. Dan Dailey	R.	*Dames*
19. Ann Sheridan	S.	*If I'm Lucky*
20. Ray Bolger	T.	*Follow the Fleet*

95 Photo 40

WITH ENEMIES LIKE THESE . . .

Listed below on the left are villains and villainesses who appeared on *Batman* and on the right are the actors and actresses who portrayed these roles. Match the stars with their roles.

1. The Penguin	A. Frank Gorshin
2. Lola Lasagne	B. Barbara Nichols
3. The Joker	C. Vincent Price
4. Dawn Robbins	D. Glynnis Johns
5. The Catwoman	E. Maurice Evans
6. The Riddler	F. Joan Crawford
7. The Archer	G. Ida Lupino
8. Maid Marilyn	H. Milton Berle
9. Lady Penelope Peasoup	I. Michael Rennie
10. Lord Marmaduke Flogg	J. Zsa Zsa Gabor
11. The Black Widow	K. Cesar Romero
12. Egghead	L. Shelley Winters
13. Dr. Cassandra	M. Burgess Meredith
14. The Sandman	N. Van Johnson
15. The Puzzler	O. Tallulah Bankhead
16. Ma Parker	P. Leslie Parrish
17. The Devil	Q. Art Carney
18. The Minstrel	R. Rudy Vallee
19. Minerva	S. Ethel Merman
20. Louie the Lilac	T. Eartha Kitt

97   Photo 41

SMALL FRY (1)

Listed below on the left are TV child actors and on the right are the programs on which they appeared. Match the stars with the programs.

1.	Tommy Rettig	A.	The Andy Griffith Show
2.	Johnny Washbrook	B.	Family Affair
3.	Philip McKeon	C.	Make Room for Daddy
4.	Brian Morris	D.	Mickey
5.	Lindsay Greenbush	E.	Father Knows Best
6.	Kami Colter	F.	The Mary Tyler Moore Show
7.	Jerry Mathers	G.	What's Happening
8.	Ron Howard	H.	The Adventures of Ozzie and Harriet
9.	Lauren Chapin	I.	Mama
10.	Richard Keith	J.	The Waltons
11.	Kathy Garver	K.	The Dick Van Dyke Show
12.	Sherry Jackson	L.	Lassie
13.	Danielle Spencer	M.	Little House on the Prairie
14.	Tim Rooney	N.	The Adventures of Rin Tin Tin
15.	Cuffy Crabbe	O.	Maude
16.	Dick Van Patten	P.	Capt. Gallant of the Foreign Legion
17.	Lee Aaker	Q.	I Love Lucy
18.	Lisa Gerritsen	R.	My Friend Flicka
19.	Ricky Nelson	S.	Leave It to Beaver
20.	Larry Matthews	T.	Alice

99   Photo 42

SMALL FRY (2)

Listed below on the left are TV child actors and on the right are the programs on which they appeared. Match the stars with the programs.

1. Burt Ward	A. *The Paul Lynde Show*
2. Brandon DeWilde	B. *National Velvet*
3. Anna Capri	C. *Maya*
4. Johnny Crawford	D. *The Monroes*
5. Lydia Reed	E. *The Partridge Family*
6. Kim Richards	F. *Love That Bob*
7. Anthony Perez	G. *My Mother, The Car*
8. Pamelyn Ferdin	H. *Mannix*
9. Suzanne Crough	I. *Family*
10. Joey Scott	J. *Bachelor Father*
11. Tim Considine	K. *The Real McCoys*
12. Cindy Eilbacher	L. *Family Affair*
13. Richard Eyer	M. *The Rifleman*
14. Tammy Locke	N. *Jamie*
15. Jay North	O. *My Friend Flicka*
16. Noreen Corcoran	P. *Room for One More*
17. Johnny Whitaker	Q. *Poppi*
18. Kristy McNichol	R. *Batman*
19. Mark Stewart	S. *My Three Sons*
20. Dwayne Hickman	T. *Nanny and the Professor*

Photo 43

FRONT MONEY

The sponsors listed on the left produced the programs listed on the right. Match the sponsors with the shows.

1.	Philip Morris	A.	*Dragnet*
2.	Jell-O	B.	*Your Hit Parade*
3.	Fatima Cigarettes	C.	*The Life of Riley*
4.	Chesterfield	D.	*Death Valley Days*
5.	Lipton Tea	E.	*Studio One*
6.	Lucky Strike	F.	*The Ed Wynn Show*
7.	Twenty-Mule Team Borax	G.	*Cavalcade of Sports*
8.	DeSoto/Plymouth	H.	*The Children's Hour*
9.	Pabst Blue Ribbon	I.	*I Love Lucy*
10.	Gillette	J.	*Lassie*
11.	Carnation Milk	K.	*Wild Bill Hickock*
12.	Old Gold and Westinghouse	L.	*Bob Hope*
13.	Texaco	M.	*The Jack Benny Show*
14.	Camel	N.	*Original Amateur Hour*
15.	Sylvania	O.	*The George Burns and Gracie Allen Show*
		P.	*The Perry Como Show*
16.	Kellogg's Sugar Pops	Q.	*Beat the Clock*
17.	Campbell's Soup	R.	*The Milton Berle Show*
18.	Kraft	S.	*You Bet Your Life*
19.	Geritol	T.	*Arthur Godfrey's Talent Scouts*
20.	Chrysler		

SOBRIQUETS

Listed below on the left are nicknames for the characters on the right. Match them and identify the performers and the series.

1. Hondo	A. Sylvester Brockway
2. Gidget	B. Benjamin F. Pierce
3. Professor	C. Theodore Cleaver
4. Bud	D. Toni Danton
5. Grizzly	E. Dennis
6. Hawkeye	F. Dan Harrelson
7. Buddy	G. Betty Anderson
8. J. R.	H. Francine Lawrence
9. Dummy	I. Lamont Sanford
10. Beaver	J. James Anderson, Jr.
11. Dumpling	K. Letitia Lawrence
12. Princess	L. John Ewing
13. Animal	M. Kathy Anderson
14. Skipper	N. Peg Riley
15. Porky	O. Michael Stivic
16. Trapper	P. John McIntyre
17. Feather	Q. Burl Smith
18. Kitten	R. Jonas Grumby
19. Gopher	S. Harold Everett
20. Meathead	T. James Adams

SPORTIN' LIFE

The actors listed below on the left were connected to the world of sports on TV series. Match the performers with the occupations listed on the right and identify the shows.

1. Ken Howard	A. New York Sports Columnist
2. Joe Namath	B. Coach of Young Baseball Players
3. Bill Cosby	C. Retired Baseball Player/Sportswriter
4. Don Chastain	D. Racing Car Driver
5. Jim Bouton	E. Bicyclist
6. Eddie Mayehoff	F. Skydiver
7. Paul Gilbert	G. Retired Football Player
8. Robert Culp	H. Boxer/Painter
9. Shaun Cassidy	I. Los Angeles Sports Columnist
10. Brian Kelly	J. Rodeo Performer
11. Ken Curtis	K. Baseball Pitcher
12. Sheldon Leonard	L. Boxer/Cabdriver
13. Jack Lord	M. Tennis Pro
14. Christopher George	N. Sports Arena Owner
15. David Hartman	O. High School Basketball Coach
16. Jack Warden	P. Tennis Pro/Spy
17. Jack Klugman	Q. Racing Car Designer
18. Tony Danza	R. High School History Teacher/Coach
19. Ron Ely	S. Deepsea Diver
20. Robert Urich	T. Trainer/Spy

Photo 44

LATHER UP (1)

Listed below on the left are actresses who have appeared in soap operas and on the right are the characters they played. Match the stars with their roles and identify the series.

1. Susan Seaforth Hayes
2. Constance Ford
3. Elizabeth Hubbard
4. Trish Van Devere
5. Irene Dailey
6. Victoria Wyndham
7. Bibi Besch
8. Rosemary Prinz
9. Gloria DeHaven
10. Mary Fickett
11. Zina Bethune
12. Anne Jeffreys
13. Julie Adams
14. Mary Stuart
15. Beverlee McKinsey
16. Ann Flood
17. Joan Bennett
18. Haila Stoddard
19. Jill Clayburgh
20. Bethel Leslie

A. Rachel Corey
B. Eve Lawrence
C. Sara Fuller
D. Maureen Mooney
E. Nancy Carr
F. Denise Wilson
G. Grace Boulton
H. Joanne Tate
 I. Elizabeth Collins Stoddard
 J. Julie Williams
K. Iris Carrington Wheeler
L. Dr. Maggie Fielding
M. Dr. Katherine Lovell
N. Dr. Althea Davis
O. Pauline Rysdale
P. Pamela Stuart
Q. Gail Lucas
R. Meredith Lord Wolek
S. Penny Hughes Baker
T. Ada McGowan Hobson

Photo 45

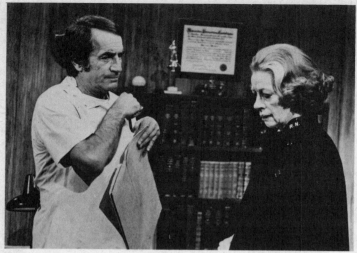

Photo 46

LATHER UP (2)

Listed below on the left are actors who have appeared in soap operas and on the right are the characters they played. Match the stars with their roles and identify the shows.

1. Bill Hayes	A. Dr. Matt Powers
2. Shepperd Strudwick	B. Ed Gibson
3. John Beal	C. Henry Barbour
4. David Birney	D. Dr. Tom Horton
5. Laurence Luckinbill	E. Luke Spencer
6. Douglass Watson	F. Gil McGowan
7. Bert Lytell	G. Dr. Tony Vincente
8. Robert Alda	H. Dr. Steve Hardy
9. Macdonald Carey	I. Dr. Jim Frazier
10. James Pritchett	J. Jim Matthews
11. Larry Hagman	K. Doug Williams
12. Nicholas Coster	L. Mackenzie Corey
13. Ted Shackleford	M. Dr. Pat Ryan
14. Dolph Sweet	N. Victor Lord
15. Anthony Geary	O. Dr. Lewis
16. Anthony George	P. Stuart Whyland
17. John Beradino	Q. Mark Elliott
18. Hugh Marlowe	R. Frank Carver
19. James Earl Jones	S. Roy Gordon
20. Malcolm Groome	T. Robert Delaney

HOME SWEET HOME

Listed below are soap opera settings with some of the characters in the shows. Identify the programs.

1. Northcross, Connecticut—the Hathaway family and friends.
2. Alden General Hospital—Liz Thorpe, Gail Lucas, and friends.
3. Springfield—the Bauer family and friends.
4. Salem—Dr. Tom Horton's family and friends.
5. Bay City—the families and friends of the Corey's, the Randolph's, and the Matthews'.
6. Pine Valley—the Tyler family and friends.
7. Hope Memorial Hospital—Dr. Althea Davis, fellow staff members, families, and friends.
8. Philadelphia—the Wolek and the Lord families and friends.
9. Henderson—Joanne Baron/Tate/Vincente families and friends.
10. Sea Cliff section of Bay City—Henry Barbour's family and friends.
11. Collinsport, Maine—Victoria Winters, the Collins family, and friends.
12. Genoa City—the Brooks and Foster families and friends.
13. Valley Hospital—the Malone family and friends.
14. Monticello—Mike Carr, Sarah Lane, Nancy Pollock et al.
15. Woodridge—the Ames family and friends.
16. Barrowsville and Rosehill—Vanessa Dale/Sterling and Meg Dale/Harper families and friends.
17. Oakdale, U.S.A.—the Hughes and the Lowell families and friends.
18. Upper West Side, NYC—the Ryan family and friends.
19. Fictitious New England town—Constance MacKenzie, the Harringtons, et al.
20. San Francisco—the Chernaks, the Donnellys, and the Garrisons, et al.

DON'T I KNOW YOU?

Listed below are groups of stars who have appeared in the same soap operas over the years (often at the start of their careers). Identify the shows.

1. John Beal, Hugh Marlowe, Irene Dailey, William Prince, Micki Grant, Ann Sheridan, Billy Dee Williams, Charles Durning.

2. Susan Flannery, John Lupton, K. T. Stevens, Peter Brown, Susan Seaforth Hayes, Kaye Stevens, Robert Clary, Mike Farrell.
3. Trish Van Devere, Al Freeman, Jr., Lillian Hayman, Shepperd Strudwick, Farley Granger, Peggy Wood.
4. Lola Albright, Mia Farrow, Ryan O'Neal, Barbara Parkins, Kent Smith, John Kerr, Ruth Warrick, Lana Wood, Ruby Dee, Lee Grant.
5. Diane Ladd, Alexander Scourby, Jane Rose, Troy Donahue, Diana Muldaur, Roy Scheider, Robert Loggia, Robert Alda.
6. Trish Van Devere, Hal Linden, Jill Clayburgh, Sandy Duncan, Don Knotts, Tom Ewell, Conrad Bain, Lee Grant, George Maharis, Andrea McArdle.
7. Gloria DeHaven, Don Scardino, Nancy Wickwire, Patty McCormick, James Earl Jones, Mark Rydell, Ruth Warrick, William Redfield.
8. Bethel Leslie, Louise Lasser, Elizabeth Hubbard, Madeleine Sherwood, John Cullum, Jean Sullivan, Ruth McDevitt, Joanna Pettit.
9. Bert Lytell, Theodore Von Eltz, Marjorie Gateson, Eva Marie Saint, Tony Randall.
10. Larry Hagman, Lynn Redgrave, Valerie French, Mary Fickett, Irene Dailey, Tony Roberts, Betty Garde, Ruby Dee, Jan Miner, Audra Lindley, Eva Marie Saint, Scott McKay.
11. Ann Burr, Jack Klugman, Anne Meara, Martin Balsam, Marvin Stephens.
12. William Prince, Barbara O'Neil, Joan Hackett, Robert Lansing, Joyce Van Patten, William Post, Dick Van Patten, Scott McKay.
13. Tom Hallick, Robert Clary, Deidre Hall, Jeanne Cooper, K. T. Stevens.
14. Joan Bennett, Grayson Hall, Anthony George, Kate Jackson, Donna McKechnie.
15. David Birney, Donna Mills, Bibi Besch, Diana Douglas, Constance Towers, Salome Jens.
16. Diana Canova, Jimmy Baio, Billy Crystal, Ted Wass, Robert Guillaume, Robert Urich.
17. Barbara Bel Geddes, Larry Hagman, David Wayne, Victoria Principal, Tina Louise, Mary Crosby.
18. Christopher Reeves, Hildy Parks, Geraldine Brooks, Zina Bethune, Robert Alda, Jessica Walter, Carl Betz, Jan Miner.
19. John Beradino, Tom Brown, Peter Hansen, K. T. Stevens, Roy Thinnes, Julie Adams, Virginia Grey, Brett Halsey, Mae Clarke, Victoria Shaw.
20. Victoria Wyndham, Barnard Hughes, James Earl Jones, Cicely Tyson, Ruby Dee, Elizabeth Hubbard, Sandy Dennis, Joseph Campanella, Diana Hyland.

IFS, ANDS, AND MUTTS (1)

Listed below on the left are TV pooches and on the right are the shows in which they appeared. Match the dogs with the programs.

1. Jack		A.	Adventures of Rin Tin Tin
2. Pete		B.	The Roy Rogers Show
3. Asta		C.	Petticoat Junction
4. Astro		D.	Border Collie
5. Daisy		E.	Shari Lewis Show
6. Rinty		F.	Pistols 'n' Petticoats
7. Snoopy		G.	Nanny and the Professor
8. Boy		H.	Topper
9. Tramp		I.	Please Don't Eat the Daisies
10. Bullet		J.	The Jetsons
11. Hush-Puppy		K.	The Partridge Family
12. Ladadog		L.	Little House on the Prairie
13. Scamp		M.	Popeye the Sailor
14. Simon		N.	No Time for Sergeants
15. Neil		O.	Yogi's Gang
16. Blue		P.	Blondie
17. Waldo		Q.	Room for One More
18. Pluto		R.	The Little Rascals
19. Bowzer		S.	Peanuts
20. Doggi Daddy		T.	The Thin Man

IFS, ANDS, AND MUTTS (2)

Listed below on the left are TV pooches and on the right are the shows in which they appeared. Match the dogs with the programs.

1. Cleo
2. Sweet Polly Purebred
3. Tramp
4. King
5. Barney
6. Sam
7. Irving
8. Tiger
9. Fugi
10. Jasper
11. Slump
12. Rebel
13. Hot Dog
14. Laddie
15. Pokey

16. Bridget
17. Tyrone
18. Happy and Walter
19. Beagle
20. Reckless

A. *My World and Welcome to It*
B. *Bachelor Father*
C. *The Adventures of Champion*
D. *The Brady Bunch*
E. *The Secret Lives of Waldo Kitty*
F. *Make Room for Daddy*
G. *The Waltons*
H. *The Archie Show*
I. *The Jack LaLanne Show*
J. *Lassie*
K. *Lucas Tanner*
L. *Lou Grant*
M. *My Three Sons*
N. *Hondo*
O. *The Tom & Jerry/Grape Ape Show*
P. *The People's Choice*
Q. *Nicohols*
R. *The Osmonds*
S. *Sergeant Preston of the Yukon*
T. *Underdog*

Photo 47

SCHIZOPHRENIA

Listed below on the left are the "professional" identities of the characters on the right. Match the names of the characters and identify the performers and the shows.

1. Bionic Woman	A. John Reid
2. Six Million Dollar Man	B. Britt Reid
3. The Incredible Hulk	C. Diana Prince
4. Spider-Man	D. Steve Austin
5. Superman	E. Simon Templar
6. Robin	F. Jaime Sommers
7. Batman	G. Oscar North
8. Wonder Woman	H. Mark Harris
9. Zorro	I. April Dancer
10. The Invisible Man (1975–76)	J. Peter Parker
11. Wonder Girl	K. Dick Grayson
12. Bat Girl	L. Drusilla Prince
13. Mr. Terrific	M. David Bruce Banner
14. Captain Nice	N. Clark Kent
15. The Lone Ranger	O. Barbara Gordon
16. The Green Hornet	P. Don Diego De La Vega
17. Man from Atlantis	Q. Dr. Daniel Westin
18. Girl from U.N.C.L.E.	R. Bruce Wayne
19. Jetman	S. Stanley Beamish
20. The Saint	T. Carter Nash

Photo 48

VOX POPULI

Listed below on the left are characters with familiar voices. Match the characters with performers on the right who provided the voices and identify the shows.

1. Oky Doky
2. Alvin
3. Bugs Bunny
4. Snidley Whiplash
5. The Colonel
6. Charlie Townsend
7. John Bracken
8. Cleo
9. Mabel King
10. Top Cat
11. Underdog
12. Carlton, the Doorman
13. John Beresford Tipton
14. "Sam"
15. Jane Jetson

16. Claude Pertwee
17. Betty Rubble
18. The Invisible Man (1958–1960)
19. Narrator of "Fractured Fairy Tales"
20. Mrs. Crabtree

A. Penny Singleton
B. Lorenzo Music
C. John Forsythe
D. Mary Jane Croft
E. Paul Lynde
F. Arnold Stang
G. Mary Tyler Moore
H. Dayton Allen
I. Mel Blanc
J. Bea Benadaret
K. Paul Frees
L. Warren Stevens
M. Anonymous
N. Hans Conreid
O. David Seville
   (Ross Bagdasarian)
P. Grace Carney
Q. Freeman Gosden
R. Ann Sothern
S. Tony Bennett

T. Edward Everett Horton

VERBATIM (1)

Listed below are well known phrases used on various TV programs. Identify the performers who spoke these lines and the shows on which they were heard.

1. One of these days, Alice . . .
2. Ooh, ooh, ooh!
3. Kiss mah grits!
4. What a revoltin' development this is . . .
5. 'Round and 'round it goes . . .
6. Ah love the waaaahd open spaces.
7. And now for something completely different . . .
8. A-one-a, a-two-a, a-three-a . . .
9. Right here on our stage . . .
10. Goodnight, Mrs. Calabash, wherever you are.
11. . . . And the ever popular Mae Busch . . .
12. Strange things are happening.
13. That's right, you're wrong.
14. Na nu, na nu . . .
15. New York, this is your last chance!
16. Oscar, Oscar, Oscar!
17. See the U.S.A. in your Chevrolet . . .
18. Did I ever tell you about my uncle?
19. Sorry about that, Chief.
20. Don't call me Chief.

Photo 49

VERBATIM (2)

Listed below are well known phrases used on various TV programs. Identify the performers who spoke these lines and the shows on which they were heard.

1. Just the facts, ma'am.
2. Well, I'll be a dirty bird!
3. And away we go!
4. And may the good Lord take a liking to you.
5. Will the mystery guest sign in, please?
6. And he—eer—ree's Johnny!
7. Did you hear that, Elizabeth?
8. God will get you for that!
9. This is Carlton, your doorman.
10. Dy—no—mite!
11. Sit on it!
12. Stifle yourself, Edith.
13. I've got a problem, believe me. I've got a problem.
14. And that's the way it is.
15. Not my job, man.
16. We—ll, gol—ly gee!
17. To put a little fun in your life, try dancing.
18. It just goes to show you, it's always something.
19. Yoo hoo, Mrs. Bloom!
20. You rang?

MOUTHPIECES

The stars listed on the left have appeared in commercials for the products listed on the right. Match up stars with the products.

1. Laurence Olivier
2. Robert Young
3. Vivian Vance
4. James Stewart
5. Lorne Greene
6. Ricardo Montalban
7. Orson Welles

A. Alpo
B. Canada Dry
C. Maxwell House
D. Crest
E. Gallo Wine
F. British Airways
G. Good Seasons Salad Dressings

8.	Louis Jourdan	H.	Wesson Oil
9.	Ann Miller	I.	Scott Towels
10.	Margaret Hamilton	J.	Comet
11.	Jan Miner	K.	Purina
12.	Robert Morley	L.	Bounty Towels
13.	Florence Henderson	M.	Maxwell House Instant Coffee
14.	Arthur O'Connell	N.	Paul Masson Wine
15.	Jane Withers	O.	Palmolive Liquid
16.	Barbara Bel Geddes	P.	Polaroid
17.	Peggy Cass	Q.	Campbell Soups
18.	Peter Ustinov	R.	Silhouette Books
19.	Mae Questel	S.	Sanka
20.	Nancy Walker	T.	Firestone Tires

THE PEN IS MIGHTIER . . .

Listed below on the left are authors whose works have been seen on TV. Listed on the right are the names of stars who have appeared in these works. Match the authors with the stars and identify the programs.

1.	Irwin Shaw	A.	Judith Anderson
2.	Grace Metalious	B.	Claudette Colbert
3.	Charles Schultz	C.	Robert Wagner
4.	James Clavell	D.	Ron Ely
5.	Henry James	E.	Mary Martin
6.	William Shakespeare	F.	Edmond O'Brien
7.	Noel Coward	G.	Pamela Sue Martin
8.	Mary Roberts Rinehardt	H.	John Amos
9.	James Barrie	I.	Peter Strauss
10.	Tennessee Williams	J.	Jackie Gleason
11.	James Jones	K.	Kirk Douglas
12.	Carolyn Keene	L.	Frank Sinatra
13.	Edgar Rice Burroughs	M.	Richard Chamberlain
14.	William Faulkner	N.	Susan Hampshire
15.	Robert Louis Stevenson	O.	Dorothy Malone
16.	William Thackery	P.	William Devane
17.	Arthur Hailey	Q.	Ingrid Bergman
18.	William Saroyan	R.	Robert Newton
19.	Thorton Wilder	S.	Pettermint Patty
20.	Alex Haley	T.	Helen Hayes

TO BE CONTINUED . . .

The term, soap operas, stems from the fact that in the early days of radio, most of the continuing dramas were sponsored by makers of soap or soap by-products. The appellation caught hold and is still with us today.

The first successful TV soap opera that caught the public's fancy was *One Man's Family*, which debuted on November 4, 1949. Bert Lytell and Marjorie Gateson were the original TV parents on the show which ran until April 1, 1955.

The second oldest soap is *Search for Tomorrow*, which debuted on September 3, 1951. Its original heroine, played by Mary Stuart, has, to date, had three husbands. The show is still running—maybe until Mary runs out of husbands.

A few days after *Search for Tomorrow* aired, the third oldest soap debuted—*Love of Life*—September 9, 1951. The show is still running.

On April 2, 1956 two other popular soaps originated, which are still running today. They are *As the World Turns* and *The Edge of Night*.

So many familiar stars have appeared in soaps over the years, either as a stepping stone up the ladder or as a "safe harbor" after an initial successful career. These include:

One Man's Family: Eva Marie Saint, Tony Randall.

Search for Tomorrow: Trish Van Devere, Jill Clayburgh, Virginia Gilmore, Jeanne Carson, Sandy Duncan, Don Knotts, Robert Mandan, Anthony George, Conrad Bain, Lee Grant, Nita Talbot, Roy Scheider, Barbara Baxley, Hal Linden, Anne Revere, George Maharis, Robert Rockwell, Andrea McArdle, Brett Halsey, Ross Martin, Margaret Hamilton, Audry Lindley.

Love of Life: Christopher Reeve, Hildy Parks, Marsha Mason, Zina Bethune, Geraldine Brooks, Jane Rose, Paul Michael Glaser, Tony Lo Bianco, Robert Alda, Nancy Marchand, Beatrice Straight, Jessica Walter, Carl Betz, Jan Miner.

As the World Turns: Gloria De Haven, James Earl Jones, Mark Rydell, Ruth Warrick, Patricia Benoit, Patty McCormick.

The Edge of Night: Larry Hagman, Lynn Redgrave, Mary Fickett, Irene Dailey, Tony Roberts, Barry Newman, Scott McKay, Ruby Dee, Jan Miner, Audra Lindley, Eva Marie Saint.

Another World: Wesley Addy, John Beal, Shepperd Strudwick, Hugh Marlowe, Irene Dailey, William Prince, Ann Sheridan, Billy Dee Williams, Nancy Marchand, Constance Ford, Charles Durning.

All My Children: Ruth Warrick, Mary Fickett, Frances Heflin, Richard Hatch, Eileen Herlie, Rosemary Murphy.

Dark Shadows: Joan Bennett, Anthony George, Kate Jackson, Donna McKechnie.

Days of Our Lives: Macdonald Carey, Susan Flannery, Susan Oliver, Rosemary Forsyth, John Lupton, K. T. Stevens, Peter Brown, Bill Hayes, Susan Seaforth, Colleen Gray, Robert Clary, Deidre Hall.

The Doctors: Bethel Leslie, Louise Lasser, Madeleine Sherwood, John Cullum, Jean Sullivan, Ruth McDevitt, Joanna Pettet.

General Hospital: John Bernadino, Tom Brown, Peter Hansen, K. T. Stevens, Patricia Breslin, Julie Adams, Mae Clark, Virginia Grey, Victoria Shaw, Brett Halsey.

The Guiding Light: Judy Lewis (Loretta Young's daughter), Victoria Wyndham, Madeleine Sherwood, Barnard Hughes, James Earl Jones, Cicely Tyson, Ruby Dee, Zina Bethune, Anne Jeffreys, Sandy Dennis, Joseph Campanella, Diana Hyland.

One Life to Live: Trish Van Devere, Lee Patterson, Shepperd Strudwick, Al Freeman, Jr., Lillian Hayman, Farley Granger, Peggy Wood.

Peyton Place: Dorothy Malone, Lola Albright, Mia Farrow, Ryan O'Neal, Warner Anderson, Barbara Parkins, Kent Smith, John Kerr, George Macready, Ruth Warrick, Lana Wood, Diana Hyland, Barbara Rush, Ruby Dee, Erin O'Brien-Moore, Lee Grant, Gena Rowlands, Dan Duryea, Heather Angel, Joan Blackman, Leigh Taylor-Young.

Ryan's Hope: Helen Gallagher, Frank Latimore.

The Secret Storm: Warren Berlinger, Haila Stoddard, Russell Hicks, Diane Ladd, Alexander Scourby, Jane Rose, Troy Donahue, Don Galloway, Diana Muldaur, Roy Scheider, Rosemary Murphy, Robert Loggia, Laurence Luckinbill, Robert Alda.

Where the Heart Is: James Mitchell, Bibi Osterwald, Tracy Brooks Swope, Rue McClanahan, Barbara Baxley, Zohra Lampert, Laurence Luckinbill.

Young Doctor Malone: William Prince, Barbara O'Neil, Robert Lansing, Joan Hackett, Zina Bethune, Ruth McDevett, Dick Van Patten, Scott McKay.

Photo 50

Photo 51

119   Photo 52

Photo 53

Photo 54

Photo 55

121

Photo 56

Photo 57

122

Photo 58

123

Photo 59   **124**

the
YOUNG
and the
RESTLESS

125 Photo 60

SCANDALS IN VIDEOLAND

In 1955, the *$64,000 Question* first aired, with Hal March as emcee. In record-breaking time, it became a top show. A year later, CBS launched its spin-off, the *$64,000 Challenge* and within months, the two shows were number one and number two in the ratings. That same fall, NBC brought forth a comparable quiz show, *Twenty-One*, with Jack Barry as emcee. Charles Van Doren, of the literary family, was one of the big winners on *Twenty-One* defeating Herbert Stempel. Stempel claimed he was told to lose to Van Doren and tried to peddle his story of foul play to the newspapers but it was squashed. In 1958, NCB inaugurated another quiz show called *Dotto*, with Jack Narz as emcee. A standby contestant, Edward Hilgemeier, contacted the *New York Post* with the story that the show was rigged. The *Post* called in the FCC and the district attorney's office. *Dotto* was promptly canceled and the *New York Journal-American* finally printed Herbert Stempel's story regarding Van Doren and the *Twenty-One* show. D.A. Frank Hogan ordered a grand jury to hear the cases. Congress probed show-rigging and "payola" and in 1959 legislature was passed making it a felony. The powers-that-be behind the shows were summarily fired and everyone connected went down in disgrace. It took years before Hal March, Jack Barry, and Jack Narz were employable. The only one to emerge unscathed was Dr. Joyce Brothers, an early winner before the rigging began.

Senator Joseph McCarthy was in the midst of his Red "witch-hunting" in the early 1950s and it had long been rumored that Lucille Ball, then at the height of her *I Love Lucy* fame, had been affiliated with the Communist Party. Finally, in the fall of 1953, it was revealed that she had registered to vote on the Communist ticket in 1936. Lucy and Desi Arnaz had known for a year and a half that she had been under investigation. On September 4, 1953, Lucy, her mother, and brother Fred all testified before committee investigator William Wheeler. They all corroborated the fact that the entire family had registered to vote the Communist ticket to please their grandfather, who had been a socialist since the days of Eugene V. Debs. "Anything to keep him happy," was their story. Lucy, who was 24 in 1936, claimed she couldn't recall if she had voted that year but if she had, it would have been for Franklin D. Roosevelt, whom she had always admired. When it was pointed out that she had twice, in 1947, appeared on broadcasts sponsored by the Committee of the First Amendment, she claimed that she had been sent by the studio as a last-minute replacement and, since the studio had sent her, she felt it was okay. Because of the sensationalism surrounding TV's top star, the House Committee on Un-American Activities, through Representative Donald L. Jackson of California, released a full transcription of Lucy's testimony. That night, Desi introduced Lucy to the studio audience (a packed house) by saying, "Here's my favorite redhead, and that's the only thing red about Lucy and even that is not legitimate." Washington was satisfied, the public was satisfied, and so was the press, with the exception of right-wing columnist Westbrook Pegler, who continued to villify the "kind" treatment accorded her. Later that fall, the B'nai B'rith named her "Woman of the Year" for her "untiring efforts for charitable causes."

JUST FOLLOW THE SIMPLE DIRECTIONS . . .

With the birth of TV came a number of "how-to" shows that were experimental and short-lived. Only those avid viewers with remarkable memories will recall these "flashes in the pan":

Practice Tee
Photographic Horizons
Let's Rhumba
Hollywood Backstage—makeup tips from Ern Westmore
R.F.D. America—help caring for animals and plants
Science Circus
The Wifesaver—household hints

Some others had a bit more staying power:

You Are an Artist (1946–50)—Jon Gnagy instructed the viewers in the fundamentals of drawing.
And Everything Nice (1949–50)—Maxine Barrat was the hostess for this program which provided fashion advice for the viewers.
Dr. Fix-Um (1949–50)—Arthur Youngquist provided his viewers with helpful household hints.
Arthur Godfrey and His Ukulele (1950)—for three months Arthur Godfrey gave ukulele lessons on the air twice a week.
The Better Home Show (1951–52)—Norman Brokenshire shared his tips for making home improvements.

Cooking shows have been a popular TV staple. In 1946–47 James Beard had a show called *I Love to Eat*. This was followed by Alma Kitchells' *In the Kelvinator Kitchen* (1947–48). Chef Dione Lucas taught cooking on the air in 1948–49 in a program entitled *To the Queen's Taste*.

We've had the Video Chef (Jean Holt), the Mystery Chef (John McPherson), the Galloping Gourmet (Graham Kerr), and of course, the very popular, often parodied, French Chef (Julia Child).

Talk/variety shows like Dinah Shore's and Mike Douglas' have featured cooking segments and from 1973 to 1977 our Saturday night woman in an

127

apron was Sue Ann Nivens. Betty White portrayed Sue Ann on the *Mary Tyler Moore Show*. Known as the "Happy Homemaker," Ms. Nivens had a cooking/homemaking program on the fictional WJM. The frilly, somewhat promiscuous Ms. Nivens was played for laughs,—spoofing cooking programs. Beneath Sue Ann's overly domesticated facade was a lusty lady who was forever pursuing Ed Asner's character, Lou Grant.

After the viewers prepared and ate the dishes served up by the on-the-air cooking teachers, it was time to take it off by getting up off the couch and exercising with Jack LaLanne or the currently popular, Richard Simmons. Or for those into more spiritual exercises, there has been yoga with Lilias or Richard Hittleman. Educational and cable stations always have their share of instructional programs featuring shows dealing with growing vegetables to repairing automobiles.

WOULD YOU BELIEVE . . .?

Modern-day mother, daughter, and granddaughter witches whose "powers" create lighthearted havoc for those around them . . .
> *Bewitched* and *Tabitha*

A staid banker's home inhabited by the ghosts of its dead occupants who materialize only for his eyes . . .
> *Topper*

The ghost of a nineteenth-century sea captain who shares his home with a lovely twentieth-century widow and her children . . .
> *The Ghost and Mrs. Muir*

A show business agent who, along with her husband, provides a home for three chimpanzees whose antics provide confusion and humor . . .
> *The Hathaways*

A crime fighting team made up of a bumbling cop and a robot . . .
> *Holmes and Yoyo*

A gorgeous woman robot . . .
> *My Living Doll*

A philosophizing dog . . .
> *The People's Choice*

A talking horse . . .
> *Mr. Ed*

An infant who thought aloud . . .
> *Happy*

128

A beautiful genie who used her "powers" to get her astronaut "master" into and out of a variety of jams . . .

I Dream of Jeannie

A visitor from another planet finding a home on Earth with a newspaper reporter . . .

My Favorite Martian

A visitor from another planet finding a home on Earth with a TV reporter . . .

Mork and Mindy

The comedic adventures of a bizarre, ghoulish family . . .

The Addams Family

The comedic adventures of a bizarre, ghoulish family . . .

The Munsters

Space Age astronauts in the Stone Age returning to contemporary Los Angeles with a family of prehistoric cave people in tow . . .

It's About Time

A cleric who flew through the air like a human pelican . . .

The Flying Nun

ONLY THE NAMES HAVE BEEN CHANGED . . .

When *Having Babies,* a group of TV movies, was converted into a series for possible regular scheduling, its title became *Julie Farr, M.D.* Many shows have acquired new titles with sponsor changes, format changes, or introduction into syndication. Here's a sampling of TV programs that have been known by more than one name. There are many others; this partial list will probably get you digging into the recesses of your memory to come up with others.

You Bet Your Life/The Best of Groucho/The Groucho Show
Inside Photoplay/Photoplay Time/The Wendy Barrie Show
Disneyland/Walt Disney Presents/Walt Disney's Wonderful World of Color/The Wonderful World of Disney
Strictly for Laughs/The Kirby Stone Quintet
Variety/NBC Playhouse/The Players
To the Queen's Taste/The Dione Lucas Show
The Vise/Uncovered
The Tonight Show/Tonight/Tonight! America After Dark/The Jack Paar Show/The Tonight Show Starring Johnny Carson

Photo 61

Bon Voyage/Treasure Quest
Tony Orlando and Dawn/The Tony Orlando and Dawn Rainbow Hour
Bob Hope Presents the Chrysler Theatre/Universal Star Time
The Sheriff of Cochise/U.S. Marshal
This is Broadway/This is Show Business
Tex and Jinx/At Home with Tex and Jinx/The Tex and Jinx Film/Preview
    with Tex and Jinx
Cross Question/They Stand Accused
Take it from Me/Talent Jackpot
Stump the Stars/Pantomime Quiz
Sugar Hill Times/Uptown Jubilee/Harlem Jubilee
Life with the Erwins/The Trouble with Father/The Stu Erwin Show/The
    New Stu Erwin Show
You'll Never Get Rich/The Phil Silvers Show
The Gale Storm Show/Oh, Susanna
Harbormaster/Adventures at Scott Island
The Art Baker Show/You Asked for It
Dragnet/Badge 714
It Could Be You/This Could Be You/The Bill Gwinn Show/This is My
    Song

The Bob Cummings Show/Love That Bob
Bonanza/Ponderosa
The Little People/The Brian Keith Show
Burke's Law/Amos Burke—Secret Agent
Richard Diamond, Private Detective/Call Mr. D
Make Room for Daddy/The Danny Thomas Show
Alcoa Presents/One Step Beyond
The Andy Griffith Show/Andy of Mayberry
The Aquanauts/Malibu Run
The Arrow Show/The Phil Silvers Arrow Show/Arrow Comedy Theatre

. . . AND YOU WERE THERE!

A popular series of the 1950s was the innovative, *You Are There*, narrated and hosted by Walter Cronkite. The show was composed of dramatic simulations of historical events. The series was launched in 1953 and ran for four years. Typical episodes included: "The Assassination of Julius Caesar"; "The Mystery of Amelia Earhart"; "Ordeal of a President" (Woodrow Wilson); "Paul Revere's Ride"; "The Siege of the Alamo"; "The Landing of the Hindenburg"; "The Salem Witchcraft Trials"; "The Gettysburg Address"; "The Fall of Troy"; and "The Scuttling of the Graf Spee." Starring in some of these episodes were such familiar names as Geraldine Brooks, Ronny Cox, E. G. Marshall, William Prince, and Fred Gwynne. The series was revived again in the 1971/72 season. The program closed with the lines, "What kind of a day was it? A day like all days, filled with those unexpected events which alter our lives—and you were there!"

BITS AND PIECES

The three wives of Ben Cartwright (Lorne Greene) on *Bonanza* were:
   Elizabeth, played by Geraldine Brooks
   Inger, played by Inge Swenson
   Marie, played by Felicia Farr
The pilot film on which *The Dick Van Dyke Show* was based was called *Head of the Family*. The cast was:
   Rob Petrie, played by Carl Reiner
   Laura Petrie, played by Barbara Britton
   Buddy Sorrell, played by Morty Gunty
131

Sally Rogers, played by Sylvia Miles

Alan Sturdy (later renamed Alan Brady), played by Jack Wakefield. When the program finally became *The Dick Van Dyke show*, Carl Reiner played the Alan Brady role.

Madge The Manicurist in the Palmolive Liquid commercials (played by Jan Miner) is known as Francoise in France, as Tilly in Germany and as Marissa in Finland.

Little Ricky Ricardo was played by: James John Gouzer (as a newborn), Richard Lee Simmons, the Mayer twins, and Richard Keith.

The first Academy Award telecast was in 1954. Bob Hope was the host and the show ran too long. It was cut off before it was over.

The idea for *All in the Family* came from a British show entitled *Till Death Do Us Part*. Similarly *Sanford and Son* grew out of an English program called *Steptoe and Son*.

Mel Brooks, Neil Simon, and Woody Allen were all writers for *Your Show of Shows*.

Ralph Edwards threatened his entire staff with a mass firing if they ever turned the tables on him and made the host the subject on *This Is Your Life*.

Two well-known TV performers who are real-life sisters, Jayne and Audrey Meadows, were born in China.

Arthur Godfrey lost his pilot's license for buzzing a tower at a New Jersey airport.

Arlene Francis played a hooker in a 1930s movie thriller, *Murders in the Rue Morgue*, loosely based on an Edgar Allen Poe story.

The identity of the actor who played the *Invisible Man* in the original TV series was never revealed.

United States Senator and former astronaut John Glenn was a contestant on *Name That Tune* in the 1950s when he was a major in the Marine Corps.

Walt Disney gave Annette Funicello the opportunity to portray Anita Cabrillo on *Zorro* as a birthday present.

In 1960 "Mr. Television" hosted a show called *Jackpot Bowling* Starring *Milton Berle*.

In 1954 Johnny Carson hosted a quiz show, *Earn Your Vacation*, in which contestants attempted to win their dream vacations.

Actor Jess Cain played a character named Jeff on the 1953–54 show *Marge and Jeff*. Fans confused Jess's name with that of his character so the actor legally changed his name to Jeff.

133   Photo 62

THE BRITISH ARE COMING . . . AND COMING . . . AND COMING . . .

Masterpiece Theatre, an anthology series of British produced serials, first aired on PBS in January 1971 and was hosted by Alistaire Cooke. The most popular of the series was *Upstairs, Downstairs*, which was a 15-part dramatization of the lives of an Edwardian family, the Bellamys, and also the lives of their servants. Jean Marsh, as Rose, the maid, stood out in a fine cast.

Glenda Jackson starred in *Masterpiece Theatre*'s 6-part story *Elizabeth R*, a tale of the first Queen Elizabeth who ruled from 1558 to 1603. John Neville and Susan Hampshire starred in the 12-part drama, *The First Churchills*, set in Restoration England. A 16-part romantic adventure, *Poldark*, based on four novels by Winston Graham, starred Robin Ellis as Ross Poldark. A 5-part dramatization of the Honore de Balzac novel, *Cousin Bette*, starred Margaret Tyzack in the title role. Susan Hampshire also starred in the 5-part series, *Vanity Fair*, playing the heroine, Becky Sharp, based on the novel by William Thackeray. Ian Carmichael and Rachel Herbert played Lord and Lady Wimsey in the 5-part adaptation, *Clouds of Witness*, from the story by Dorothy Sayers. A 6-part dramatization of Lewis Grassic Gibbons' novel, *Sunset Song*, starred Vivien Heilbron.

Other fine dramas presented by *Masterpiece Theatre* include:

The Last of the Mohicans	*Tom Brown's Schooldays*
The Moonstone	*Madame Bovary*
How Green Was My Valley	*Anna Karenina*
I, Claudius	

Commercial network television's attempt to cash in on the success of *Masterpiece Theatre* was a series entitled *Beacon Hill*. Set in Boston in the 1920s, this drama focused on the lives of the wealthy Lassiters and their servants. It ran for thirteen episodes. American television has been more succesful with the presentation of mini-series like *Rich Man, Poor Man* and *Shogun* and is no longer trying to imitate the English. Public television continues to offer British dramas on *Masterpiece Theatre*.

NUMERO UNO

Here are each season's top rated shows:

1950/51
    Texaco Star Theatre (NBC)

1951/52
    Arthur Godfrey's Talent Scouts (CBS)

1952/53
I Love Lucy (CBS)
1953/54
I Love Lucy (CBS)
1954/55
I Love Lucy (CBS)
1955/56
The $64,000 Question (CBS)
1956/57
I Love Lucy (CBS)
1957/58
Gunsmoke (CBS)
1958/59
Gunsmoke (CBS)
1959/60
Gunsmoke (CBS)
1960/61
Gunsmoke (CBS)
1961/62
Wagon Train (NBC)
1962/63
The Beverly Hillbillies (CBS)
1963/64
The Beverly Hillbillies (CBS)
1964/65
Bonanza (NBC)
1965/66
Bonanza (NBC)
1966/67
Bonanza (NBC)

1967/68
The Andy Griffith Show (CBS)
1968/69
Rowan and Martin's Laugh-In (NBC)
1969/70
Rowan and Martin's Laugh-In (NBC)
1970/71
Marcus Welby, M.D. (ABC)
1971/72
All in the Family (CBS)
1972/73
All in the Family (CBS)
1973/74
All in the Family (CBS)
1974/75
All in the Family (CBS)
1975/76
All in the Family (CBS)
1976/77
Happy Days (ABC)
1977/78
Laverne & Shirley (ABC)
1978/79
Laverne & Shirley (ABC)
1979/80
60 Minutes (CBS)
1980/81
Dallas (CBS)

Photo 63

IT'S A LIVING

The occupations listed on the left were portrayed by the performers listed on the right. Match the jobs with the stars and identify the shows.

1.	Sewer Worker	A.	Jackie Gleason
2.	Train Engineer	B.	Nancy Walker
3.	Unemployment Officer	C.	Tom Ewell
4.	Building Superintendant	D.	Henry Winkler
5.	Landlady	E.	Redd Foxx
6.	Shoe Salesman	F.	Gardner McKay
7.	Orthodontist	G.	Vic Tayback
8.	Hollywood Press Agent	H.	Ted Knight
9.	Baseball Pitcher	I.	Alan Hale, Jr.
10.	Deepsea Diver	J.	Sally Field
11.	Junkman	K.	Jack Albertson
12.	Loading Platform Foreman	L.	Betty Garrett
13.	Bus Driver	M.	Art Carney
14.	Diner Owner	N.	Adam Arkin
15.	Hotel Detective	O.	Richard Castellano
16.	Escort Service Owner	P.	Carroll O'Connor
17.	Nun	Q.	Ron Ely
18.	Garage Owner	R.	Peter Bonerz
19.	Schooner Skipper	S.	Jim Bouton
20.	Auto Mechanic	T.	James Coco

Photo 64

GET THE SCOOP (1)

Listed below on the left are fictional TV journalists and on the right are the actors and actresses who portrayed these roles. Match the roles with the performers and identify the shows.

1. R. B. Kingston	A. Dan Dailey
2. John Michael O'Toole	B. Peter Lawford
3. Bob Major	C. Jim Sutorius
4. Celeste Anders	D. Gloria Henry
5. Ray Whitehead	E. George Reeves
6. Tim Collier	F. George Brent
7. Michael Powers	G. Margaret Hayes
8. Michele Malone	H. Pippa Scott
9. Phoebe Goodheart	I. Donald May
10. Casey	J. Richard Crenna
11. Steve Wilson	K. Celeste Holm
12. Mike Andros	L. Audie Murphy
13. Richard Barrington III	M. Ted Bessell
14. Clark Kent	N. Raymond Burr
15. Lorelei Kilbourne	O. Patrick McVey
16. Dean Evans	P. Darren McGavin
17. Tom Smith	Q. Jim Backus
18. Molly Wood	R. Gig Young
19. Don Hollinger	S. James Daly
20. Pat Garrison	T. Robert Sterling

GET THE SCOOP (2)

Listed below on the left are fictional TV journalists and on the right are the actors and actresses who portrayed these roles. Match the roles with the performers and identify the shows.

1. Mickey Riley		A.	Phyllis Coates
2. Steve Wilson		B.	Mercedes McCambridge
3. Hiram Holliday		C.	Jane Nigh
4. Dan Miller		D.	Lee Tracey
5. Ann Williams		E.	Ed Asner
6. Scott Novis		F.	Jack Klugman
7. Danny Taylor		G.	Tony Franciosa
8. Elliott Carson		H.	Henry Jones
9. Lorelei Kilbourne		I.	Gary Merrill
10. Oscar Madison		J.	Jackie Cooper
11. Lee Cochran		K.	George Chandler
12. Lois Lane		L.	Marcia Henderson
13. Lou Grant		M.	Linda Kelsey
14. Lou Sheldon		N.	Rex Reason
15. Jeff Dillon		O.	Wally Cox
16. Pete Campbell		P.	Mark Stevens
17. Billie Newman		Q.	Warren Stevens
18. The Obit Editor		R.	Dane Clark
19. Icabod Adams		S.	Harry Guardino
20. Katherine Wells		T.	Jan Miner

Photo 65

WOMEN IN WHITE

Listed below on the left are the names of characters portrayed by the actresses on the right. Match the characters with the performers and identify the shows.

1. Nurse Wills
2. Gail Lucas
3. Consuelo Lopez
4. Zoe Lawton
5. Molly Gibbons
6. Janet Scott
7. Julia Baker
8. Dixie McCall
9. Nurse Puni
10. Jill Danko
11. Vera Wales
12. Annie Carlisle
13. Nurse Chambers
14. Janet Dean
15. Martha Hale
16. Mary Ellen Walton
17. Nancy Remington
18. Margaret Houlihan
19. Nurse Bradley
20. Rosa Santiago

A. Jayne Meadows
B. Patricia Benoit
C. Ella Raines
D. Kate Jackson
E. Jeanne Bates
F. Elena Verdugo
G. Diahann Caroll
H. Zina Bethune
I. Aneta Corsaut
J. Abby Dalton
K. Loretta Swit
L. Judy Norton-Taylor
M. Rosana Soto
N. Joan Van Ark
O. Millie Slavin
P. Julie London
Q. Lee Kurty
R. Victoria Young
S. Audra Lindley
T. Dena Dietrich

Photo 66

FLYING HIGH

The stars on the left have portrayed pilots or astronauts on the TV shows listed on the right. Match the stars with the shows.

1. Kirby Grant
2. Frankie Thomas
3. Ed Bishop
4. Martin Landau
5. Robert Lansing
6. Robert Conrad
7. William Shatner
8. Sam Elliott
9. Warner Scott
10. Al Hodge
11. Kem Dibbs
12. Bob Denver
13. Steve Holland
14. Richard Denning
15. Larry Hagman

16. Frank Aletter
17. Richard Webb
18. Gary Conway
19. Guy Williams
20. William Lundigan

A. Star Trek
B. Twelve O'Clock High
C. Buck Rogers in the 25th Century
D. The Flying Doctor
E. Once an Eagle
F. Far Out Space Nuts
G. Lost in Space
H. It's About Time
I. Tom Corbett, Space Cadet
J. I Dream of Jeannie
K. Men Into Space
L. Jet Jackson, Flying Commando
M. Sky King
N. Land of the Giants
O. Captain Video and His Video Rangers
P. Space: 1999
Q. Baa Baa Black Sheep
R. Flash Gordon
S. The Blue Angels
T. U.F.O.

Photo 67

PLEASE BE BRIEF (1)

Listed below on the left are TV lawyers and on the right are the performers who played these roles. Match the roles with the stars and identify the programs.

1.	Perry Mason	A.	Robert Reed
2.	John J. Malone	B.	William Shatner
3.	John Egan	C.	Ken Howard
4.	Paul Ryan	D.	Burl Ives
5.	Lawrence Preston	E.	Ron Liebman
6.	Feather Danton	F.	Gary Merrill
7.	David Koster	G.	Jerry Van Dyke
8.	Clinton Judd	H.	Chuck Connors
9.	Jason Tyler	I.	William Talman
10.	Abraham Lincoln Jones	J.	Arthur Hill
11.	Kate McShane	K.	Raymond Burr
12.	Kenneth Preston	L.	Barry Newman
13.	Adam Bonner	M.	James Farentino
14.	Martin Kazinsky	N.	Anne Meara
15.	Walter Nichols	O.	Lee Tracy
16.	Dave Crabtree	P.	Carl Betz
17.	Owen Marshall	Q.	James Whitmore
18.	Hamilton Burger	R.	Robert Conrad
19.	Tony Petrocelli	S.	Stephanie Powers
20.	Neil Darrell	T.	E. G. Marshall

Photo 68

PLEASE BE BRIEF (2)

Listed below on the left are TV lawyers and on the right are the performers who played those roles. Match the roles with the stars and identify the programs.

1. Clay Culhane		A.	Tony Roberts
2. Daniel O'Brien		B.	Jim Backus
3. Willa Dodger		C.	Tony Randall
4. David Barrett		D.	Meredith Baxter Birney
5. George Baxter		E.	Peter Breck
6. Joyce Davenport		F.	Ben Gazzara
7. Bentley Gregg		G.	Paul Lynde
8. Herbert Maris		H.	Eddie Albert
9. Beth Davenport		I.	Gretchen Corbett
10. Roy Markham		J.	Macdonald Carey
11. Paul Bryan		K.	Blythe Danner
12. Nancy Lawrence Maitland		L.	Ray Milland
13. Oliver Wendell Douglas		M.	John Forsythe
14. Walter Franklin		N.	Stephen Young
15. Jess Brandon		O.	Lee Majors
16. Bradley Stevens		P.	Veronica Hamel
17. Ben Caldwell		Q.	Don DeFore
18. Amanda Bonner		R.	Peter Falk
19. Joseph Rosetti		S.	Lee J. Cobb
20. Paul Simms		T.	June Havoc

Photo 69   **143**

IS THERE A DOCTOR IN THE HOUSE? (1)

Listed below on the left are characters in series and on the right are the performers who played them. Match the roles with the stars and identify the programs.

1. Dr. "Kentucky" Jones
2. Dr. Benjamin Franklin Pierce
3. Dr. David Zorba
4. Dr. Quincy
5. Dr. Joe Bogert
6. Doc Corkle
7. Dr. Benjamin Elliot
8. Dr. Leonard Gillespie
9. Dr. Sam Marsh
10. Dr. Norah Purcell
11. Dr. Roland Caine
12. Dr. Sean Jamison
13. Dr. Jules Bedford
14. Dr. Peter Goldstone
15. Dr. Mike Rogers
16. Dr. David Craig
17. Dr. Ted Stuart
18. Dr. Jake Goodwin
19. Dr. Paul Hunter
20. Dr. David Bedford

A. Brian Keith
B. Ben Piazza
C. Zohra Lampert
D. Danny Thomas
E. Broderick Crawford
F. David Hartman
G. David Spielberg
H. George Peppard
I. John Saxon
J. Sam Jaffe
K. Dennis Weaver
L. Alan Alda
M. E. G. Marshall
N. John Byner
O. Eddie Mayehoff
P. Raymond Massey
Q. James Franciscus
R. Mike Farrell
S. Barnard Hughes
T. Jack Klugman

IS THERE A DOCTOR IN THE HOUSE? (2)

Listed below on the left are characters from series and on the right are the performers who played them. Match the roles with the stars and identify the programs.

1. Dr. Maggie Graham	A.	Susan Sullivan
2. Dr. Julie Farr	B.	Joan Hotchkiss
3. Dr. Michael Rossi	C.	Cleavon Little
4. Dr. Nancy Cunningham	D.	Corinne Camacho
5. Dr. Janet Craig	E.	George Nader
6. Dr. Anne Jamison	F.	Belinda Montgomery
7. Dr. Jerry Noland	G.	Ralph Bellamy
8. Dr. Lydia Thorpe	H.	Linda Carlson
9. Dr. Jeanne Bartlett	I.	Tom Bower
10. Dr. Claire Morton	J.	Mariette Hartley
11. Dr. Janet Cottrell	K.	Harry Morgan
12. Dr. Glenn Barton	L.	Ed Nelson
13. Dr. James Whitman	M.	Ann Burr
14. Dr. Elizabeth Merrill	N.	June Lockhart
15. Dr. Dave Kelsey	O.	Larry Gelman
16. Dr. Bernie Tupperman	P.	Shelley Fabares
17. Dr. Kate Morrow	Q.	Bob Crane
18. Dr. L. Richard Starke	R.	Sandra Smith
19. Dr. Amos Coogan	S.	Roy Thinnes
20. Dr. Curtis Willard	T.	Mariette Hartley

CLOAKS AND DAGGERS

Listed below on the left are the names of TV spies and on the right are the actors and actresses who portrayed these roles. Match the performers with their roles and identify the shows.

1. John Drake
2. Jonathan Steed
3. Nick Bianco
4. James Phelps
5. Peter Murphy/
   Mark Wainwright
6. Napoleon Solo
7. Kelly Robinson
8. Bart Adams
9. James Hunter
10. April Dancer
11. Maxwell Smart
12. Illya Kuryakin
13. Alexander Scott
14. Victor Sebastian
15. Henry Wadsworth Phyfe
16. Agent 99
17. Doug Carter
18. Emma Peel
19. Matt Anders
20. Cinnamon Carter

A. Robert Vaughn
B. Bill Cosby
C. James Franciscus
D. Don Adams
E. Stefanie Powers

F. David McCallum
G. Red Buttons
H. David Hedison
I. Patrick Macnee
J. Barbara Feldon
K. Brian Keith
L. Grant Richards
M. Diana Rigg
N. Patrick McGoohan
O. Barbara Bain
P. Peter Graves
Q. Barry Nelson
R. Robert Lansing
S. Robert Culp
T. Tony Franciosa

146

SCHOOL DAYS, SCHOOL DAYS . . .

Listed below on the left are the names of characters portrayed by the performers listed on the right. Match the stars with their roles and identify the programs.

1. Connie Brooks	A. James Stewart
2. Charles W. Kingsfield	B. Gabe Kaplan
3. Robinson J. Peepers	C. Richard Long
4. Lucas Tanner	D. Tony Randall
5. Pete Dixon	E. Andy Griffith
6. Philip Boynton	F. Ronald Colman
7. Mike Stivic	G. John McGiver
8. Prof. McKillup	H. Ray Milland
9. Harold Everett	I. Don Porter
10. Alice Johnson	J. David Doyle
11. Harvey Weskitt	K. James Franciscus
12. James K. Howard	L. David Hartman
13. William Todhunter Hall	M. Eve Arden
14. Russ Lawrence	N. Wally Cox
15. Gabe Kotter	O. Karen Valentine
16. Andy Thompson	P. Lloyd Corrigan
17. John Novack	Q. Rob Reiner
18. McCutcheon	R. Robert Rockwell
19. Ray McNulty	S. Lloyd Haynes
20. Luther Quince	T. John Houseman

LAW AND ORDER (1)

Match the characters listed on the left with the performers listed on the right and identify the programs.

1. Rocky King	A. James Garner
2. Amy Prentiss	B. Robert Forster
3. Lew Archer	C. Hal Linden
4. Nick Anderson	D. Angie Dickinson
5. Thomas Banacek	E. Gene Barry
6. Tony Baretta	F. William Conrad
7. Jim Rockford	G. Buddy Ebsen
8. Bumper Morgan	H. Kate Jackson
9. Alex Bronkov	I. Joe E. Ross
10. Pepper Martin	J. Mitchell Ryan
11. Amos Burke	K. Roscoe Karns
12. Miles C. Banyon	L. Victor French
13. Barnaby Jones	M. Brian Keith
14. Sam Cade	N. George Kennedy
15. Frank Cannon	O. Glenn Ford
16. Gunther Toody	P. Jessica Walter
17. Roy Mobey	Q. Jack Palance
18. Sabrina Duncan	R. Ben Gazarra
19. Chase Reddick	S. Robert Blake
20. Barney Miller	T. George Peppard

Photo 70

LAW AND ORDER (2)

Match the characters listed on the left with the performers listed on the right and identify the programs.

1. Francis Muldoon	A. Wayne Rogers	
2. Ben Logan	B. Burt Reynolds	
3. Jill Munroe	C. Judd Hirsch	
4. Frank Poncherello	D. Jack Webb	
5. Jake Axminster	E. Skip Homeier	
6. Lt. Columbo	F. Dan Dailey	
7. Dan August	G. Lorne Greene	
8. Matt Holbrook	H. David Janssen	
9. Joe Friday	I. Teresa Graves	
10. Lewis Erskine	J. Fred Gwynne	
11. Sam Stone	K. Van Williams	
12. Christie Love	L. Jack Lord	
13. Dan Raven	M. Robert Conrad	
14. Britt Reid	N. Farrah Fawcett	
15. Steve McGarrett	O. Howard Duff	
16. Dominck Delvecchio	P. Erik Estrada	
17. Tom Lopaka	Q. Efrem Zimbalist, Jr.	
18. Harry Ordwell	R. Robert Taylor	
19. Wade Griffith	S. Stacy Keach	
20. Frank Faraday	T. Peter Falk	

Photo 71

149

LAW AND ORDER (3)

Match the characters listed on the left with the performers listed on the right and identify the programs.

1. Ben Guthrie
2. Robert Ironside
3. Paul Duval
4. Russ Andrews
5. Bobby Crocker
6. Honey West
7. Gregory Yoyonovich
8. Sam McCloud
9. Barney Fife
10. Gregg MacKenzie
11. Barney Marcus
12. Philip Gerard
13. Ben Manfred
14. Dan Briggs
15. Danny Williams
16. Frank Ballinger
17. Ellery Queen
18. Nick Charles
19. Steve Carella
20. Phil Fish

A. John Schuck
B. Grant Williams
C. Barry Morse
D. Dennis Weaver
E. Ben Alexander
F. James McArthur
G. Peter Lawford
H. Jack Hawkins
I. Lee Marvin
J. Anne Francis
K. Abe Vigoda
L. Charles Korvin
M. George Nader
N. Warner Anderson
O. Robert Lansing
P. Vic Tayback
Q. Raymond Burr
R. James Franciscus
S. Don Knotts
T. Kevin Dobson

LAW AND ORDER (4)

Match the characters listed on the left with the performers listed on the right and identify the programs.

1. Ed Brown		A.	Charles Haid
2. Alexander Holmes		B.	Max Gail
3. Charles Enright		C.	John Ericson
4. Jim Briggs		D.	Rod Cameron
5. Ellery Queen		E.	Boris Karloff
6. Matt Grebb		F.	Richard Anderson
7. Stan Wojohowicz		G.	Charles Durning
8. Andy Renko		H.	Linda Lavin
9. Sam Bolt		I.	William Hopper
10. Frank Smith		J.	Richard B. Shull
11. Steve Nelson		K.	Larry Wilcox
12. George Untermyer		L.	Don Galloway
13. Paul Drake		M.	Cheryl Ladd
14. Dan Adams		N.	Al Molinaro
15. Frank Murphy		O.	Tom Tully
16. Colonel March		P.	Adam West
17. Jon Baker		Q.	Jim Hutton
18. Kris Munroe		R.	John Schuck
19. Janet Wentworth		S.	Ben Alexander
20. Murray Grechner		T.	Dennis Cole

IN A NUTSHELL (1)

Identify the TV series from one sentence descriptions.

1. Daily events of husband, wife, and two sons who live at 822 Sycamore Lane, Hillsdale.
2. Exploits of the Special Weapons and Tactics Unit of the West California Police Department.
3. Comedy capers of Vernon Albright, widower, and his 21-year-old daughter.
4. Trials and tribulations of a young idealist staff worker for "Open America."
5. Adventures of three co-owners of private detective agency in exotic setting.
6. Queens, N.Y. family (father, mother, daughter, son-in-law) in constant generation gap problems.
7. Experiences of Western marshal, his deputies, and the townsfolk.
8. Doctor on the run because he is falsely accused of murdering his wife.
9. Family of three con-artists who bilk the wealthy of their treasures.
10. Harassments faced by father with a large brood of children.
11. Realistic crime drama, drawn from actual files, noted for its laconic and sparse dialogue.
12. Panelists try to guess contestants' occupations.
13. Adventures of a boy and his beloved horse.
14. Adventures of a boy and his beloved dog.
15. Homesteader, wife, and three daughters struggle against nature and neighbors to eke out a living.
16. Young politician is abetted by a talking dog.
17. Young architect is abetted by a talking horse.
18. Astronaut is injured; an operation gives him super power.
19. Medical cases of older G.P. and his motorcyclist assistant.
20. Medical cases of young hospital intern and his older doctor/mentor.

IN A NUTSHELL (2)

Identify the TV series from one sentence descriptions.

1. Wife of band leader yearns to be in show business.
2. Exploits of hospital unit in Korea.
3. Widow with two children works in a bank as a secretary.

4. Junk dealers, father and son, constantly clash over life and the junk business.
5. Widow with two children works for an employment agency.
6. Trials and tribulations of a California lawyer, his wife, and children.
7. Widow and daughter leave Minneapolis for San Francisco and live with in-laws.
8. Widow and son settle in Phoenix, where she is employed as a waitress.
9. Two girls and a boy share platonic relationship and apartment.
10. Adventures in the West with two brothers—one serious, one fun-loving.
11. Bus driver and sewer worker battle life and their wives.
12. Life in the Blue Ridge Mountains during depression seen through one family.
13. Private eye, who lives in trailer, and his Dad fight crime and City Hall.
14. Private eye fights crime and spends most of his time in nightclub called "Mother's."
15. Private eye and gal Friday, Peggy Fair, combat crime in Los Angeles.
16. Criminal lawyer and staff constantly outwit District Attorney Burger.
17. Ozark family strikes oil in frontyard and moves to California.
18. Young husband has trouble with his wife and mother-in-law, both of whom are witches.
19. Manhattan lawyer moves to country and faces woes of rural living amidst livestock.
20. Police commissioner and wife fight crime in San Francisco.

IN A NUTSHELL (3)

Identify the TV series from one sentence descriptions.

1. Medical cases of young surgeon and his older doctor/mentor.
2. Misadventures of three high-schoolers—Roger, Rerun, and Dwayne.
3. Satire concerning the Tate and Campbell families.
4. Two elderly sisters, both mystery writers, get constantly involved in real-life crimes.
5. Schoolroom drama about a black teacher and his co-workers.
6. "Rock Around the Clock" in the '50s with high-schoolers of Milwaukee.
7. More '50s in Milwaukee with two beer bottle cappers.
8. Susie's problems with her boss and her job.

9. Melodramas covered by the newspaper, *The Illustrated Press.*
10. Family life of insurance agent, his wife and their children, two daughters and one son.
11. Widowed mother-in-law and her life with daughter and son-in-law.
12. Steve, Dan-O, Kono, and Chin Ho battle with Wo Fat.
13. Brooklyn teacher vs. the "Sweathogs" and the principal.
14. Police captain and his staff fight crime, real and comedic, in Greenwich Village.
15. Tuckahoe matron and her amusing trials with family and friends.
16. The hilarious and heart-warming stories of the staff of TV station WJM in Minneapolis.
17. Exploits of Pepper, a female cop, and her cohorts.
18. Two divorced men share an apartment and adventures in Manhattan.
19. Jewish princess marries "goy" but can't escape her family.
20. Home-spun tale of small-town sheriff, his son, his aunt, and his inept deputy.

IN A NUTSHELL (4)

Identify the TV series from one sentence descriptions.

1. Greek police lieutenant battles crime in Manhattan's 13th Precinct.
2. Divorcee with two teen-age daughters faces life in Indianapolis.
3. Garage owner and assistant adjust to one another in a Los Angeles barrio.
4. Owner of dry cleaning establishments moves his family from Queens to Manhattan high-rise apartment.
5. Detective, with cockatoo, battles crime in California.
6. Two patrol-car police officers battle crime in Los Angeles.
7. Two patrol-car police officers try, hilariously, to battle crime in the Bronx, N.Y.
8. Weird family consists of Morticia, Gomez, Uncle Fester, and Grandmama.
9. Weird family consists of Herman, Lily, Grandpa, Edward, and Marilyn.
10. West Virginia mountain family moves to ranch in San Fernando Valley.
11. Western gunslinger for hire, no matter where.
12. Western marshal "cleans up" Dodge City and Tombstone.
13. Three-man detective team works in Hollywood.

14. Two men in a Corvette search for adventure in mid-USA.
15. People are given $1,000,000 by anonymous donor.
16. Little boy annoys next door neighbor.
17. Animated adventures of stone-age family and friends.
18. Household maid solves all of the family's problems, but adds a few of her own.
19. Famed U.S. agent battles crime in Chicago in the 1930s.
20. POWs in German stalag create havoc for the Nazis.

¿QUIÉNES?

Listed below on the left are performers who have portrayed the characters listed on the right. Match the stars with their roles and identify the programs.

1. Duncan Renaldo	A. Consuelo Lopez
2. Gregory Sierra	B. Joe Rivera
3. Jose Perez	C. Hey Soos Patines
4. Freddie Prinze	D. Jose Jimenez
5. Elena Verdugo	E. Don Diego de la Vega
6. Liz Torrez	F. Nurse Rose Santiago
7. Ned Romero	G. Thomas Alcala
8. Ricardo Montalban	H. Ricky Ricardo
9. Bill Dana	I. Elena Torres
10. Robert Cabal	J. Chico Rodriquez
11. Robert Hegyes	K. Pancho
12. Guy Williams	L. Recruit Rodriquez
13. Erik Estrada	M. The Cisco Kid
14. Desi Arnaz	N. Teresa Ortega
15. Eugenia Paul	O. Juan Epstein
16. Leo Carillo	P. Mr. Roarke
17. Rosana Soto	Q. Sgt. Chano
18. Richard Beaucamp	R. Francis Poncherello
19. Anthony Quinn	S. Teresa Betancourt
20. Lisa Mordente	T. Hector Fuentez

IT'S GREEK TO ME (1)

Listed below are the scrambled names of TV celebrities. Unscramble and identify the stars.

1. SDI RSAACE
2. LILELCU LABL
3. KJAC NYNEB
4. GONEMIE OACC
5. DE NYWN
6. SMEAJ SNERSA
7. LEGA MORTS
8. ERTEP SAVRGE
9. SORID ADY
10. LIPH VISSERL

11. TENTENA BRYAAF
12. NITMOL REEBL
13. LACOR NUBTERT
14. MIJ BROANS
15. ERIEVAL RERPHA
16. OBB NACRE
17. ROLCSI HAAMELCN
18. ADEN TRIMNA
19. YARM TREYL OMREO
20. DE NILVASUL

IT'S GREEK TO ME (2)

Listed below are the scrambled names of TV celebrities. Unscramble and identify the stars.

1. YNNDA STAHMO
2. NAHID ROSHE
3. RYPER OMCO
4. ZAIL NIIMELLN
5. VAHRYE MOKARN
6. NEJA PNEATTLOS
7. ROCRALL NOOCRON
8. DOYRAMN RURB
9. IDES RAANZ
10. YTETB HEWTI

11. LALNE DUNELD
12. DANAMA KLEAB
13. AJIECK AGLENOS
14. RYEUDA WAMSEDO
15. TRA NYCREA
16. EJUIL EWSANER
17. TREEP KALF
18. HERC
19. YTELL VLAAASS
20. CRIBEETA RHURAT

IT'S GREEK TO ME (3)

Listed below are the scrambled names of TV celebrities. Unscramble and identify the stars.

1. TERBRO DRONCA
2. KHUCC SNORCNO
3. EANN REAMA
4. RHOZA PEMTRAL
5. ROGGEE DAPPERP
6. NAN DREASHIN
7. AJNO NEBTENT
8. ACJK GLAMKUN
9. YOTN DLARNAL
10. SAM FEAJF
11. TEARLOT WIST
12. GRINPS GOINYNTB
13. AITNSSABE OTABC
14. DORYNAM SMESYA
15. TEAK SNOCKAJ
16. NEAZNUS MORESS
17. CEAJISS TRAWLE
18. DUBYD BEENS
19. CREOSO RANKS
20. LHA DINNEL

IT'S GREEK TO ME (4)

Listed below are the scrambled names of TV celebrities. Unscramble and identify the stars.

1. SMAJE SNEARS
2. TEBORR GUONY
3. ANDON DERE
4. CIVIK CLERAWEN
5. NEERI SKACVO
6. APT OBOEN
7. BLYLI RHAGMA
8. NOR DRAWHO
9. HAIRS SWEIL
10. NAN HORNETS
11. LOARM STOMAH
12. TEARLOT GUNOY
13. DRACHIR MOSTAH
14. RONEL EGNEER
15. CLIMAHE DRAENEL
16. DRAW DOBN
17. RABARAB WACKSTYN
18. DERD XOFX
19. BRO NERRIE
20. NCYID LIWIMASL

BIG SCREEN, LITTLE SCREEN

The performers listed on the left all originated roles in films which were portrayed on TV by the performers on the right. Match the performers and identify the shows.

1.	Loretta Young	A.	Clarence Muse
2.	Lew Ayres	B.	Roger Moore
3.	James Stewart	C.	Jack Kelly
4.	Sandra Dee	D.	Marilyn Maxwell
5.	Dooley Wilson	E.	John Gavin
6.	Warner Baxter	F.	Natalie Wood
7.	Lana Turner	G.	Ken Howard
8.	Betty Field	H.	Sally Field
9.	Robert Cummings	I.	Mitchell Ryan
10.	Gene Tierney	J.	Phyllis Kirk
11.	Deborah Kerr	K.	Inger Stevens
12.	Ralph Bellamy	L.	Richard Chamberlain
13.	Spencer Tracy	M.	Tommy Rettig
14.	Myrna Loy	N.	Linda Lavin
15.	Lionel Barrymore	O.	Pamela Sue Martin
16.	Bonita Granville	P.	Raymond Massey
17.	William Holden	Q.	Dorothy Malone
18.	Roddy McDowall	R.	George Nader
19.	Ellen Burstyn	S.	Hope Lange
20.	Louis Hayward	T.	Duncan Renaldo

159 Photo 72

REGARDS TO BROADWAY

The performers on the left all originated roles on the stage which the performers on the right portrayed on TV. Match the performers and identify the shows.

1.	Tallulah Bankhead	A.	Sammy Jackson
2.	Frank Craven	B.	Roger Smith
3.	Katharine Hepburn	C.	Diana Lynn
4.	Alfred Lunt	D.	Alfred Lunt
5.	Barbara Bel Geddes	E.	Elaine Stritch
6.	Andy Griffith	F.	Scoey Mitchell
7.	Margalo Gilmore	G.	Dorothy McGuire
8.	Lloyd Nolan	H.	Jeanmaire
9.	Henry Fonda	I.	Judith Anderson
10.	Margaret Sullavan	J.	Leon Ames
11.	Otto Kruger	K.	Mary Martin
12.	Robert Redford	L.	Claudette Colbert
13.	Gertrude Lawrence	M.	Natalie Wood
14.	Louis Calhern	N.	Joan McCracken
15.	Ethel Merman	O.	Samantha Eggar
16.	Howard Lindsay	P.	Frank Sinatra
17.	Shirley Booth	Q.	Fredric March
18.	Peggy Wood	R.	Lloyd Nolan
19.	Judith Anderson	S.	Larry Blyden
20.	Dorothy McGuire	T.	Ruth Hussey

161   Photo 73

WHEN IN ROME . . .

Listed below on the left are performers who have portrayed the roles listed on the right. Match the performers with their roles and identify the shows.

1. Barry Newman	A.	Frank Lorenzo
2. Robert Blake	B.	Ann Romano
3. Peter Falk	C.	Joey Delucca
4. Joe Sirola	D.	Joe Pizo
5. Vincent Gardenia	E.	Vinnie Barbarino
6. Phil Foster	F.	Pvt. Frankie Lombardi
7. Henry Winkler	G.	Joe Calucci
8. Bonnie Franklin	H.	Esmee Belotti
9. John Travolta	I.	Sgt. Dominick Delvecchio
10. Paul Sorvino	J.	Tony Petrocelli
11. Eddie Mekka	K.	Joe Girelli
12. James Coco	L.	Arthur Fonzarelli
13. Paul Regina	M.	Johnny Staccato
14. Joseph Mascolo	N.	Tony Baretta
15. Judd Hirsch	O.	Frank De Fazio
16. Ted Bessell	P.	Karen Angelo
17. Charlotte Rae	Q.	Lt. Columbo
18. Richard Castellano	R.	Mayor Paul Santoni
19. John Cassavetes	S.	Bert D'Angelo
20. Karen Valentine	T.	Tony Montefusco

Photo 74

MISSING LINKS (1)

Find the missing word/s in each pair of titles and forty TV shows will be identified.

1. The Mothers-In _____ less Years.
2. Mr. and Mrs. _____ West Passage.
3. Chico and the _____ from Atlantis
4. All in the _____ Affair
5. Accidental _____ Holvak
6. Slattery's _____ Are Funny
7. The _____ Circus
8. Take It from _____ and the Chimp
9. Bachelor _____ Knows Best
10. Movin' _____ The Rocks
11. Gentle _____ Casey
12. Honey _____ Point
13. December _____ and Groom
14. The Awakening _____ of the Lost
15. The $1.98 Beauty _____ offs
16. Run, Buddy, _____ for Your Life
17. Most _____ Dead or Alive
18. The Flying _____ Kildare
19. Mobile _____ Day at a Time
20. To Rome with _____ on a Rooftop

MISSING LINKS (2)

Find the missing word/s in each pair of titles and forty TV shows will be identified.

1. Big _____ Five-O
2. The Restless _____ smoke
3. Portia Faces _____ with Luigi
4. Operation _____ Junction
5. Peter Loves _____ Hartline Show
6. The Partridge _____ Feud
7. Information _____ Don't Eat the Daisies
8. Nothing But the _____ or Consequences
9. Naked _____ of Angels
10. My Partner _____ and Mrs. Muir
11. My Three _____ and Daughters
12. Cimarron _____ Hospital
13. Mr. _____ Partners
14. Monty Python's Flying _____ Boy
15. Men Into _____ Patrol
16. The Man Against _____ Photographer
17. Love That _____ Newhart Show
18. The Blue _____
19. One Man's _____
20. My Little _____

164

Photo 75

AND THE WINNER WAS . . . DRAMA (1)

Listed below on the left are actors who have won Emmies for Drama (leading role, supporting role, single performance, or series) and on the right are the programs for which they won. Match the actors with the shows.

1.	Robert Cummings	A.	*The Life of Samuel Johnson*
2.	Lloyd Nolan	B.	*The Moon and Sixpence*
3.	Daniel J. Trivanti	C.	*The Invincible Mr. Disraeli*
4.	Jack Palance	D.	*The Price of Tomatoes*
5.	Peter Ustinov	E.	*The Game*
6.	Raymond Burr	F.	*Macbeth*
7.	Dennis Weaver	G.	*The Poppy Is Also a Flower*
8.	Laurence Olivier	H.	*The Defenders*
9.	Robert Stack	I.	*The Magnificent Yankee*
10.	Maurice Evans	J.	*The Caine Mutiny Court Martial*
11.	Roddy McDowall	K.	*Eagle in a Cage*
12.	Peter Falk	L.	*Blacklist*
13.	E. G. Marshall	M.	*I Spy*
14.	Trevor Howard	N.	*Hill Street Blues*
15.	Jack Klugman	O.	*Twelve Angry Men*
16.	Alfred Lunt	P.	*Perry Mason*
17.	Cliff Robertson	Q.	*The Untouchables*
18.	James Daly	R.	*Requiem for a Heavyweight*
19.	Bill Cosby	S.	*Not Without Honor*
20.	Eli Wallach	T.	*Gunsmoke*

AND THE WINNER WAS . . . DRAMA (2)

Listed below on the left are actors who have won Emmies for Drama (leading role, supporting role, single performance, or series) and on the right are the programs for which they won. Match the actors with the shows.

1.	Peter Ustinov	A.	*The Price*
2.	Melvyn Douglas	B.	*Catherine Howard* (*Henry VIII* series)
3.	Milburn Stone	C.	*Long Day's Journey into Night*
4.	Paul Scofield	D.	*That Certain Summer*
5.	Carl Betz	E.	*The Blue Knight*
6.	Robert Young	F.	*Rich Man, Poor Man*
7.	George C. Scott	G.	*The Glass Menagerie*
8.	Hal Holbrook	H.	*Barefoot in Athens*
9.	Keith Mitchell	I.	*The Waltons*
10.	Peter Falk	J.	*Kojak*
11.	Jack Warden	K.	*The Male of the Species*
12.	Laurence Olivier	L.	*Baretta*
13.	Richard Thomas	M.	*Do Not Go Gentle into That Good Night*
14.	Scott Jacoby	N.	*QB VII*
15.	Telly Savalas	O.	*Brian's Song*
16.	William Holden	P.	*Judd, For the Defense*
17.	Michael Moriarty	Q.	*The Senator*
18.	Robert Blake	R.	*Columbo*
19.	Anthony Quayle	S.	*Marcus Welby, M.D.*
20.	Ed Asner	T.	*Gunsmoke*

AND THE WINNER WAS . . . DRAMA (3)

Listed below on the left are actresses who have won Emmies for Drama (leading role, supporting role, single performance, or series) and on the right are the programs for which they won. Match the actresses with the shows.

1. Judith Anderson		A.	Hill Street Blues
2. Mary Martin		B.	Perry Mason
3. Ellen Corby		C.	The Turn of the Screw
4. Claire Trevor		D.	Two Is the Number
5. Barbara Babcock		E.	Little Moon of Alban
6. Polly Bergen		F.	Victoria Regina
7. Barbara Hale		G.	Peyton Place
8. Julie Harris		H.	A Small Rebellion
9. Ingrid Bergman		I.	The Magnificent Yankee
10. Barbara Stanwyck		J.	A Christmas Morning
11. Kim Stanley		K.	Dodsworth
12. Shelley Winters		L.	Mission Impossible
13. Lynn Fontanne		M.	Macbeth
14. Simone Signoret		N.	Night of the Vicious Valentine
15. Lee Grant		O.	The Helen Morgan Story
16. Geraldine Page		P.	Peter Pan
17. Barbara Bain		Q.	A Cardinal Act of Mercy
18. Agnes Moorehead		R.	Among the Paths to Eden
19. Pamela Brown		S.	The Big Valley
20. Maureen Stapleton		T.	The Waltons

Photo 76

AND THE WINNER WAS . . . DRAMA (4)

Listed below on the left are actresses who have won Emmies for Drama (leading role, supporting role, single performance, or series) and on the right are the programs for which they won. Match the actresses with the shows.

1. Glenda Farrell	A. *My Sweet Charlie*
2. Julie Harris	B. *Hamlet*
3. Barbara Anderson	C. *The Waltons*
4. Geraldine Page	D. *Mannix*
5. Anne Calder-Marshall	E. *The Snow Goose*
6. Susan Saint James	F. *The Neon Ceiling*
7. Patty Duke	G. *Shadow in the Sun (Elizabeth R series)*
8. Susan Hampshire	H. *Upstairs, Downstairs*
9. Gail Fisher	I. *Victoria Regina*
10. Lee Grant	J. *A Brand New Life*
11. Margaret Leighton	K. *The Glass Menagerie*
12. Glenda Jackson	L. *A Cardinal Act of Mercy*
13. Jenny Agutter	M. *The Name of the Game*
14. Cloris Leachman	N. *Love Among the Ruins*
15. Michael Learned	O. *The Male of the Species*
16. Joanna Miles	P. *Amy Prentiss*
17. Jean Marsh	Q. *Ironside*
18. Katharine Hepburn	R. *Queen of the Gypsies*
19. Jessica Walter	S. *The Forsythe Saga*
20. Zohra Lampert	T. *The Thanksgiving Visitor*

AND THE WINNER WAS . . . DIRECTORS (1)

The directors listed on the left won Emmies for the programs listed on the right. Match the directors with the shows.

1. David Green		A.	*Eleanor and Franklin*
2. George Cukor		B.	*Liza with a Z*
3. John Corty		C.	*Peggy Fleming at Sun Valley*
4. Dwight Hemion		D.	*An Evening with John Denver*
5. Bob Fosse		E.	*Movin' With Nancy*
6. Joseph Sargent		F.	*The Game*
7. Daniel Petrie		G.	*The People Next Door*
8. Marvin J. Chomsky		H.	*Car 54, Where Are You?*
9. Mark Warren		I.	*Death of a Salesman*
10. Sterling Johnson		J.	*The Mary Tyler Moore Show*
11. Bill Davis		K.	*The Defenders*
12. Paul Bogart		L.	*Barbra Streisand and Other Musical Instruments*
13. Jay Sandrich		M.	*The Dick Van Dyke Show*
14. Jack Haley, Jr.		N.	*Love Among the Ruins*
15. Alex Segal		O.	*Macbeth*
16. Sidney Pollack		P.	*Rowan and Martin's Laugh-In*
17. Jerry Paris		Q.	*Shadow Game*
18. Franklin Schaffner		R.	*The Marcus-Nelson Murders*
19. Nat Hiken		S.	*The Autobiography of Miss Jane Pittman*
20. George Schaefer		T.	*Holocaust*

AND THE WINNER WAS . . . DIRECTORS (2)

The directors listed on the left won Emmies for the programs listed on the right. Match the directors with the shows.

1. Robert Mulligan

2. George Schaefer
3. Bob Banner
4. Bud Yorkin
5. Ralph Levy and Bud Yorkin

6. Robert Stevens

7. Jackie Cooper
8. Nat Hiken

9. Franklin Schaffner
10. Alan Alda
11. Ralph Nelson
12. Paul Bogart
13. Gene Reynolds
14. Sheldon Leonard
15. Dwight Hemion

16. David Lowell Rich
17. Dave Wilson
18. Dave Powers
19. Robert Butler
20. Bill Davis

A. *The Glass Eye (Alfred Hitchcock Presents)*
B. *The Phil Silvers Show*
C. *Requiem for a Heavyweight*
D. *Dear Sigmund (M*A*S*H)*
E. *Edith's 50th Birthday (All in the Family)*
F. *Sentry Collection Presents Ben Vereen*
G. *Little Moon of Alban*
H. *Danny's Comeback (The Danny Thomas Show)*
I. *NBC's Saturday Night*
J. *The Blue Knight, Part III*
K. *The Moon and Sixpence*
L. *The Defection of Simas Kudirka*
M. *Carry On, Hawkeye (M*A*S*H)*
N. *The Dinah Shore Chevy Show*
O. *The Carol Burnett Show (with Alan Alda)*
P. *The Jack Benny Show*
Q. *The Julie Andrews Hour*
R. *The Caine Mutiny Court Martial*
S. *Welcome to Korea (M*A*S*H)*
T. *An Evening with Fred Astaire*

AND THE WINNER WAS . . . COMEDY OR MUSICAL VARIETY (1)

Listed below on the left are actors who have won Emmies for Comedy or Musical Variety (leading, supporting, single performance, or series) and on the right are the programs for which they won. Match the actors with the shows.

1. Carroll O'Connor
2. Tim Conway
3. Gary Burghoff
4. Jack Albertson
5. Ted Knight
6. Jack Klugman
7. Michael Constantine
8. William Windom
9. Don Adams
10. Werner Klemperer
11. Don Knotts
12. Phil Silvers

13. Danny Thomas
14. Chevy Chase
15. Jack Lemmon
16. Tom Poston
17. Donald O'Connor
18. Judd Hirsh
19. Art Carney
20. Carl Reiner

A. *The Andy Griffith Show*
B. *NBC's Saturday Night*
C. *Hogan's Heroes*
D. *Colgate Comedy Hour*
E. *You'll Never Get Rich*
F. *The Steve Allen Show*
G. *Taxi*
H. *Make Room for Daddy*
I. *Caesar's Hour*
J. *The Jackie Gleason Show*
K. *All in the Family*
L. *'S Wonderful, 'S Marvelous, 'S Gershwin*
M. *M*A*S*H*
N. *Room 222*
O. *Get Smart*
P. *The Mary Tyler Moore Show*
Q. *My World and Welcome to It*
R. *The Carol Burnett Show*
S. *The Odd Couple*
T. *Chico and the Man*

Photo 77

Photo 78   174

AND THE WINNER WAS . . . COMEDY OR MUSICAL VARIETY (2)

Listed below on the left are actresses who have won Emmies for Comedy or Musical Variety (leading, supporting, single performance, or series) and on the right are the programs for which they won. Match the actresses with the shows.

1.	Julie Kavner	A.	*The Jeffersons*
2.	Beatrice Arthur	B.	*Hazel*
3.	Alice Pearce	C.	*Father Knows Best*
4.	Mildred Natwick	D.	*The Andy Griffith Show*
5.	Karen Valentine	E.	*Your Show of Shows*
6.	Jean Stapleton	F.	*Mary Hartman, Mary Hartman*
7.	Hope Lange	G.	*The Muppet Show*
8.	Isabel Sanford	H.	*Caesar's Hour*
9.	Eileen Brennan	I.	*Our Miss Brooks*
10.	Frances Bavier	J.	*The Robert Cummings Show*
11.	Shirley Booth	K.	*Bewitched*
12.	Mary Kay Place	L.	*The Goldbergs*
13.	Ann B. Davis	M.	*Rhoda*
14.	Jane Wyatt	N.	*The Ghost and Mrs. Muir*
15.	Rita Moreno	O.	*The Jackie Gleason Show*
16.	Nanette Fabray	P.	*Maude*
17.	Imogene Coca	Q.	*Private Benjamin*
18.	Eve Arden	R.	*Room 222*
19.	Audrey Meadows	S.	*The Snoop Sisters*
20.	Gertrude Berg	T.	*All in the Family*

Photo 79

176

177   Photo 80

Photo 81

179   Photo 82

Photo 83

Photo 84

Photo 85

Photo 86

Photo 87   **184**

Photo 88

Photo 89

Photo 90

MAJOR EMMY AWARDS NOMINEES AND WINNERS FROM 1948–1981

MAJOR EMMY AWARDS NOMINEES
AND WINNERS FROM 1948–1981

1948
Most Outstanding Personality:
*Shirley Dinsdale, Rita LeRoy, Patricia Morison, Mike Stokey, Bill Welsh
Most Popular Television Program:
Armchair Detective, Don Lee Music Hall, Felix De Cola Show, Judy
Splinters, Mabel's Fables, *Pantomime Quiz*, Treasure of Literature, Tuesday
Varieties, What's the Name of That Song?
Best Film Made for Television:
Christopher Columbus, Hollywood Brevities, It Could Happen to You, *The
Necklace*, Telltale Heart, Time Signal

1949
Best Live Show:
The Ed Wynn Show, Pantomime Quiz, Your Witness
Best Kinescope Show:
Fred Waring, The Goldbergs, Studio One, *Texaco Star Theater*
Best Outstanding Live Personality:
Tom Harmon, Mike Stokey, Bill Welsh, *Ed Wynn
Best Film Made for and Viewed on Television:
Guiding Star, *The Life of Riley*, The Lone Ranger, Time Bomb, Vain Glory,
Your Showtime
Most Outstanding Kinescoped Personality:
Fran Allison, *Milton Berle, Arthur Godfrey

1950
Best Actor:
Sid Caesar, Jose Ferrer, Stan Freberg, Charles Ruggles, *Alan Young
Best Actress:
Judith Anderson, *Gertrude Berg, Imogene Coca, Helen Hayes, Betty White

*denotes winner

189

Most Outstanding Personality:
Sid Caesar, Faye Emerson, Dick Lane, *Groucho Marx, Alan Young
Best Variety Show:
*The Alan Young Show, Four Star Revue, Ken Murray, Show of Shows,
Texaco Star Theater
Best Dramatic Show:
Fireside Theater, Mama, Philco TV Playhouse, *Pulitzer Prize Playhouse,
Studio One
Best Games and Audience Participation Show:
Kay Kyser's Kollege of Musical Knowledge, Life With Linkletter, Pantomime
Quiz, *Truth or Consequences, You Bet Your Life

1951
Best Dramatic Show:
Celanese Theatre, Philco-Goodyear TV Playhouse, Pulitzer Prize Playhouse,
Robert Montgomery Presents, *Studio One
Best Comedy Show:
Burns and Allen, Groucho Marx, Herb Shriner, I Love Lucy, *Red Skelton
Show
Best Variety Show:
All Star Revue, Comedy Hour, Fred Waring, Toast of the Town, *Your Show
of Shows
Best Actor:
*Sid Caesar, Walter Hampden, Charlton Heston, Robert Montgomery,
Thomas Mitchell, Vaughn Taylor
Best Actress:
*Imogene Coca, Helen Hayes, Maria Riva, Mary Sinclair, Margaret Sullavan
Best Comedian or Comedienne:
Lucille Ball, Sid Caesar, Imogene Coca, Jimmy Durante, Martin and Lewis,
Herb Shriner, *Red Skelton

1952
Best Dramatic Program:
Celanese Theatre, Kraft Television Theatre, Philco-Goodyear TV Playhouse,
*Robert Montgomery Presents, Studio One
Best Variety Program:
Arthur Godfrey and His Friends, Colgate Comedy Hour, Jackie Gleason
Show, Toast of the Town, *Your Show of Shows
Best Actor:
John Forsythe, Charlton Heston, *Thomas Mitchell, John Newland, Vaughn
Taylor, Jack Webb
Best Actress:
Sarah Churchill, *Helen Hayes, June Lockhart, Maria Riva, Peggy Wood

*denotes winner

Best Comedian:

Sid Caesar, Wally Cox, *Jimmy Durante, Jackie Gleason, Herb Shriner

Best Comedienne:

Eve Arden, *Lucille Ball, Imogene Coca, Joan Davis, Martha Raye

Most Outstanding Personality:

Lucille Ball, Arthur Godfrey, Jimmy Durante, Edward R. Murrow, Donald O'Connor, *Bishop Fulton J. Sheen, Adlai Stevenson

1953

Best Dramatic Program:

Kraft Television Theatre, Philco-Goodyear TV Playhouse, Robert Montgomery Presents, Studio One, *U.S. Steel Hour

Best Situation Comedy:

Burns and Allen, *I Love Lucy, Mr. Peepers, Our Miss Brooks, Topper

Best Variety Program:

Colgate Comedy Hour, Jackie Gleason Show, *Omnibus, Toast of the Town, Your Show of Shows

Best Male Star of Regular Series:

Sid Caesar for Your Show of Shows, Wally Cox for Mr. Peepers, Jackie Gleason for Jackie Gleason Show, *Donald O'Connor for Colgate Comedy Hour, Jack Webb for Dragnet

Best Female Star of Regular Series:

*Eve Arden for Our Miss Brooks, Lucille Ball for I Love Lucy, Imogene Coca for Your Show of Shows, Dinah Shore for Dinah Shore Show, Loretta Young for Letter to Loretta

Best Series Supporting Actor:

Ben Alexander for Dragnet, *Art Carney for Jackie Gleason Show, William Frawley for I Love Lucy, Tony Randall for Mr. Peepers, Carl Reiner for Your Show of Shows

Best Series Supporting Actress:

Bea Benadaret for Burns and Allen, Ruth Gilbert for Milton Berle Show, Marion Lorne for Mr. Peepers, Audrey Meadows for Jackie Gleason Show, *Vivian Vance for I Love Lucy

Most Outstanding Personality:

Arthur Godfrey, *Edward R. Murrow, Martha Raye, Bishop Fulton J. Sheen, Jack Webb

1954

Most Outstanding New Personality:

Richard Boone, Walt Disney, Tennessee Ernie Ford, Preston Foster, *George Gobel, Michael O'Shea, Fess Parker

*denotes winner

191

Best Actor in a Single Performance:

*Robert Cummings for *Twelve Angry Men*, Frank Lovejoy for *Double Indemnity*, Fredric March for *A Christmas Carol*, Fredric March for *Royal Family*, Thomas Mitchell for *Good of His Soul*, David Niven for *The Answer*

Best Actress in a Single Performance:

*Judith Anderson for *Macbeth*, Ethel Barrymore for *The 13th Chair*, Beverly Garland for *White Is the Color*, Ruth Hussey for *Craig's Wife*, Dorothy McGuire for *The Giaconda Smile*, Eva Marie Saint for *Middle of the Night*, Claire Trevor for *Ladies in Retirement*

Best Male Singer:

*Perry Como, Eddie Fisher, Frankie Laine, Tony Martin, Gordon MacRae

Best Female Singer:

Jane Froman, Peggy King, Gisele Mackenzie, *Dinah Shore, Jo Stafford

Best Supporting Actor in a Regular Series:

Ben Alexander for *Dragnet*, *Art Carney for *Jackie Gleason Show*, Don DeFore for *The Adventures of Ozzie and Harriet*, William Frawley for *I Love Lucy*, Gale Gordon for *Our Miss Brooks*

Best Supporting Actress in a Regular Series:

Bea Benadaret for *Burns and Allen*, Jean Hagen for *Make Room for Daddy*, Marion Lorne for *Mr. Peepers*, *Audrey Meadows for *Jackie Gleason Show*, Vivian Vance for *I Love Lucy*

Best Actor Starring in a Regular Series:

Richard Boone for *Medic*, Robert Cummings for *My Hero*, Jackie Gleason for *Jackie Gleason Show*, *Danny Thomas for *Make Room for Daddy*, Jack Webb for *Dragnet*

Best Actress Starring in a Regular Series:

Eve Arden for *Our Miss Brooks*, Gracie Allen for *Burns and Allen*, Lucille Ball for *I Love Lucy*, Ann Sothern for *Private Secretary*, *Loretta Young for *Loretta Young Show*

1955

Best Comedy Series:

Jack Benny Show, Bob Cummings Show, Caesar's Hour, George Gobel Show, Make Room for Daddy, *Phil Silvers Show: You'll Never Get Rich*

Best Variety Series:

Ed Sullivan Show, Dinah Shore Show, Ford Star Jubilee, Perry Como Show, Shower of Stars

Best Dramatic Series:

Alcoa-Goodyear TV Playhouse, Climax, *Producers Showcase*, Studio One, U.S. Steel Hour

Best Single Program of the Year:

The American West, Caine Mutiny Court Martial, Davy Crockett and River Pirates, No Time for Sergeants, *Peter Pan Meets Rusty Williams*, The Sleeping Beauty

*denotes winner

Best Actor—Single Performance:

Ralph Bellamy for *Fearful Decision*, Jose Ferrer for *Cyrano de Bergerac*, *Lloyd Nolan for *Caine Mutiny Court Martial*, Everett Sloane for *Patterns*, Barry Sullivan for *Caine Mutiny Court Martial*

Best Actress—Single Performance:

Julie Harris for *Wind from the South*, *Mary Martin for *Peter Pan*, Eva Marie Saint for *Our Town*, Jessica Tandy for *The Fourposter*, Loretta Young for *Christmas Stopover*

Best Actor—Continuing Performance:

Bob Cummings for *Bob Cummings Show*, Jackie Gleason for *The Honeymooners*, *Phil Silvers for *You'll Never Get Rich*, Danny Thomas for *Make Room for Daddy*, Robert Young for *Father Knows Best*

Best Actress—Continuing Performance:

Gracie Allen for *Burns and Allen*, Eve Arden for *Our Miss Brooks*, *Lucille Ball for *I Love Lucy*, Jean Hagen for *Make Room for Daddy*, Ann Sothern for *Private Secretary*

Best Actor in a Supporting Role:

Ed Begley for *Patterns*, *Art Carney for *The Honeymooners*, William Frawley for *I Love Lucy*, Carl Reiner for *Caesar's Hour*, Cyril Ritchard for *Peter Pan*

Best Actress in a Supporting Role:

Ann B. Davis for *Bob Cummings Show*, *Nanette Fabray for *Caesar's Hour*, Jean Hagen for *Make Room for Daddy*, Audrey Meadows for *The Honeymooners*, Thelma Ritter for *A Catered Affair*

Best Comedian:

Jack Benny, Sid Caesar, Art Carney, George Gobel, *Phil Silvers

Best Comedienne:

Gracie Allen, Eve Arden, Lucille Ball, *Nanette Fabray, Ann Sothern

Best Male Singer:

Harry Belafonte, *Perry Como, Eddie Fisher, Gordon MacRae, Frank Sinatra

Best Female Singer:

Rosemary Clooney, Judy Garland, Peggy Lee, Giselle Mackenzie, *Dinah Shore

1956

Best Single Program of the Year:

A Night to Remember, Leonard Bernstein, *Requiem for a Heavyweight*, *Secret Life of Danny Kaye*, *Victor Borge Show*

Best Continuing Performance by an Actor in a Dramatic Series:

James Arness for *Gunsmoke*, Charles Boyer for *Four Star Playhouse*, David Niven for *Four Star Playhouse*, Hugh O'Brian for *Wyatt Earp*, *Robert Young for *Father Knows Best*

Best Continuing Performance by an Actress in a Dramatic Series:

Jan Clayton for *Lassie*, Ida Lupino for *Four Star Playhouse*, Peggy Wood for

*denotes winner

Mama, Jane Wyman for *Jane Wyman Show*, ***Loretta Young** for *Loretta Young Show*

Best Continuing Performance by a Comedian in a Series:

Jack Benny in *Jack Benny Show*, ***Sid Caesar** in *Caesar's Hour*, Bob Cummings in *Bob Cummings Show*, Ernie Kovacs in *Ernie Kovacs Show*, Phil Silvers in *Phil Silvers Show*

Best Continuing Performance by a Comedienne in a Series:

Edie Adams in *Ernie Kovacs Show*, Gracie Allen in *Burns and Allen*, Lucille Ball in *I Love Lucy*, ***Nanette Fabray** in *Caesar's Hour*, Ann Sothern for *Private Secretary*

Best Single Performance by an Actor:

Lloyd Bridges for *Tragedy in a Temporary Town*, Fredric March for *Dodsworth*, Sal Mineo for *Dino*, ***Jack Palance** for *Requiem for a Heavyweight*, Red Skelton for *The Big Slide*

Best Single Performance by an Actress:

Edna Best for *This Happy Breed*, Gracie Fields for *Old Lady Shows Her Medals*, Nancy Kelly for *The Pilot*, Evelyn Rudie for *Eloise*, ***Claire Trevor** for *Dodsworth*

Best Supporting Performance by an Actor:

Art Carney for *Jackie Gleason Show*, Paul Ford for *Phil Silvers Show*, William Frawley for *I Love Lucy*, ***Carl Reiner** for *Caesar's Hour*, Ed Wynn for *Requiem for a Heavyweight*

Best Supporting Performance by an Actress:

Ann B. Davis for *Bob Cummings Show*, ***Pat Carroll** for *Caesar's Hour*, Audrey Meadows for *Jackie Gleason Show*, Mildred Natwick for *Blithe Spirit*, Vivian Vance for *I Love Lucy*

Best Male Personality—Continuing Performance

Steve Allen, Leonard Bernstein, ***Perry Como**, Tennessee Ernie Ford, Alfred Hitchcock, Bishop Fulton J. Sheen

Best Female Personality—Continuing Performance:

Rosemary Clooney, Faye Emerson, Arlene Francis, Gisele Mackenzie, ***Dinah Shore**

1957

Best Single Program of the Year:

* *The Comedian*, Edsel Show, Green Pastures, Helen Morgan Story

Best Continuing Performance by an Actor in a Leading Role in a Dramatic or Comedy Series:

James Arness for *Gunsmoke*, Bob Cummings for *Bob Cummings Show*, Phil Silvers for *Phil Silvers Show*, Danny Thomas for *Danny Thomas Show*, ***Robert Young** for *Father Knows Best*

Best Continuing Performance by an Actress in a Leading Role in a Dramatic or Comedy Series:

*denotes winner

194

Eve Arden for *Eve Arden Show*, Spring Byington for *December Bride*, Jan
Clayton for *Lassie*, Ida Lupino for *Mr. Adams and Eve*, *__Jane Wyatt__* for
Father Knows Best

**Best Continuing Performance (Male) in a Series by a Comedian, Singer,
Host, Dancer, Emcee, Announcer, Narrator, Panelist, or Any Person Who
Essentially Plays Himself:**

Steve Allen for *Steve Allen Show*, *__Jack Benny__* for ***Jack Benny Show***, Sid
Caesar for *Caesar's Hour*, Perry Como for *Perry Como Show*, Jack Paar for
Tonight

**Best Continuing Performance (Female) in a Series by a Comedienne,
Singer, Hostess, Dancer, Emcee, Announcer, Narrator, Panelist, or Any
Person Who Essentially Plays Herself:**

Gracie Allen for *Burns and Allen*, Lucille Ball for *I Love Lucy*, Dody
Goodman for *Tonight*, *__Dinah Shore__* for ***Dinah Shore Chevy Show***, Loretta
Young for *Loretta Young Show*

Actor—Best Single Performance—Lead or Support:

Lee J. Cobb for *No Deadly Medicine*, Mickey Rooney for *The Comedian*,
__Peter Ustinov__ for ***The Life of Samuel Johnson***, David Wayne for *Heartbeat*,
Ed Wynn for *On Borrowed Time*

Actress—Best Single Performance—Lead or Support:

Julie Andrews for *Cinderella*, *__Polly Bergen__* for ***Helen Morgan Story***, Helen
Hayes for *Mrs. Gilling and the Skyscraper*, Piper Laurie for *The Deaf Heart*,
Teresa Wright for *The Miracle Worker*

Best Continuing Performance by an Actor in a Dramatic or Comedy Series:

Paul Ford for *Phil Silvers Show*, William Frawley for *I Love Lucy*, Louis Nye
for *Steve Allen Show*, *__Carl Reiner__* for ***Caeser's Hour***, Dennis Weaver for
Gunsmoke

**Best Continuing Performance by an Actress in a Dramatic or Comedy
Series:**

Pat Carroll for *Caesar's Hour*, *__Ann B. Davis__* for ***Bob Cummings Show***, Verna
Felton for *December Bride*, Marion Lorne for *Sally*, Vivian Vance for *I Love
Lucy*

1958/59

Most Outstanding Single Program of the Year:

Child of Our Time, *__*An Evening with Fred Astaire*__*, *Little Moon of Alban*,
The Old Man

Best Actor in a Leading Role (Continuing Character) in a Dramatic Series:

James Arness for *Gunsmoke*, Richard Boone for *Have Gun, Will Travel*,
__Raymond Burr__ for ***Perry Mason***, James Garner for *Maverick*, Craig Stevens
for *Peter Gunn*, Efrem Zimbalist, Jr. for *77 Sunset Strip*

*denotes winner

195

Best Actress in a Leading Role (Continuing Character) in a Dramatic Series:
Phyllis Kirk for *The Thin Man*, June Lockhart for *Lassie*, Jane Wyman for *Jane Wyman Show*, *Loretta Young for *Loretta Young Show*

Best Actor for a Leading Role (Continuing Character) in a Comedy Series:
*Jack Benny for *Jack Benny Show*, Walter Brennan for *The Real McCoys*, Bob Cummings for *Bob Cummings Show*, Phil Silvers for *Phil Silvers Show*, Danny Thomas for *Danny Thomas Show*, Robert Young for *Father Knows Best*

Best Actress in a Leading Role (Continuing Character) in a Comedy Series:
Gracie Allen for *Burns and Allen*, Spring Byington for *December Bride*, Ida Lupino for *Mr. Adams and Eve*, Donna Reed for *Donna Reed Show*, Ann Sothern for *Ann Sothern Show*, *Jane Wyatt for *Father Knows Best*

Best Supporting Actor (Continuing Character) in a Dramatic Series:
Herschel Bernardi for *Peter Gunn*, Johnny Crawford for *The Rifleman*, William Hopper for *Perry Mason*, *Dennis Weaver for *Gunsmoke*

Best Supporting Actress (Continuing Character) in a Comedy Series:
Lola Albright for *Peter Gunn*, Amanda Blake for *Gunsmoke*, Hope Emerson for *Peter Gunn*, *Barbara Hale for *Perry Mason*

Best Supporting Actor (Continuing Role) in a Comedy Series:
Richard Crenna for *The Real McCoys*, Paul Ford for *Phil Silvers Show*, Maurice Gosfield for *Phil Silvers Show*, Billy Gray for *Father Knows Best*, Harry Morgan for *December Bride*, *Tom Poston for *Steve Allen Show*

Best Supporting Actress (Continuing Role) in a Comedy Series:
Rosemary DeCamp for *Bob Cummings Show*, *Ann B. Davis for *Bob Cummings Show*, Elinor Donahue for *Father Knows Best*, Verna Felton for *December Bride*, Kathy Nolan for *The Real McCoys*, ZaSu Pitts for *Oh, Susanna*

Best Performance by an Actor (Continuing Character) in a Musical or Variety Series:
Steve Allen for *Steve Allen Show*, *Perry Como for *Perry Como Show*, Jack Paar for *Jack Paar Show*

Best Performance by an Actress (Continuing Character) in a Musical or Variety Series:
Patti Page for *Patti Page Show*, *Dinah Shore for *Dinah Shore Chevy Show*

Best Single Performance by an Actor:
*Fred Astaire for *An Evening with Fred Astaire*, Robert Crawford for *Child of Our Time*, Paul Muni for *Last Clear Chance*, Christopher Plummer for *Little Moon of Alban*, Mickey Rooney for *Eddie*, Rod Steiger for *A Town Has Turned to Dust*

Best Single Performance by an Actress:
Judith Anderson for *Bridge of San Luis Rey*, *Julie Harris for *Little Moon of Alban*, Helen Hayes for *One Red Rose for Christmas*, Piper Laurie for *Days of*

*denotes winner

Wine and Roses, Geraldine Page for *The Old Man*, Maureen
Stapleton for *All the King's Men*

1959/60
Outstanding Program Achievement in the Field of Humor:
  *Art Carney VIP, *Danny Thomas Show*, *Father Knows Best*, *Jack Benny*
  Show, *Red Skelton Show*
Outstanding Program Achievement in the Field of Drama:
  Ethan Frome, *The Moon and Sixpence*, *Playhouse 90, *The Turn of the*
  Screw, *The Untouchables*
Outstanding Program Achievement in the Field of Variety:
  Another Evening with Fred Astaire, *Dinah Shore Chevy Show*, *Fabulous
  Fifties, *Garry Moore Show*, *Tonight with Belafonte*
Outstanding Single Performance by an Actor (Lead or Support):
  Lee J. Cobb for *Project Immortality*, Alec Guinness for *The Wicked Scheme of*
  Jebel Deeks, ***Laurence Olivier** for *The Moon and Sixpence*
Outstanding Single Performance by an Actress (Lead or Support):
  ***Ingrid Bergman** for *The Turn of the Screw*, Julie Harris for *Ethan Frome*,
  Teresa Wright for *Margaret Bourke-White Story*
Outstanding Performance by an Actor in a Series (Lead or Support):
  Richard Boone for *Have Gun, Will Travel*, Raymond Burr for *Perry Mason*,
  ***Robert Stack** for *The Untouchables*
Outstanding Performance by an Actress in a Series (Lead or Support):
  Donna Reed for *Donna Reed Show*, ***Jane Wyatt** for *Father Knows Best*,
  Loretta Young for *Loretta Young Show*
Outstanding Performance in a Variety or Musical Program or Series:
  Fred Astaire for *Another Evening with Fred Astaire*, ***Harry Belafonte** for
  Tonight with Belafonte, Dinah Shore for *Dinah Shore Chevy Show*

1960/61
Outstanding Program Achievement in the Field of Humor:
  Andy Griffith Show, *Bob Hope Buick Show*, *Candid Camera*, *Flintstones*,
  *Jack Benny Show
Outstanding Program Achievement in the Field of Drama:
  *Macbeth, *Naked City*, *Sacco-Vanzetti*, *Twilight Zone*, *The Untouchables*
Outstanding Program Achievement in the Field of Variety:
  *Astaire Time, *Belafonte, N.Y. 19*, *Garry Moore Show*, *An Hour with Danny*
  Kaye, *Jack Paar Show*
Outstanding Single Performance by an Actor in a Leading Role:
  ***Maurice Evans** for *Macbeth*, Cliff Robertson for *The Two Worlds of Charlie*,
  Ed Wynn for *The Man in the Funny Suit*
  *denotes winner

197

Outstanding Single Performance by an Actress in a Leading Role:
*Judith Anderson for *Macbeth*, Ingrid Bergman for *24 Hours in a Woman's Life*, Elizabeth Montgomery for *The Rusty Heller Story*

Outstanding Performance by an Actor in a Series (Lead):
*Raymond Burr for *Perry Mason*, Jackie Cooper for *Hennesey*, Robert Stack for *The Untouchables*

Outstanding Performance by an Actress in a Series (Lead):
Donna Reed for *Donna Reed Show*, *Barbara Stanwyck for *Barbara Stanwyck Show*, Loretta Young for *Loretta Young Show*

Outstanding Performance in a Supporting Role by an Actor or Actress in a Single Program:
Charles Bronson for *Memory in White*, Peter Falk for *Cold Turkey*, *Roddy McDowall for *Not Without Honor*

Outstanding Performance in a Supporting Role by an Actor or Actress in a Series:
Abby Dalton for *Hennesey*, Barbara Hale for *Perry Mason*, *Don Knotts for *Andy Griffith Show*

Outstanding Performance in a Variety or Musical Program or Series:
*Fred Astaire for *Astaire Time*, Harry Belafonte for *Belafonte N.Y. 19*, Dinah Shore for *Dinah Shore Chevy Show*

Program of the Year:
Astaire Time, Convention Coverage, An Hour with Danny Kaye, *Macbeth*, Sacco-Vanzetti

1961/62
Outstanding Program Achievement in the Field of Humor:
Andy Griffith Show, *Bob Newhart Show*, Car 54, Where Are You?, Hazel, Red Skelton Show

Outstanding Program Achievement in the Field of Drama:
Ben Casey, *The Defenders*, Dick Powell Show, Naked City, People Need People, Victoria Regina

Outstanding Program Achievement in the Fields of Variety or Music:
Variety:
Garry Moore Show, Here's Edie, Judy Garland Show, Perry Como's Kraft Music Hall, Walt Disney's Wonderful World of Color
Music:
Bell Telephone Hour, *Leonard Bernstein and the New York Philharmonic in Japan*, NBC Opera, The Thief and the Hangman

Outstanding Single Performance by an Actor in a Leading Role:
Milton Berle for *Against the House*, James Donald for *Victoria Regina*, *Peter Falk for *The Price of Tomatoes*, Lee Marvin for *People Need People*, Mickey Rooney for *Somebody's Waiting*

Outstanding Single Performance by an Actress in a Leading Role:
Geraldine Brooks for *Call Back Yesterday*, *Julie Harris for *Victoria Regina*,

*denotes winner

Suzanne Pleshette for *Shining Image*, Inger Stevens for *The Price of Tomatoes*, Ethel Waters for *Goodnight Sweet Blues*

Outstanding Continued Performance by an Actor in a Series (Lead):

Paul Burke for *Naked City*, Jackie Cooper for *Hennesey*, Vincent Edwards for *Ben Casey*, George Maharis for *Route 66*, *E. G. Marshall for *The Defenders*

Outstanding Continued Performance by an Actress in a Series (Lead):

Gertrude Berg for *Gertrude Berg Show*, *Shirley Booth for *Hazel*, Donna Reed for *Donna Reed Show*, Mary Stuart for *Search for Tomorrow*, Cara Williams for *Pete and Gladys*

Outstanding Performance in a Supporting Role by an Actor:

Sam Jaffe for *Ben Casey*, Barry Jones for *Victoria Regina*, *Don Knotts for *Andy Griffith Show*, Horace McMahon for *Naked City*, George C. Scott for *I Remember a Lemon Tree*

Outstanding Performance in a Supporting Role by an Actress:

*Pamela Brown in *Victoria Regina*, Jeanne Cooper for *But Linda Only Smiled*, Colleen Dewhurst for *Focus*, Joan Hackett for *A Certain Time, A Certain Darkness*, Mary Wickes for *Gertrude Berg Show*

Outstanding Performance in a Variety or Musical Program or Series:

Edie Adams for *Here's Edie*, *Carol Burnett for *Garry Moore Show*, Perry Como for *Perry Como's Kraft Music Hall*, Judy Garland for *Judy Garland Show*, Yves Montand for *Yves Montand on Broadway*

1962/63

The Program of the Year:

The Danny Kaye Show with Lucille Ball, *The Madman*, **The Tunnel*, *The Voice of Charlie Pont*

Outstanding Program Achievement in the Field of Humor:

The Beverly Hillbillies, *The Danny Kaye Show*, **The Dick Van Dyke Show*, *McHale's Navy*

Outstanding Program Achievement in the Field of Drama:

Alcoa Premiere, **The Defenders*, *The Dick Powell Show*, *The Eleventh Hour*, *Naked City*

Outstanding Program Achievement in the Field of Music:

Bell Telephone Hour, *Judy Garland and Her Guests Phil Silvers and Robert Goulet*, **Julie and Carol at Carnegie Hall*, *The Lively Ones*, *NBC Opera*

Outstanding Achievement in the Field of Variety:

**Andy Williams Show*, *Carol and Company*, *The Garry Moore Show*, *Here's Edie*, *The Red Skelton Show*

Outstanding Single Performance by an Actor in a Single Role:

Bradford Dillman for *The Voice of Charlie Pont*, Don Gordon for *The Madman*, *Trevor Howard for *The Invincible Mr. Disraeli*, Walter Matthau for *Big Deal in Laredo*, Joseph Schildkraut for *Hear the Mellow Wedding Bells*

Outstanding Performance by an Actress in a Leading Role:

Diahann Carroll for *A Horse Has a Big Head, Let Him Worry*, Diana Hyland

**denotes winner*

199

for *The Voice of Charlie Pont*, Eleanor Parker for *Why Am I Grown So Cold?*, Sylvia Sidney for *The Madman*, *****Kim Stanley** for *A Cardinal Act of Mercy*

Outstanding Continued Performance by an Actor in a Series (Lead):
Ernest Borgnine for *McHale's Navy*, Paul Burke for *Naked City*, *****E. G. Marshall** for *The Defenders*, Vic Morrow for *Combat*, Dick Van Dyke for *The Dick Van Dyke Show*

Outstanding Continued Performance by an Actress in a Series (Lead):
Lucille Ball for *The Lucille Ball Show*, *****Shirley Booth** for *Hazel*, Shirl Conway for *The Nurses*, Mary Tyler Moore for *The Dick Van Dyke Show*, Irene Ryan for *The Beverly Hillbillies*

Outstanding Performance in a Supporting Role by an Actor:
Tim Conway for *McHale's Navy*, Paul Ford for *Teahouse of the August Moon*, Hurd Hatfield for *The Invincible Mr. Disraeli*, *****Don Knotts** for *The Andy Griffith Show*, Robert Redford and George Laurents for *The Voice of Charlie Pont*

Outstanding Performance in a Supporting Role by an Actress:
Davey Davison for *Roses and Nightingales and Other Lovely Things*, *****Glenda Farrell** for *A Cardinal Act of Mercy*, Nancy Malone for *Naked City*, Rose Marie for *The Dick Van Dyke Show*, Kate Reid for *The Invincible Mr. Disraeli*

Outstanding Performance in a Variety or Musical Program or Series:
Edie Adams for *Here's Edie*, *****Carol Burnett** for *Julie and Carol at Carnegie Hall*, Merv Griffin for *The Merv Griffin Show*, Danny Kaye for *The Danny Kaye Show with Lucille Ball*, Andy Williams for *The Andy Williams Show*

1963/64

The Program of the Year:
American Revolution of '63, *Blacklist (The Defenders)*, *The Kremlin Story*, *****The Making of the President 1960*, *Town Meeting of the World*

Outstanding Program Achievement in the Field of Comedy:
The Bill Dana Show, *****The Dick Van Dyke Show*, *The Farmer's Daughter*, *McHale's Navy*, *That Was the Week That Was*

Outstanding Achievement in the Field of Variety:
The Andy Williams Show, *****The Danny Kaye Show*, *The Garry Moore Show*, *The Judy Garland Show*, *The Tonight Show Starring Johnny Carson*

Outstanding Single Performance by an Actor in a Leading Role:
James Earl Jones for *Who Do You Kill?*, *****Jack Klugman** for *Blacklist (The Defenders)*, Roddy McDowall for *Journey Into Darkness*, Jason Robards, Jr. for *Abe Lincoln in Illinois*, Rod Steiger for *A Slow Fade to Black*, Harold J. Stone for *Nurse Is a Feminine Noun*

Outstanding Single Performance by an Actress in a Leading Role:
Ruby Dee for *Express Stop from Lenox Avenue*, Bethel Leslie for *Statement of Fact*, Jeanette Nolan for *Vote No on 11!*, Diana Sands for *Who Do You Kill?*, *****Shelley Winters** for *Two Is the Number*

*denotes winner

200

Outstanding Continued Performance by an Actor in a Series (Lead):
Richard Boone for *The Richard Boone Show*, Dean Jagger for *Mr. Novak*, David Janssen for *The Fugitive*, George C. Scott for *East Side/West Side*, *Dick Van Dyke** for ***The Dick Van Dyke Show***

Outstanding Continued Performance by an Actress in a Series (Lead):
Shirley Booth for *Hazel*, Patty Duke for *The Patty Duke Show*, ***Mary Tyler Moore** for ***The Dick Van Dyke Show***, Irene Ryan for *The Beverly Hillbillies*, Inger Stevens for *The Farmer's Daughter*

Outstanding Performance in a Supporting Role by an Actor:
Sorrell Booke for *What's God to Julius?*, Conlan Carter for *The Hostages*, Carl Lee for *Express Stop from Lenox Avenue*, ***Albert Paulsen** for ***One Day in the Life of Ivan Denisovich***

Outstanding Performance in a Supporting Role by an Actress:
Martine Bartlett for *Journey into Darkness*, Anjanette Comer for *Journey into Darkness*, Rose Marie for *The Dick Van Dyke Show*, Claudia McNeill for *Express Stop from Lenox Avenue*, ***Ruth White** for ***Little Moon of Alban***

Outstanding Performance in a Variety or Musical Program or Series:
Judy Garland for *The Judy Garland Show*, ***Danny Kaye** for ***The Danny Kaye Show***, Barbra Streisand for *The Judy Garland Show*, Burr Tillstrom for *The Week That Was*, Andy Williams for *The Andy Williams Show*

1964/65

Outstanding Achievement in Entertainment:
*Dick Van Dyke Show, **The Magnificent Yankee*, **My Name Is Barbra*, **What Is Sonata Form?*, The Andy Williams Show, Bob Hope Presents the Chrysler Theatre, The Defenders, Hallmark Hall of Fame, The Man from U.N.C.L.E., Mr. Novak, Profiles in Courage, Walt Disney's Wonderful World of Color, The Wonderful World of Burlesque, Xerox Specials

Outstanding Individual Achievement in Entertainment: Actors and Performers:
*Leonard Bernstein for ***New York Philharmonic Young People's Concerts***, **Lynn Fontanne* for ***The Magnificent Yankee***, **Alfred Lunt* for ***The Magnificent Yankee***, **Barbra Streisand* for ***My Name Is Barbra***, **Dick Van Dyke* for ***The Dick Van Dyke Show***, Julie Andrews for *The Andy Williams Show*, Johnny Carson for *The Tonight Show Starring Johnny Carson*, Gladys Cooper for *The Rogues*, Robert Cootes for *The Rogues*, Julie Harris for *The Holy Terror*, Bob Hope for *Chrysler Presents a Bob Hope Comedy Special*, Dean Jagger for *Mr. Novak*, Danny Kaye for *The Danny Kaye Show*, David McCallum for *The Man from U.N.C.L.E.*, Red Skelton for *The Red Skelton Hour*

1965/66

Outstanding Comedy Series:
Batman, Bewitched, **Dick Van Dyke Show*, Get Smart, Hogan's Heroes

*denotes winner

Outstanding Variety Series:
 Andy Williams Show, Danny Kaye Show, The Hollywood Palace, Red
 Skelton Show, Tonight Show Starring Johnny Carson
Outstanding Variety Special:
 An Evening with Carol Channing, *Chrysler Presents Bob Hope Christmas
 Special*, Jimmy Durante Meets the Lively Arts, The Julie Andrews Show, The
 Swinging World of Sammy Davis, Jr.
Outstanding Dramatic Series:
 Bonanza, *The Fugitive*, I Spy, The Man from U.N.C.L.E., Slattery's People
**Outstanding Single Performance by an Actor in a Leading Role in a
Drama:**
 Ed Begley for Inherit the Wind, Melvyn Douglas for Inherit the Wind,
 Trevor Howard for *Eagle in a Cage*, Christopher Plummer for Hamlet, Cliff
 Robertson for The Game
**Outstanding Single Performance by an Actress in a Leading Role in a
Drama:**
 Eartha Kitt for The Loser, Margaret Leighton for Behold the Great Man; A
 Life for a Life; Web of Hate; Horizontal Hero, *Simone Signoret* for *A Small
 Rebellion*, Shelley Winters for Back to Back
**Outstanding Continued Performance by an Actor in a Leading Role in a
Dramatic Series:**
 Bill Cosby for *I Spy*, Richard Crenna for Slattery's People, Robert Culp for I
 Spy, David Janssen for The Fugitive, David McCallum for The Man from
 U.N.C.L.E.
**Outstanding Continued Performance by an Actress in a Leading Role in a
Dramatic Series:**
 Anne Francis for Honey West, Barbara Parkins for Peyton Place, *Barbara
 Stanwyck* for *The Big Valley*
**Outstanding Continued Performance by an Actor in a Leading Role in a
Comedy Series:**
 Don Adams for Get Smart, Bob Crane for Hogan's Heroes, *Dick Van Dyke*
 for *The Dick Van Dyke Show*
**Outstanding Continued Performance by an Actress in a Leading Role in a
Comedy Series:**
 Lucille Ball for The Lucy Show, Elizabeth Montgomery for Bewitched, *Mary
 Tyler Moore* for *The Dick Van Dyke Show*
Outstanding Performance by an Actor in a Supporting Role in a Drama:
 David Burns for Trials of O'Brien, Leo G. Carroll for The Man from
 U.N.C.L.E., *James Daly* for *Eagle in a Cage*
Outstanding Performance by an Actress in a Supporting Role in a Drama:
 Diane Baker for Inherit the Wind, Pamela Franklin for Eagle in a Cage, *Lee
 Grant* for *Peyton Place*, Jeanette Nolan for The Conquest of Maude Murdock
Outstanding Performance by an Actor in a Suppporting Role in a Comedy:
 Morey Amsterdam for The Dick Van Dyke Show, Frank Gorshin for Hi
 Diddle Riddle, Werner Klemperer for Hogan's Heroes, *Don Knotts* for *The
 Andy Griffith Show*

*denotes winner

Outstanding Performance by an Actress in a Supporting Role in a Comedy:

Agnes Moorehead for Bewitched, Rose Marie for The Dick Van Dyke Show, *Alice Pearce for **Bewitched**

1966/67

Outstanding Comedy Series:

Bewitched, Get Smart, The Andy Griffith Show, Hogan's Heroes, *The Monkees*

Outstanding Variety Series:

The Andy Williams Show, The Dean Martin Show, The Jackie Gleason Show, The Smothers Brothers Comedy Hour, The Tonight Show Starring Johnny Carson

Outstanding Variety Special:

The Bob Hope Christmas Special, *The Sid Caesar, Imogene Coca, Carl Reiner, Howard Morris Special Hour*, A Time for Laughter: A Look at Negro Humor in America, Dick Van Dyke

Outstanding Dramatic Series:

The Avengers, I Spy, *Mission: Impossible*, Run for Your Life, Star Trek

Outstanding Dramatic Program:

A Christmas Memory, *Death of a Salesman*, The Final War of Olly Winter, The Glass Menagerie, The Love Story of Barney Kempinski, Mark Twain Tonight!

Outstanding Musical Program:

Brigadoon, Frank Sinatra: A Man and His Music, Toscanini: The Maestro Revisited

Outstanding Single Performance by an Actor in a Leading Role in a Drama:

Alan Arkin for The Love Song of Barney Kempinski, Lee J. Cobb for Death of a Salesman, Ivan Dixon for The Final War of Olly Winter, Hal Holbrook for Mark Twain Tonight!, *Peter Ustinov for *Barefoot in Athens**

Outstanding Single Performance by an Actress in a Leading Role in a Drama:

Shirley Booth for The Glass Menagerie, Mildred Dunnock for Death of a Salesman, Lynn Fontanne for Anastasia, Julie Harris for Anastasia, *Geraldine Page for *A Christmas Memory**

Outstanding Continued Performance by an Actor in a Leading Role in a Dramatic Series:

*Bill Cosby for *I Spy**, Robert Culp for I Spy, Ben Gazzara for Run for Your Life, David Janssen for The Fugitive, Martin Landau for Mission: Impossible

Outstanding Continued Performance by an Actress in a Leading Role in a Dramatic Series:

*Barbara Bain for *Mission: Impossible**, Diana Rigg for The Avengers, Barbara Stanwyck for The Big Valley

*denotes winner

Outstanding Continued Performance by an Actor in a Leading Role in a Comedy Series:

*Don Adams for *Get Smart*, Bob Crane for *Hogan's Heroes*, Brian Keith for *Family Affair*, Larry Storch for *F Troop*

Outstanding Continued Performance by an Actress in a Leading Role in a Comedy Series:

*Lucille Ball for *The Lucy Show*, Elizabeth Montgomery for *Bewitched*, Agnes Moorehead for *Bewitched*, Marlo Thomas for *That Girl*

Outstanding Performance by an Actor in a Supporting Role in a Drama:

Leo G. Carroll for *The Man from U.N.C.L.E.*, Leonard Nimoy for *Star Trek*, *Eli Wallach for *The Poppy Is Also a Flower*

Outstanding Performance by an Actress in a Supporting Role in a Drama:

Tina Chen for *The Final War of Olly Winter*, *Agnes Moorehead for *Night of the Viciou Valentine*, Ruth Warrick for *Peyton Place*

Outstanding Performance by an Actor in a Supporting Role in a Comedy:

Gale Gordon for *The Lucy Show*, Werner Klemperer for *Hogan's Heroes*, *Don Knotts for *The Andy Griffith Show*

Outstanding Performance by an Actress in a Supporting Role in a Comedy:

*Frances Bavier for *The Andy Griffith Show*, Nancy Kulp for *The Beverly Hillbillies*, Marion Lorne for *Bewitched*

1967/68

Outstanding Comedy Series:

Bewitched, *Hogan's Heroes*, *Get Smart*, *Family Affair*, *The Lucy Show*

Outstanding Dramatic Series:

The Avengers, *I Spy*, *Mission: Impossible*, *NET Playhouse*, *Run for Your Life*, *Star Trek*

Outstanding Dramatic Program:

Dear Friends, *Do Not Go Gentle into That Good Night*, *Elizabeth the Queen*, *The Strange Case of Dr. Jekyll and Mr. Hyde*, *Uncle Vanya*, *Luther*

Outstanding Musical or Variety Series:

Bell Telephone Hour, *The Carol Burnett Show*, *The Dean Martin Show*, *Rowan and Martin's Laugh-In*, *The Smothers Brothers Comedy Hour*

Outstanding Musical or Variety Special:

A Man and His Music + Ella + Jobim, *The Bob Hope Christmas Special*, *Five Ballets of the Five Senses*, *The Fred Astaire Show*, *Herb Alpert and the Tijuana Brass*, *Rowan and Martin's Laugh-In Special*

Outstanding Single Performance by an Actor in a Leading Role in a Drama:

Raymond Burr for *Ironside World Premiere*, *Melvyn Douglas for *Do Not Go Gentle into That Good Night*, Van Heflin for *A Case of Libel*, George C. Scott for *The Crucible*, Eli Wallach for *Dear Friends*

Outstanding Single Performance by an Actress in a Leading Role in a Drama:

*denotes winner

Judith Anderson for *Elizabeth the Queen*, Genevieve Bujold for *Saint Joan*, Colleen Dewhurst for *The Crucible*, Anne Jackson for *Dear Friends*, *Maureen Stapleton** for ***Among the Paths to Eden***

Outstanding Continued Performance by an Actor in a Leading Role in a Dramatic Series:

Raymond Burr for *Ironside*, *Bill Cosby** for *I Spy*, Robert Culp for *I Spy*, Ben Gazzara for *Run for Your Life*, Martin Landau for *Mission: Impossible*

Outstanding Continued Performance by an Actress in a Leading Role in a Dramatic Series:

*Barbara Bain** for ***Mission: Impossible***, Diana Rigg for *The Avengers*, Barbara Stanwyck for *The Big Valley*

Outstanding Continued Performance by an Actor in a Leading Role in a Comedy Series:

*Don Adams** for ***Get Smart***, Richard Benjamin for *He and She*, Sebastian Cabot for *Family Affair*, Brian Keith for *Family Affair*, Dick York for *Bewitched*

Outstanding Continued Performance by an Actress in a Leading Role in a Comedy Series:

*Lucille Ball** for ***The Lucy Show***, Barbara Feldon for *Get Smart*, Elizabeth Montgomery for *Bewitched*, Paula Prentiss for *He and She*, Marlo Thomas for *That Girl*

Outstanding Performance by an Actor in a Supporting Role in a Drama:

Joseph Campanella for *Mannix*, Lawrence Dobkin for *Do Not Go Gentle Into That Good Night*, Leonard Nimoy for *Star Trek*, *Milburn Stone** for ***Gunsmoke***

Outstanding Performance by an Actress in a Supporting Role in a Drama:

*Barbara Anderson** for ***Ironside***, Linda Cristal for *The High Chaparral*, Tessie O'Shea for *The Strange Case of Dr. Jekyll and Mr. Hyde*

Outstanding Performance by an Actor in a Supporting Role in a Comedy:

Jack Cassidy for *He and She*, William Demarest for *My Three Sons*, Gale Gordon for *The Lucy Show*, *Werner Klemperer** for ***Hogan's Heroes***,

Outstanding Performance by an Actress in a Supporting Role in a Comedy:

*Marion Lorne** for ***Bewitched***, Agnes Moorehead for *Bewitched*, Marge Redmond for *The Flying Nun*, Nita Talbot for *The Hostage*

1968/69

Outstanding Comedy Series:

Bewitched, *Family Affair*, **Get Smart**, *The Ghost and Mrs. Muir*, *Julia*

Outstanding Dramatic Program:

The Execution, *Heidi*, *A Midsummer Night's Dream*, *The People Next Door*, *Talking to a Stranger*, ***Teacher, Teacher***

Outstanding Dramatic Series:

The FBI, *Ironside*, *Judd, For the Defense*, *Mission: Impossible*, *The Name of the Game*, ***NET Playhouse***

*denotes winner

205

Outstanding Variety or Musical Series:

The Carol Burnett Show, The Dean Martin Show, *Rowan and Martin's Laugh-In*, The Smothers Brothers Comedy Hour, That's Life

Outstanding Variety or Musical Program:

Barbra Streisand: A Happening in Central Park, *The Bill Cosby Special*, Duke Ellington: Concert of Sacred Music, Francis Albert Sinatra Does His Thing, The Rite of Spring, Rowan and Martin's Laugh-In (with Marcel Marceau), Vladimir Horowitz: A Television Concert at Carnegie Hall

Outstanding Single Performance by an Actor in a Leading Role:

Ossie Davis for Teacher, Teacher, David McCallum for Teacher, Teacher, *Paul Scofield for *Male of the Species*, Bill Travers for The Admirable Crichton

Outstanding Single Performance by an Actress in a Leading Role:

Anne Baxter for The Bobbie Currier Story, Lee Grant for The Gates of Cerberus, *Geraldine Page for *The Thanksgiving Visitor*

Outstanding Continued Performance by an Actor in a Leading Role in a Dramatic Series:

*Carl Betz for *Judd, For the Defense*, Raymond Burr for Ironside, Peter Graves for Mission: Impossible, Martin Landau for Mission: Impossible, Ross Martin for The Wild, Wild West

Outstanding Continued Performance by an Actress in a Leading Role in a Dramatic Series:

*Barbara Bain for *Mission: Impossible*, Joan Blondell for Here Come the Brides, Peggy Lipton for The Mod Squad

Outstanding Continued Performance by an Actor in a Leading Role in a Comedy Series:

*Don Adams for *Get Smart*, Brian Keith for Family Affair, Edward Mulhare for The Ghost and Mrs. Muir, Lloyd Nolan for Julia

Outstanding Continued Performance by an Actress in a Leading Role in a Comedy Series:

Diahann Carroll for Julia, Barbara Feldon for Get Smart, *Hope Lange for *The Ghost and Mrs. Muir*, Elizabeth Montgomery for Bewitched

Outstanding Single Performance by an Actor in a Supporting Role (no award given):

Ned Glass for A Little Chicken Soup Never Hurt Anybody, Hal Holbrook for The Whole World Is Watching, Billy Schulman for Teacher, Teacher

Outstanding Single Performance by an Actress in a Supporting Role:

Pamela Brown for The Admirable Mr. Crichton, *Anna Calder-Marshall for *Male of the Species*, Irene Hervey for The O'Casey Scandal, Nancy Kovak for The Girl Who Came in with the Tide

Outstanding Continued Performance by an Actor in a Supporting Role in a Series:

*Werner Klemperer for *Hogan's Heroes*, Greg Morris for Mission: Impossible, Leonard Nimoy for Star Trek

*denotes winner

206

Outstanding Continued Performance by an Actress in a Supporting Role in a Series:

Barbara Anderson for *Ironside*, Agnes Moorehead for *Bewitched*, *Susan Saint James for *The Name of the Game*

1969/70
Outstanding Comedy Series:

**My World and Welcome to It*, The Bill Cosby Show, The Courtship of Eddie's Father, Love American Style, Room 222

Outstanding Dramatic Series:

**Marcus Welby, M.D.*, The Forsyte Saga, The Mod Squad, The Name of the Game, NET Playhouse

Outstanding Single Dramatic Program:

**A Storm in Summer*, David Copperfield, Hello Goodbye Hello, My Sweet Charlie

Outstanding Variety or Musical Series:

The Carol Burnett Show, *The David Frost Show*, The Dean Martin Show, The Dick Cavett Show, Rowan and Martin's Laugh-In

Outstanding Variety or Musical Program (Popular):

**Annie, The Women in the Life of a Man*, The Friars Club "Roasts" Jack Benny, The Second Bill Cosby Special, Sinatra, The Sound of Burt Bacharach

Outstanding Variety or Musical Program (Classical):

**Cinderella* (National Ballet of Canada), S. Hurok Presents—Part 3, Sounds of Summer, The Switched-On Symphony

Outstanding New Series:

The Bill Cosby Show, The Forsyte Saga, Marcus Welby, M.D., *Room 222*, Sesame Street

Outstanding Single Performance by an Actor in a Leading Role:

Al Freeman, Jr. for *My Sweet Charlie*, Laurence Olivier for *David Copperfield*, *Peter Ustinov for *A Storm in Summer*

Outstanding Single Performance by an Actress in a Leading Role:

*Patty Duke for *My Sweet Charlie*, Edith Evans for *David Copperfield*, Shirley Jones for *Silent Night, Lonely Night*

Outstanding Continued Performance by an Actor in a Leading Role in a Dramatic Series:

Raymond Burr for *Ironside*, Mike Connors for *Mannix*, Robert Wagner for *It Takes a Thief*, *Robert Young for *Marcus Welby, M.D.*

Outstanding Continued Performance by an Actress in a Leading Role in a Dramatic Series:

Joan Blondell for *Here Comes the Brides*, Peggy Lipton for *The Mod Squad*, *Susan Hampshire for *The Forsyte Saga*

*denotes winner

207

Outstanding Continued Performance by an Actor in a Leading Role in a Comedy Series:
> Bill Cosby for *The Bill Cosby Show*, Lloyd Haynes for *Room 222*, *William Windom for *My World and Welcome to It*

Outstanding Continued Performance by an Actress in a Leading Role in a Comedy Series:
> *Hope Lange for *The Ghost and Mrs. Muir*, Elizabeth Montgomery for *Bewitched*, Marlo Thomas for *That Girl*

Outstanding Performance by an Actor in a Supporting Role in a Drama:
> *James Brolin for *Marcus Welby, M.D.*, Tige Andrews for *The Mod Squad*, Greg Morris for *Mission: Impossible*

Outstanding Performance by an Actress in a Supporting Role in a Drama:
> Barbara Anderson for *Ironside*, *Gail Fisher for *Mannix*, Susan Saint James for *The Name of the Game*

Outstanding Performance by an Actor in a Supporting Role in a Comedy:
> *Michael Constantine for *Room 222*, Werner Klemperer for *Hogan's Heroes*, Charles Nelson Reilly for *The Ghost and Mrs. Muir*

Outstanding Performance by an Actress in a Supporting Role in a Comedy:
> Agnes Moorehead for *Bewitched*, Lurene Tuttle for *Julia*, *Karen Valentine for *Room 222*

1970/71

Outstanding Series—Comedy:
> **All in the Family*, Arnie, Love, American Style, The Mary Tyler Moore Show, The Odd Couple

Outstanding Series—Drama:
> The First Churchills—Masterpiece Theatre, Ironside, NET Playhouse, Marcus Welby, M.D., **The Senator—The Bold Ones*

Outstanding Single Program—Drama or Comedy:
> **The Andersonville Trial*, Hamlet, The Price, They're Tearing Down Tim Riley's Bar, Vanished—Parts 1 and 2

Outstanding Variety Series—Musical:
> The Carol Burnett Show, **The Flip Wilson Show*, Rowan and Martin's Laugh-In

Outstanding Variety Show—Talk:
> The Dick Cavett Show, **The David Frost Show*, The Tonight Show Starring Johnny Carson

Outstanding Single Program—Variety or Musical:
> Popular:
> Another Evening with Burt Bacharach, Harry and Lena, **Singer Presents Burt Bacharach*

*denotes winner

Classical:

*__Leopold Stokowski__, Queen of Spades, Swan Lake

Outstanding New Series:

*__All in the Family__, The Flip Wilson Show, The Mary Tyler Moore Show, The Odd Couple, The Senator—The Bold Ones

Outstanding Single Performance by an Actor in a Leading Role:

Jack Cassidy for The Andersonville Trial, Hal Holbrook for A Clear and Present Danger, *__George C. Scott__ for __The Price__, Richard Widmark for Vanished, Parts 1 and 2, Gig Young for The Neon Ceiling

Outstanding Single Performance by an Actress in a Leading Role:

Colleen Dewhurst for The Price, *__Lee Grant__ for __The Neon Ceiling__, Lee Grant for Ransom for a Dead Man

Outstanding Continued Performance by an Actor in a Leading Role in a Dramatic Series:

Raymond Burr for Ironside, Mike Connors for Mannix, *__Hal Holbrook__ for __The Senator—The Bold Ones__, Robert Young for Marcus Welby, M.D.

Outstanding Continued Performance by an Actress in a Leading Role in a Dramatic Series:

Linda Cristal for The High Chaparral, *__Susan Hampshire__ for __The First Churchills__, Peggy Lipton for The Mod Squad

Outstanding Performance by an Actor in a Leading Role in a Comedy Series:

Ted Bessell for That Girl, Bill Bixby for The Courtship of Eddie's Father, *__Jack Klugman__ for __The Odd Couple__, Carroll O'Connor for All in the Family, Tony Randall for The Odd Couple

Outstanding Continued Performance by an Actress in a Leading Role in a Comedy Series:

Mary Tyler Moore for The Mary Tyler Moore Show, *__Jean Stapleton__ for __All in the Family__, Marlo Thomas for That Girl

Outstanding Performance by an Actor in a Supporting Role in a Drama:

James Brolin for Marcus Welby, M.D., *__David Burns__ for __The Price__, Robert Young for Vanished, Parts 1 and 2

Outstanding Performance by an Actress in a Supporting Role in a Drama:

Gail Fisher for Mannix, *__Margaret Leighton__ for __Hamlet__, Susan Saint James for The Name of the Game, Elena Verdugo for Marcus Welby, M.D.

Outstanding Performance by an Actor in a Supporting Role in a Comedy:

*__Edward Asner__ for __The Mary Tyler Moore Show__, Michael Constantine for Room 222, Gale Gordon for Here's Lucy

Outstanding Performance by an Actress in a Supporting Role in a Comedy:

*__Valerie Harper__ for __The Mary Tyler Moore Show__, Agnes Moorehead for Bewitched, Karen Valentine for Room 222

*denotes winner

1971/72

Outstanding Series–Comedy

All in the Family, The Mary Tyler Moore Show, The Odd Couple, Sanford and Son

Outstanding Series–Drama:

Columbo, *Elizabeth R*, Mannix, Marcus Welby, M.D., The Six Wives of Henry VIII

Outstanding Single Program–Comedy or Drama:

Brian's Song, Jane Seymour (The Six Wives of Henry VIII), The Lion's Club, Sammy's Quest, The Snow Goose

Outstanding Variety Series–Musical:

The Carol Burnett Show, The Dean Martin Show, The Flip Wilson Show, The Sonny and Cher Comedy Hour

Outstanding Variety Series–Talk:

The Dick Cavett Show, The David Frost Show, The Tonight Show Starring Johnny Carson

Outstanding Single Program–Variety or Musical:

Popular:

Jack Lemmon in 'S Wonderful, 'S Marvelous, 'S Gershwin, The Flip Wilson Show, Julie and Carol at Lincoln Center, The Sonny and Cher Comedy Hour

Classical Music:

Beethoven's Birthday—A Celebration in Vienna with Leonard Bernstein, Heifeitz, The Peking Ballet, The Trial of Mary Lincoln

Outstanding New Series:

Elizabeth R, Columbo, Sanford and Son, The Six Wives of Henry VIII, The Sonny and Cher Comedy Hour

Outstanding Single Performance by an Actor in a Leading Role:

James Caan for Brian's Song, Richard Harris for The Snow Goose, *Keith Mitchell for Catherine Howard (The Six Wives of Henry VIII)*, George C. Scott for Jane Eyre, Billy Dee Williams for Brian's Song

Outstanding Single Performance by an Actress in a Leading Role:

Helen Hayes for Do Not Fold, Spindle or Mutilate, Glenda Jackson for The Lions' Club, *Glenda Jackson for Shadow in the Sun*, Patricia Neal for The Homecoming—A Christmas Story, Susannah York for Jane Eyre

Outstanding Continued Performance by an Actor In a Leading Role in a Dramatic Series:

Raymond Burr for Ironside, Mike Connors for Mannix, *Peter Falk for Columbo*, Keith Mitchell for The Six Wives of Henry VIII, Robert Young for Marcus Welby, M.D.

Outstanding Continued Performance by an Actress in a Leading Role in a Dramatic Series:

Glenda Jackson for Elizabeth R, Peggy Lipton for The Mod Squad, Susan Saint James for McMillan and Wife

*denotes winner

Outstanding Continued Performance by an Actor in a Leading Role in a Comedy Series:
Redd Foxx for *Sanford and Son*, Jack Klugman for *The Odd Couple*, ***Carroll O'Connor** for *All in the Family*, Tony Randall for *The Odd Couple*

Outstanding Continued Performance by an Actress in a Leading Role in a Comedy Series:
Sandy Duncan for *Funny Face*, Mary Tyler Moore for *The Mary Tyler Moore Show*, ***Jean Stapleton** for *All in the Family*

Outstanding Performance by an Actor in a Supporting Role in Drama:
James Brolin for *Marcus Welby, M.D.*, Greg Morris for *Mission: Impossible*, ***Jack Warden** for *Brian's Song*

Outstanding Performance by an Actress in a Supporting Role in Drama:
*Jenny Agutter for *The Snow Goose*, Gail Fisher for *Mannix*, Elena Verdugo for *Marcus Welby, M.D.*

Outstanding Performance by an Actor in a Supporting Role in Comedy:
*Edward Asner for *The Mary Tyler Moore Show*, Ted Knight for *The Mary Tyler Moore Show*, Rob Reiner for *All in the Family*

Outstanding Performance by an Actress in a Supporting Role in Comedy (Tie):
*Valerie Harper for *The Mary Tyler Moore Show*, ***Sally Struthers** for *All in the Family*, Cloris Leachman for *The Mary Tyler Moore Show*

Outstanding Achievement by a Performer in Music or Variety:
Ruth Buzzi for *Rowan and Martin's Laugh-In*, ***Harvey Korman** for *The Carol Burnett Show*, Lily Tomlin for *Rowan and Martin's Laugh-In*

1972/73
Outstanding Comedy Series:
*All in the Family, The Mary Tyler Moore Show, M*A*S*H, Maude, Sanford and Son

Outstanding Dramatic Series—Continuing:
Cannon, Columbo, Hawaii Five-O, Kung Fu, Mannix, **The Waltons*

Outstanding Drama/Comedy—Limited Episodes:
The Last of the Mohicans, Parts 1 through 8, The Life of Leonardo da Vinci, Parts 1 through 5, **Tom Brown's Schooldays, Parts 1 through 5*

Outstanding Variety Musical Series:
*The Julie Andrews Hour, The Carol Burnett Show, The Dick Cavett Show, The Flip Wilson Show, The Sonny and Cher Comedy Hour

Outstanding Single Program—Drama or Comedy:
Long Day's Journey into Night, The Marcus-Nelson Murders, The Red Pony, That Certain Summer, **A War of Children*

Outstanding Single Program—Variety or Popular Music:
Applause, Once Upon a Mattress, **Singer Presents Liza with a "Z"*

Outstanding Single Program—Classical Music:
Bernstein in London, The Metropolitan Salute to Sir Rudolf Bing, **The Sleeping Beauty*

*denotes winner

Outstanding New Series:
America, The Julie Andrews Hour, Kung Fu, M*A*S*H, Maude, The
Waltons

Outstanding Program Achievement in Daytime Drama:
Days of Our Lives, *The Edge of Night*, The Doctors, One Life to Live

Outstanding Program Achievement in Daytime:
Dinah's Place, The Hollywood Squares, Jeopardy, The Mike Douglas Show,
Password

Outstanding Single Performance by an Actor in a Leading Role:
Henry Fonda for The Red Pony, Hal Holbrook for That Certain Summer,
Laurence Oliver for *Long Day's Journey into Night*, Telly Savalas for The
Marcus-Nelson Murders

Outstanding Single Performance by an Actress in a Leading Role:
Lauren Bacall for Applause, Hope Lange for That Certain Summer, *Cloris
Leachman* for *A Brand New Life*

Outstanding Continued Performance by an Actor in a Leading Role:
Continuing:
David Carradine for Kung Fu, Mike Connors for Mannix, William Conrad for
Cannon, Peter Falk for Columbo, *Richard Thomas* for *The Waltons*
Limited:
John Abineri for The Last of the Mohicans, Phillipe LeRoy for The Life of
Leonardo da Vinci, *Anthony Murphy* for *Tom Brown's Schooldays*

Outstanding Continued Performance by an Actress in a Leading Role:
Continuing:
Linda Day George for Mission: Impossible, Susan Saint James for McMillan
and Wife, *Michael Learned* for *The Waltons*
Limited:
Susan Hampshire for *Vanity Fair*, Vivien Heilbron for The Moonstone,
Margaret Tyzack for Cousin Bette

**Outstanding Continued Performance by an Actor in a Leading Role in a
Comedy Series:**
Alan Alda for M*A*S*H, Redd Foxx for Sanford and Son, *Jack Klugman*
for *The Odd Couple*, Carroll O'Connor for All in the Family, Tony Randall
for The Odd Couple

**Outstanding Continued Performance by an Actress in a Leading Role in a
Comedy Series:**
Beatrice Arthur for Maude, *Mary Tyler Moore* for *The Mary Tyler Moore
Show*, Jean Stapleton for All in the Family

Outstanding Performance by an Actor in a Supporting Role in Drama:
James Brolin for Marcus Welby, M.D., Will Geer for The Waltons, *Scott
Jacoby* for *That Certain Summer*

Outstanding Performance by an Actress in a Supporting Role in Drama:
Ellen Corby for *The Waltons*, Gail Fisher for Mannix, Nancy Walker for
McMillan and Wife

Outstanding Performance by an Actor in a Supporting Role in Comedy:

*denotes winner

212

Edward Asner for *The Mary Tyler Moore Show*, Gary Burghoff for M*A*S*H,
*Ted Knight for *The Mary Tyler Moore Show*, Rob Reiner for *All in
the Family*, McLean Stevenson for M*A*S*H
Outstanding Performance by an Actress in a Supporting Role in Comedy:
*Valerie Harper for *The Mary Tyler Moore Show*, Cloris Leachman for *The
Mary Tyler Moore Show*, Sally Struthers for *All in the Family*
Outstanding Achievement by a Supporting Performer in Music or Variety:
*Tim Conway for *The Carol Burnett Show*, Harvey Korman for *The Carol
Burnett Show*, Liza Minnelli for *A Royal Gala Variety Performance*, Lily
Tomlin for *Rowan and Martin's Laugh-In*

1973/74
Outstanding Comedy Series:
All in the Family, *The Mary Tyler Moore Show*, **M*A*S*H*, *The Odd
Couple*
Outstanding Drama Series:
Kojak, *Police Story*, *The Streets of San Francisco*, *The Waltons*, **Upstairs,
Downstairs*
Outstanding Music-Variety Series:
**The Carol Burnett Show*, *The Sonny and Cher Comedy Hour*, *The Tonight
Show Starring Johnny Carson*
Outstanding Limited Series:
The Blue Knight, *Columbo, *McCloud*
Oustanding Special–Comedy or Drama:
**The Autobiography of Miss Jane Pittman*, *The Execution of Private Slovik*,
The Migrants, *Steambath*, *6 Rms Riv Vu*
Outstanding Comedy-Variety, Variety or Music Special:
Barbra Streisand . . . and Other Musical Instruments, *Lily, *Magnavox
Presents Frank Sinatra*, *The John Denver Show*
Best Lead Actor in a Comedy Series:
*Alan Alda for M*A*S*H, Redd Foxx for *Sanford and Son*, Jack Klugman
for *The Odd Couple*, Carroll O'Connor for *All in the Family*, Tony Randall
for *The Odd Couple*
Best Lead Actor in a Drama Series:
William Conrad for *Cannon*, Karl Malden for *The Streets of San Francisco*,
*Telly Savalas for *Kojak*, Richard Thomas for *The Waltons*
Best Lead Actor in a Limited Series:
Peter Falk for *Columbo*, ***William Holden** for *The Blue Knight*, Dennis
Weaver for *McCloud*
Best Lead Actor in a Drama:
Alan Alda for *6 Rms Riv Vu*, ***Hal Holbrook** for *Pueblo*, Laurence Olivier for
The Merchant of Venice, Martin Sheen for *The Execution of Private Slovik*,
Dick Van Dyke for *The Morning After*
Actor of the Year–Series:
*Alan Alda for *M*A*S*H*

*denotes winner

213

Actor of the Year–Special:
*Hal Holbrook for *Pueblo*
Best Lead Actress in a Comedy Series:
Beatrice Arthur for *Maude*, *Mary Tyler Moore for *The Mary Tyler Moore Show*, Jean Stapleton for *All in the Family*
Best Lead Actress in a Drama Series:
*Michael Learned for *The Waltons*, Jean Marsh for *Upstairs, Downstairs*, Jeanette Nolan for *Dirty Sally*
Best Lead Actress in a Limited Series:
Helen Hayes for *The Snoop Sisters*, *Mildred Natwick for *The Snoop Sisters*, Lee Remick for *The Blue Knight*
Best Lead Actress for a Drama:
Carol Burnett for *6 Rms Riv Vu*, Katharine Hepburn for *The Glass Menagerie*, Cloris Leachman for *The Migrants*, Elizabeth Montgomery for *A Case of Rape*, *Cicely Tyson for *The Autobiography of Miss Jane Pittman*
Actress of the Years–Series:
*Mary Tyler Moore for *The Mary Tyler Moore Show*
Actress of the Year–Special:
*Cicely Tyson for *The Autobiography of Miss Jane Pittman*
Best Supporting Actor in Comedy:
Edward Asner for *The Mary Tyler Moore Show*, Gary Burghoff for *M*A*S*H*, Ted Knight for *The Mary Tyler Moore Show*, *Rob Reiner for *All in the Family*, McLean Stevenson for *M*A*S*H*
Best Supporting Actor in Drama:
Michael Douglas for *The Streets of San Francisco*, Will Geer for *The Waltons*, *Michael Moriarty for *The Glass Menagerie*, Sam Waterston for *The Glass Menagerie*
Best Supporting Actor in Comedy-Variety, Variety or Music:
Foster Brooks for *The Dean Martin Comedy Hour*, Tim Conway for *The Carol Burnett Show*, *Harvey Korman for *The Carol Burnett Show*
Supporting Actor of the Year:
*Michael Moriarty for *The Glass Menagerie*
Best Supporting Actress in Comedy:
Valerie Harper for *The Mary Tyler Moore Show*, *Cloris Leachman for *The Mary Tyler Moore Show*, Sally Struthers in *All in the Family*, Loretta Swit for *M*A*S*H*
Best Supporting Actress in Drama:
Ellen Corby for *The Waltons*, *Joanna Miles for *The Glass Menagerie*, Nancy Walker for *McMillan and Wife*
Best Supporting Actress in Comedy-Variety, Variety or Music:
Ruth Buzzi for *The Dean Martin Comedy Hour*, Lee Grant for *The Shape of Things*, Vicki Lawrence for *The Carol Burnett Show*, *Brenda Vaccaro for *The Shape of Things*
Supporting Actress of the Year:
*Joanna Miles for *The Glass Menagerie*

*denotes winner

1974/75

Outstanding Comedy Series:

All in the Family, *The Mary Tyler Moore Show*, M*A*S*H, Rhoda

Outstanding Drama Series:

Kojak, Police Story, The Streets of San Francisco, *Upstairs, Downstairs*, The Waltons

Outstanding Comedy, Variety or Music Series:

The Carol Burnett Show, Cher

Outstanding Limited Series:

Benjamin Franklin, Columbo, McCloud

Outstanding Special–Drama or Comedy:

The Law, Love Among the Ruins, The Missiles of October, QB VII, Queen of the Stardust Ballroom

Outstanding Special–Comedy-Variety or Music:

An Evening with John Denver, Lily, Shirley MacLaine: If They Could See Me Now

Outstanding Lead Actor in a Comedy Series:

Alan Alda for M*A*S*H, Jack Albertson for Chico and the Man, Jack Klugman for The Odd Couple, Carroll O'Connor for All in the Family, *Tony Randall* for *The Odd Couple*

Outstanding Lead Actor in a Drama Series:

Robert Blake for *Baretta*, Karl Malden for The Streets of San Francisco, Barry Newman for Petrocelli, Telly Savalas for Kojak

Outstanding Lead Actor in a Limited Series:

Peter Falk for *Columbo*, Dennis Weaver for McCloud

Outstanding Lead Actor in a Special Program–Drama or Comedy:

Richard Chamberlain for The Count of Monte Cristo, William Devane for The Missiles of October, Charles Durning for Queen of the Stardust Ballroom, Henry Fonda for IBM Presents Clarence Darrow, *Laurence Olivier* for *Love Among the Ruins*

Outstanding Lead Actress in a Comedy Series:

Valerie Harper for *Rhoda*, Mary Tyler Moore for The Mary Tyler Moore Show, Jean Stapleton for All in the Family

Outstanding Lead Actress in a Drama Series:

Angie Dickinson for Police Woman, Michael Learned for The Waltons, *Jean Marsh* for *Upstairs, Downstairs*

Outstanding Lead Actress in a Limited Series:

Susan Saint James for McMillan and Wife, *Jessica Walter* for *Amy Prentiss*

Outstanding Lead Actress in a Special Program–Drama or Comedy:

Jill Clayburgh for Hustling, *Katharine Hepburn* for *Love Among the Ruins*, Elizabeth Montgomery for The Legend of Lizzie Borden, Diana Rigg for In This Hour of Brede, Maureen Stapleton for Queen of the Stardust Ballroom

Outstanding Continuing Performance by a Supporting Actor in a Comedy Series:

*denotes winner

*Edward Asner for *The Mary Tyler Moore Show*, Gary Burghoff for M*A*S*H, Ted Knight for *The Mary Tyler Moore Show*, Rob Reiner for *All in the Family*, McLean Stevenson for M*A*S*H

Outstanding Continuing Performance by a Supporting Actor in a Drama Series:

J. D. Cannon for *McCloud*, Michael Douglas for *The Streets of San Francisco*, *Will Geer for *The Waltons*

Outstanding Continuing or Single Performance by a Supporting Actor in Variety or Music:

*Jack Albertson for *Cher*, Tim Conway for *The Carol Burnett Show*, John Denver for *Doris Day Today*

Outstanding Single Performance by a Supporting Actor in a Comedy or Drama Special:

Ralph Bellamy for *The Missiles of October*, Jack Hawkins for *QB VII*, Trevor Howard for *The Count of Monte Cristo*, *Anthony Quayle for *QB VII*

Outstanding Single Performance by a Supporting Actor in a Comedy or Drama Series:

Lew Ayres for *The Vanishing Image (Kung Fu)*, Harold Gould for *Fathers and Sons (Police Story)*, *Patrick McGoohan for *By Dawn's Early Light (Columbo)*, Harry Morgan for *The General Flipped at Dawn (M*A*S*H)*

Outstanding Continuing Performance by a Supporting Actress in a Comedy Series:

Julie Kavner for *Rhoda*, Loretta Swit for M*A*S*H, Nancy Walker for *Rhoda*, *Betty White for *The Mary Tyler Moore Show*

Outstanding Continuing Performance by a Supporting Actress in a Drama Series:

Angela Baddeley for *Upstairs, Downstairs*, *Ellen Corby for *The Waltons*, Nancy Walker for *McMillan and Wife*

Outstanding Continuing or Single Performance by a Supporting Actress in Variety or Music:

Vicki Lawrence for *The Carol Burnett Show*, *Cloris Leachman for *Cher*, Rita Moreno for *Out to Lunch*

Outstanding Single Performance by a Supporting Actress in a Comedy or Drama Special:

Eileen Heckart for *Wedding Band*, *Juliet Mills for *QB VII*, Charlotte Rae for *Queen of the Stardust Ballroom*, Lee Remick for *QB VII*

Outstanding Single Performance by a Supporting Actress in a Comedy or Drama Series (Tie):

*Zohra Lampert for *Queen of the Gypsies (Kojak)*, *Cloris Leachman for *Phyllis Whips Inflation (The Mary Tyler Moore Show)*, Shelley Winters for *The Barefoot Ladies of Bleecker Street (McCloud)*

Outstanding Classical Musical Program:

Bernstein at Tanglewood, Evening at Pops, *Profile in Music: Beverly Sills*, Rubinstein

*denotes winner

216

1975/76

Outstanding Comedy Series:

All in the Family, *The Mary Tyler Moore Show*, M*A*S*H, Barney Miller, Welcome Back, Kotter

Outstanding Drama Series:

Baretta, Columbo, *Police Story*, The Streets of San Francisco

Outstanding Comedy-Variety or Music Series:

The Carol Burnett Show, *NBC's Saturday Night*

Outstanding Limited Series:

The Adams Chronicles, Jennie: Lady Randolph Churchill, The Law, *Upstairs, Downstairs*, Rich Man, Poor Man

Outstanding Special—Drama or Comedy:

Babe, *Eleanor and Franklin*, Fear on Trial, The Lindbergh Kidnapping Case, A Moon for the Misbegotten

Outstanding Special—Comedy-Variety or Music:

Gypsy in My Soul (Shirley MacLaine), John Denver Rocky Mountain Christmas, Monty Python's Flying Circus, Lily Tomlin, Steve and Edie: Our Love Is Here to Stay

Outstanding Classical Music Program:

Arthur Rubinstein—Chopin, *Bernstein and the New York Philharmonic*, Dance in America: The City Center Joffrey Ballet, Live from Lincoln Center, Three by Balanchine with the New York City Ballet

Outstanding Lead Actor in a Comedy Series:

*Jack Albertson for *Chico and the Man*, Alan Alda for M*A*S*H, Hal Linden for Barney Miller, Henry Winkler for Happy Days

Outstanding Lead Actor in a Drama Series:

*Peter Falk for *Columbo*, James Garner for The Rockford Files, Karl Malden for The Streets of San Francisco

Outstanding Lead Actor in a Limited Series:

George Grizzard for The Adams Chronicles, *Hal Holbrook for *Sandburg's Lincoln*, Nick Nolte for Rich Man, Poor Man, Peter Strauss for Rich Man, Poor Man

Outstanding Lead Actor in a Drama or Comedy Special:

William Devane for Fear on Trial, Edward Herrmann for Eleanor and Franklin, *Anthony Hopkins for *The Lindbergh Kidnapping Case*, Jack Lemmon for The Entertainer, Jason Robards for A Moon for the Misbegotten

Outstanding Lead Actor for a Single Appearance in a Drama or Comedy Series:

*Edward Asner for *Rich Man, Poor Man*, Bill Bixby for Police Bluff (The Streets of San Francisco), Tony Musante for The Quality of Mercy (Medical Story), Robert Reed for The Fourth Sex (Medical Center)

Outstanding Lead Actress in a Comedy Series:

Beatrice Arthur for Maude, Lee Grant for Fay, Valerie Harper for Rhoda,

**denotes winner*

Cloris Leachman for *Phyllis*, *****Mary Tyler Moore** for *The Mary Tyler Moore Show*

Outstanding Lead Actress in a Drama Series:

Angie Dickinson for *Police Woman*, *****Michael Learned** for *The Waltons*, Anne Meara for *Kate McShane*, Brenda Vaccaro for *Sara*

Outstanding Lead Actress in a Limited Series:

Susan Blakely for *Rich Man, Poor Man*, *****Rosemary Harris** for *Notorious Woman*, Jean Marsh for *Upstairs, Downstairs*, Lee Remick for *Jennie: Lady Randolph Churchill*

Outstanding Lead Actress in a Drama or Comedy Special:

Jane Alexander for *Eleanor and Franklin*, *****Susan Clark** for *Babe*, Colleen Dewhurst for *A Moon for the Misbegotten*, Sada Thompson for *The Entertainer*

Outstanding Lead Actress for a Single Appearance in a Drama or Comedy Series:

Helen Hayes for *Retire in Sunny Hawaii . . . Forever (Hawaii Five-O)*, Sheree North for *How Do You Know What Hurts Me? (Marcus Welby, M.D.)*, Pamela Payton-Wright for *John Quincy Adams, Diplomat (The Adams Chronicles)*, Martha Raye for *Greed (McMillan and Wife)*, *****Kathryn Walker** for *John Adams, Lawyer (The Adams Chronicles)*

Outstanding Continuing Performance by a Supporting Actor in a Comedy Series:

Edward Asner for *The Mary Tyler Moore Show*, Gary Burghoff for *M*A*S*H*, *****Ted Knight** for *The Mary Tyler Moore Show*, Harry Morgan for *M*A*S*H*, Abe Vigoda for *Barney Miller*

Outstanding Continuing Performance by a Supporting Actor in a Drama Series:

Michael Douglas for *The Streets of San Francisco*, Will Geer for *The Waltons*, Ray Milland for *Rich Man, Poor Man*, Robert Reed for *Rich Man, Poor Man*, *****Anthony Zerbe** for *Harry-O*

Outstanding Continuing or Single Performance by a Supporting Actor in Variety or Music:

*****Chevy Chase** for *NBC's Saturday Night*, Tim Conway for *The Carol Burnett Show*, Harvey Korman for *The Carol Burnett Show*

Outstanding Single Performance by a Supporting Actor in a Comedy or Drama Special:

Ray Bolger for *The Entertainer*, Art Carney for *Katherine*, *****Ed Flanders** for *A Moon for the Misbegotten*

Outstanding Single Performance by a Supporting Actor in a Comedy or Drama Series:

Bill Bixby for *Rich Man, Poor Man*, Roscoe Lee Browne for *The Escape Artist (Barney Miller)*, Norman Fell for *Rich Man, Poor Man*, *****Gordon Jackson** for *The Beastly Hun (Upstairs, Downstairs)*, Van Johnson for *Rich Man, Poor Man*

*denotes winner

Outstanding Continuing Performance by a Supporting Actress in a Comedy Series:

Georgia Engel for *The Mary Tyler Moore Show*, Julie Kavner for *Rhoda*, Loretta Swit for *M*A*S*H*, Nancy Walker for *Rhoda*, ***Betty White** for *The Mary Tyler Moore Show*

Outstanding Continuing Performance by a Supporting Actress in a Drama Series:

Angela Baddeley for *Upstairs, Downstairs*, ***Ellen Corby** for *The Waltons*, Susan Howard for *Petrocelli*, Dorothy McGuire for *Rich Man, Poor Man*, Sada Thompson for *Sandburg's Lincoln*

Outstanding Continuing or Single Performance by a Supporting Actress in a Variety or Music Program:

***Vicki Lawrence** for *The Carol Burnett Show*, Cloris Leachman for *Telly . . . Who Loves Ya, Baby?*

Outstanding Single Performance by a Supporting Actress in a Comedy or Drama Special:

Lois Nettleton for *Fear on Trial*, ***Rosemary Murphy** for *Eleanor and Franklin*, Lilia Skala for *Eleanor and Franklin*, Irene Tedrow for *Eleanor and Franklin*

Outstanding Single Performance by a Supporting Actress in a Comedy or Drama Series:

Kim Darby for *Rich Man, Poor Man*, ***Fionnuala Flanagan** for *Rich Man, Poor Man*, Ruth Gordon for *Kiss Your Epaulets Goodbye (Rhoda)*, Eileen Heckart for *Mary's Aunt (The Mary Tyler Moore Show)*, Kay Lenz for *Rich Man, Poor Man*

1976/77

Outstanding Comedy Series:

All in the Family, Barney Miller, * *The Mary Tyler Moore Show, M*A*S*H, The Bob Newhart Show*

Outstanding Drama Series:

Baretta, Columbo, Family, Police Story, **Upstairs, Downstairs*,

Outstanding Comedy-Variety or Music Series:

The Carol Burnett Show, Evening at Pops, The Muppet Show, NBC's Saturday Night, **Van Dyke and Company*,

Outstanding Limited Series:

The Adams Chronicles, Captains and the Kings, Madame Bovary, *Roots,

Outstanding Special—Comedy or Drama (Tie):

**Eleanor and Franklin: The White House Years*, Harry Truman: Plain Speaking, Raid on Entebbe, *Sybil, 21 Hours at Munich

Outstanding Special—Comedy-Variety or Music:

* *The Barry Manilow Special*, Doug Henning's World of Magic, The Neil Diamond Special, The Shirley MacLaine Special: Where Do We Go From Here?, Sills and Burnett at the Met

*denotes winner

Outstanding Classical Program in the Performing Arts:

American Ballet Theater—Dance in America, *American Ballet Theater: Swan Lake*, Arthur Rubinstein at 90, The Bolshoi Ballet: Romeo and Juliet, Martha Graham Dance Company

Outstanding Lead Actor in a Comedy Series:

Jack Albertson for Chico and the Man, Alan Alda for M*A*S*H, Hal Linden for Barney Miller, *Carroll O'Connor* for *All in the Family*, Henry Winkler for Happy Days

Outstanding Lead Actor in a Drama Series:

Robert Blake for Baretta, Peter Falk for Columbo, *James Garner* for *The Rockford Files*, Jack Klugman for Quincy, M.E., Karl Malden for The Streets of San Francisco

Outstanding Lead Actor in a Limited Series:

Stanley Baker for How Green Was My Valley, Richard Jordan for Captains and the Kings, *Christopher Plummer* for *The Moneychangers*

Outstanding Lead Actor in a Drama or Comedy Special:

Peter Boyle for Tailgunner Joe, Peter Finch for Raid on Entebbe, *Ed Flanders* for *Harry Truman: Plain Speaking*, Edward Herrmann for Eleanor and Franklin: The White House Years, George C. Scott for Beauty and the Beast

Outstanding Lead Actor for a Single Appearance in a Drama or Comedy Series:

John Amos for Roots, LeVar Burton for Roots, *Louis Gossett, Jr.* for *Roots*, Ben Vereen for Roots

Outstanding Lead Actress in a Comedy Series:

Beatrice Arthur for *Maude*, Valerie Harper for Rhoda, Mary Tyler Moore for The Mary Tyler Moore Show, Suzanne Pleshette for The Bob Newhart Show, Jean Stapleton for All in the Family

Outstanding Lead Actress in a Drama Series:

Angie Dickinson for Police Woman, Kate Jackson for Charlie's Angels, Michael Learned for The Waltons, Sada Thompson for Family, *Lindsay Wagner* for *The Bionic Woman*

Outstanding Lead Actress in a Limited Series:

Susan Flannery for The Moneychangers, *Patty Duke Astin* for *Captains and the Kings*, Dori Brenner for Seventh Avenue, Eva Marie Saint for How the West Was Won, Jane Seymour for Captains and the Kings

Outstanding Lead Actress in a Drama or Comedy Special:

Jane Alexander for Eleanor and Franklin: The White House Years, Susan Clark for Amelia Earhart, *Sally Field* for *Sybil*, Julie Harris for The Last of Mrs. Lincoln, Joanne Woodward for Sybil

Outstanding Lead Actress for a Single Appearance in a Drama or Comedy Series:

Susan Blakely for Rich Man, Poor Man, *Beulah Bondi* for *The Waltons*, Madge Sinclair for Roots, Leslie Uggams for Roots, Jessica Walter for The Streets of San Francisco

*denotes winner

220

Outstanding Continuing Performance by a Supporting Actor in a Comedy Series:

Edward Asner for *The Mary Tyler Moore Show*, *****Gary Burghoff** for *M*A*S*H*, Ted Knight for *The Mary Tyler Moore Show*, Harry Morgan for *M*A*S*H*, Abe Vigoda for *Barney Miller*

Outstanding Continuing Performance by a Supporting Actor in a Drama Series:

Noah Beery for *The Rockford Files*, David Doyle for *Charlie's Angels*, Tom Ewell for *Baretta*, *****Gary Frank** for *Family*, Will Geer for *The Waltons*

Outstanding Continuing or Single Performance by a Supporting Actor in Variety or Music:

John Belushi for *NBC's Saturday Night*, Chevy Chase for *NBC's Saturday Night*, *****Tim Conway** for ***The Carol Burnett Show***, Harvey Korman for *The Carol Burnett Show*, Ben Vereen for *The Bell Telephone Hour Jubilee*

Outstanding Performance by a Supporting Actor in a Comedy or Drama Special:

Martin Balsam for *Raid on Entebbe*, Mark Harmon for *Eleanor and Franklin: The White House Years*, Yaphet Kotto for *Raid on Entebbe*, Walter McGinn for *Eleanor and Franklin: The White House Years*, *****Burgess Meredith** for ***Tailgunner Joe***

Outstanding Single Performance by a Supporting Actor in a Comedy or Drama Series:

*****Edward Asner** for ***Roots***, Charles Durning for *Captains and the Kings*, Moses Gunn for *Roots*, Robert Reed for *Roots*, Ralph Waite for *Roots*

Outstanding Continuing Performance by a Supporting Actress in a Comedy Series:

Georgia Engel for *The Mary Tyler Moore Show*, Julie Kavner for *Rhoda*, *****Mary Kay Place** for ***Mary Hartman, Mary Hartman***, Loretta Swit for *M*A*S*H*, Betty White for *The Mary Tyler Moore Show*

Outstanding Continuing Performance by a Supporting Actress in a Drama Series:

Meredith Baxter Birney for *Family*, Ellen Corby for *The Waltons*, *****Kristy McNichol** for ***Family***, Lee Meriwether for *Barnaby Jones*, Jacqueline Tong for *Upstairs, Downstairs*

Outstanding Continuing or Single Performance by a Supporting Actress in Variety or Music:

Vicki Lawrence for *The Carol Burnett Show*, *****Rita Moreno** for ***The Muppet Show***, Gilda Radner for *NBC's Saturday Night*

Outstanding Performance by a Supporting Actress in a Comedy or Drama Special:

Ruth Gordon for *The Great Houdinis*, *****Diana Hyland** for ***The Boy in the Plastic Bubble***, Rosemary Murphy for *Eleanor and Franklin: The White House Years*, Patricia Neal for *Tailgunner Joe*, Susan Oliver for *Amelia Earhart*

*denotes winner

221

Outstanding Single Performance by a Supporting Actress in a Comedy or Drama Series:

*Olivia Cole for *Roots*, Sandy Duncan for *Roots*, Eileen Heckart for *Lou Proposes (The Mary Tyler Moore Show)*, Cicely Tyson for *Roots*, Nancy Walker for *The Separation (Rhoda)*

1977/78
Outstanding Comedy Series:

**All in the Family*, Barney Miller, M*A*S*H, Soap, Three's Company

Outstanding Drama Series:

Columbo, Family, Lou Grant, Quincy, **The Rockford Files*

Outstanding Limited Series:

**Holocaust*, King, Washington: Behind Closed Doors, Anna Karenina. I, Claudius

Outstanding Comedy–Variety or Music Series:

America 2Night, The Carol Burnett Show, Evening at Pops, **The Muppet Show*, NBC's Saturday Night

Outstanding Special–Comedy or Drama:

Death in Canaan, **The Gathering*, Jesus of Nazareth, Our Town, Young Joe, the Forgotten Kennedy

Outstanding Special–Comedy-Variety or Music:

**Bette Midler—Ol' Red Hair Is Back*, Doug Henning's World of Magic, The George Burns One-Man Show, Neil Diamond: I'm Glad You're Here with Me Tonight, The Second Barry Manilow Special

Outstanding Lead Actor in a Comedy Series:

Alan Alda for M*A*S*H, Hal Linden for *Barney Miller*, *Carroll O'Connor for *All in the Family*, John Ritter for *Three's Company*, Henry Winkler for *Happy Days*

Outstanding Lead Actor in a Drama Series:

*Edward Asner for *Lou Grant*, James Broderick for *Family*, Peter Falk for *Columbo*, James Garner for *The Rockford Files*, Jack Klugman for *Quincy*, Ralph Waite for *The Waltons*

Outstanding Lead Actor in a Limited Series:

Hal Holbrook for *The Awakening*, *Michael Moriarty for *Holocaust*, Jason Robards for *Washington: Behind Closed Doors*, Fritz Weaver for *Holocaust*, Paul Winfield for *King*

Outstanding Lead Actor in a Drama or Comedy Special:

*Fred Astaire for *A Family Upside Down*, Alan Alda for *Kill Me If You Can*, Hal Holbrook for *Our Town*, Martin Sheen for *Taxi!!!*, James Stacey for *Just a Little Inconvenience*

Outstanding Lead Actor for a Single Performance in a Drama or Comedy Series:

David Cassidy for *A Chance to Live (Police Story)*, Will Geer for *The Old Man and The Runaway (The Love Boat)*, Judd Hirsch for *Rhoda Likes Mike*

*denotes winner

(Rhoda), *Barnard Hughes for *Judge (Lou Grant)*, John Rubinstein for *And Baby Makes Three (Family)*, Keenan Wynn for *Good Old Uncle Ben (Police Woman)*

Outstanding Lead Actress in a Comedy Series:

Beatrice Arthur for *Maude*, Cathryn Damon for *Soap*, Valerie Harper for *Rhoda*, Katherine Helmond for *Soap*, Suzanne Pleshette for *The Bob Newhart Show*, *Jean Stapleton for *All in the Family*

Outstanding Lead Actress in a Drama Series:

Melissa Sue Anderson for *Little House on the Prairie*, Fionnuala Flanagan for *How The West Was Won*, Kate Jackson for *Charlie's Angels*, Susan Sullivan for *Julie Farr, M.D.*, *Sada Thompson for *Family*

Outstanding Lead Actress in a Limited Series:

Rosemary Harris for *Holocaust*, Elizabeth Montgomery for *The Awakening*, Lee Remick for *Wheels*, *Meryl Streep for *Holocaust*, Cicely Tyson for King

Outstanding Lead Actress for a Single Appearance in a Drama or Comedy Series:

Patty Duke Astin for *Having Babies*, Kate Jackson for *James at 15/16*, Jayne Meadows for *Meeting of Minds*, *Rita Moreno for *The Paper Palace (The Rockford Files)*, Irene Tedrow for *James at 15/16*

Outstanding Lead Actress in a Drama or Comedy Special:

Helen Hayes for *A Family Upside Down*, Eva Marie Saint for *Taxi!!!*, Maureen Stapleton for *The Gathering*, Sada Thompson for *Our Town*, *Joanne Woodward for *See How She Runs*

Outstanding Continuing Performance by a Supporting Actor in a Comedy Series:

Tom Bosley for *Happy Days*, Gary Burghoff for *M*A*S*H*, Harry Morgan for *M*A*S*H*, *Rob Reiner for *All in the Family*, Vic Tayback for *Alice*

Outstanding Continuing or Single Performance by a Supporting Actor in a Drama Series:

Ossie Davis for *King*, Will Geer for *The Waltons*, *Robert Vaughn for *Washington: Behind Closed Doors*, Sam Wanamaker for *Holocaust*, David Warner for *Holocaust*

Outstanding Continuing or Single Performance by a Supporting Actor in Variety or Music:

Dan Aykroyd in *NBC's Saturday Night*, John Belushi in *NBC's Saturday Night*, *Tim Conway for *The Carol Burnett Show*, Louis Gossett, Jr. for *Ben Vereen—His Roots*, Peter Sellers for *The Muppet Show*

Outstanding Performance by a Supporting Actor in a Comedy or Drama Special:

*Howard Da Silva for *Verna: USO Girl*, James Farentino for *Jesus of Nazareth*, Burgess Meredith for *The Last Hurrah*, Donald Pleasance for *The Defection of Simas Kudirka*, Efrem Zimbalist, Jr. for *A Family Upside Down*

*denotes winner

223

Outstanding Single Performance by a Supporting Actor in a Comedy or Drama Series:

Will Geer for *Yes, There Is a Santa Claus (Eight Is Enough)*, Larry Gelman for *Goodbye, Mr. Fish (Barney Miller)*, Harold Gould for *Happy Anniversary (Rhoda)*, *****Richardo Montalban** for ***How the West Was Won, Part 2***, Abe Vigoda for *Goodbye Mr. Fish (Barney Miller)*

Outstanding Continuing Performance by a Supporting Actress in a Comedy Series:

Polly Holliday for *Alice*, *****Julie Kavner** for ***Rhoda***, Sally Struthers for *All In The Family*, Loretta Swit for *M*A*S*H*, Nancy Walker for *Rhoda*

Outstanding Continuing Performance by a Supporting Actress in a Drama Series:

Meredith Baxter Birney for *Family*, Tovah Feldshuh for *Holocaust*, Linda Kelsey for *Lou Grant*, *****Nancy Marchand** for ***Lou Grant***, Kristy McNichol for *Family*

Outstanding Continuing or Single Performance by a Supporting Actress in Variety or Music:

Beatrice Arthur in *Laugh-In*, Jane Curtin for *NBC's Saturday Night*, Dolly Parton for *Cher . . . Special*, Bernadette Peters for *The Muppet Show*, *****Gilda Radner** for ***NBC's Saturday Night***

Outstanding Performance by a Supporting Actress in a Drama or Comedy Special:

Patty Duke Astin for *A Family Upside Down*, Tyne Daly for *Intimate Strangers*, Mariette Hartley for *The Last Hurrah, Hallmark Hall of Fame*, *****Eva LaGallienne** for ***The Royal Family***, Cloris Leachman for *It Happened One Christmas*, Viveca Lindfors for *A Question of Guilt*

Outstanding Single Performance by a Supporting Actress in a Comedy or Drama Series:

*****Blanch Baker** for ***Holocaust, Part 1***, Ellen Corby for *Grandma Comes Home (The Waltons)*, Jeanette Nolan for *The Awakening Land, Part 1*, Beulah Quo for *Meeting of Minds: Douglass, Tz'U-Hsi, Beccaria De Sade)*, Beatrice Straight for *The Dain Curse, Part 1*

1978/79

Outstanding Comedy Series:

All in the Family, Barney Miller, M*A*S*H, Mork and Mindy, ***Taxi***

Outstanding Drama Series:

Lou Grant, *The Paper Chase, The Rockford Files*

Outstanding Limited Series:

Backstairs at the White House, Blind Ambition, ***Roots: the Next Generations***

*denotes winner

224

Outstanding Comedy/Drama Special:
Dummy, First You Cry, *Friendly Fire*, The Jericho Mile, Summer of My German Soldier

Outstanding Actor (Limited Series/Special):
Ned Beatty for Friendly Fire, Louis Gossett, Jr. for Backstairs at the White House, Kurt Russell for Elvis, *Peter Strauss for *The Jericho Mile*

Outstanding Actress (Limited Series/Special):
Carol Burnett for Friendly Fire, Olivia Cole for Backstairs at the White House, *Bette Davis for *Strangers*, Katharine Hepburn for The Corn Is Green, Mary Tyler Moore for First You Cry

Outstanding Actor in a Comedy Series:
Alan Alda for M*A*S*H, Judd Hirsch for Taxi, Hal Linden for Barney Miller, *Carroll O'Connor for *All in the Family*, Robin Williams for Mork and Mindy

Outstanding Actress in a Comedy Series:
*Ruth Gordon for *Taxi*, Katherine Helmond for Soap, Linda Lavin for Alice, Isabel Sanford for The Jeffersons, Jean Stapleton for All in the Family

Outstanding Actor in a Drama Series:
Edward Asner for Lou Grant, James Garner for The Rockford Files, Jack Klugman for Quincy, M.E., *Ron Leibman for *Kaz*

Outstanding Actress in a Drama Series:
Barbara Bel Geddes for Dallas, *Mariette Hartley for *The Incredible Hulk*, Rita Moreno for The Rockford Files, Sada Thompson for Family

1979/80

Outstanding Comedy Series:
Barney Miller, M*A*S*H, Soap, *Taxi*, WKRP in Cincinnati

Outstanding Drama Series:
Dallas, Family, *Lou Grant*, The Rockford Files, The White Shadow

Outstanding Limited Series:
Disraeli: Portrait of a Romantic, *Edward and Mrs. Simpson*, The Duchess of Duke Street II, Moviola

Outstanding Drama/Comedy Special:
All Quiet on the Western Front, Amber Waves, Gideon's Trumpet, Guyana Tragedy: The Story of Jim Jones, *The Miracle Worker*

Outstanding Variety/Music Program:
The Benny Hill Show, Goldie and Liza Together, *Baryshnikov on Broadway*, The Muppet Show, Shirley MacLaine . . . Every Little Movement

Outstanding Actor in a Comedy Series:
Alan Alda for M*A*S*H, Robert Guillaume for Benson, Judd Hirsch for Taxi, Hal Linden for Barney Miller, *Richard Mulligan for *Soap*

*denotes winner

225

Outstanding Actress in a Comedy Series:
  *Cathryn Damon for *Soap*, Katherine Helmond for *Soap*, Polly Holliday for *Flo*, Sheree North for *Archie Bunker's Place*, Isabel Sanford for *The Jeffersons*

Outstanding Actress in a Drama Series:
  Lauren Bacall for *The Rockford Files*, *Barbara Bel Geddes for *Dallas*, Mariette Hartley for *The Rockford Files*, Kristy McNichol for *Family*, Sada Thompson for *Family*

Outstanding Actor in a Drama Series:
  *Edward Asner in *Lou Grant*, James Garner in *The Rockford Files*, Larry Hagman for *Dallas*, Jack Klugman for *Quincy, M.E.*

Outstanding Actor (Limited Series/Special):
  *Powers Boothe for *Guyana Tragedy: The Story of Jim Jones*, Tony Curtis for *Moviola*, Henry Fonda for *Gideon's Trumpet*, Jason Robards for *F.D.R., The Last Year*

Outstanding Actress (Limited Series/Special):
  *Patty Duke Astin for *The Miracle Worker*, Bette Davis for *White Mama*, Melissa Gilbert for *The Miracle Worker*, Lee Remick for *Haywire*

1980/81

Outstanding Comedy Series:
  Barney Miller, M*A*S*H, Soap, *Taxi*, WKRP in Cincinnati

Outstanding Drama Series:
  Dallas, *Hill Street Blues*, Lou Grant, Quincy, M.E., The White Shadow

Outstanding Limited Series:
  East of Eden, Masada, Rumpole of the Bailey, *Shogun*, Tinker, Tailor, Soldier, Spy

Outstanding Variety/Music Program:
  AFI Salute to Fred Astaire, The Benny Hill Show, *Lily: Sold Out*, The Muppet Show, The Tonight Show Starring Johnny Carson

Outstanding Drama Special:
  Evita Peron, Fallen Angel, *Playing for Time*, The Shadow Box, The Women's Room

Outstanding Actor in Comedy Series:
  Alan Alda for M*A*S*H, *Judd Hirsch for *Taxi*, Hal Linden for *Barney Miller*, Richard Mulligan for *Soap*, John Ritter for *Three's Company*

Outstanding Actress in Comedy Series:
  Eileen Brennan for *Taxi*, Cathryn Damon for *Soap*, Katherine Helmond for *Soap*, Lynn Redgraves for *House Calls*, *Isabel Sanford for *The Jeffersons*

Outstanding Actor in Drama Series:
  Edward Asner for *Lou Grant*, Jim Davis for *Dallas*, Larry Hagman for *Dallas*, Louis Gossett, Jr. for *Palmerstown, U.S.A.*, Pernell Roberts for *Trapper John, M.D.*, *Daniel J. Travanti for *Hill Street Blues*

*denotes winner

226

Outstanding Actress in Drama Series:
  *Barbara Babcock for *Hill Street Blues*, Veronica Hamel for *Hill Street Blues*, Barbara Bel Geddes for *Dallas*, Linda Gray for *Dallas*, Michael Learned for *Nurse*, Stephanie Powers for *Hart to Hart*
Outstanding Actor in Limited Series:
  Richard Chamberlain for *Shogun*, Toshiro Mifune for *Shogun*, *Anthony Hopkins for *The Bunker*, Peter O'Toole for *Masada*, Peter Strauss for *Masada*
Outstanding Actress in Limited Series:
  Ellen Burstyn for *The People vs. Jean Harris*, Catherine Hicks for *Marilyn, the Untold Story*, *Vanessa Redgrave for *Playing for Time*, Yoko Shimada for *Shogun*, Joanne Woodward for *Crisis at Central High*
Supporting Awards—Winners Only:
Outstanding Supporting Actress in a Comedy, Variety, or Music Series:
  *Eileen Brennan for *Private Benjamin*
Outstanding Supporting Actor in a Comedy, Variety, or Music Series:
  *Danny De Vito for *Taxi*
Outstanding Supporting Actor in a Drama Series:
  *Michael Conrad for *Hill Street Blues*
Outstanding Supporting Actress in a Drama Series:
  *Nancy Marchand for *Lou Grant*
Outstanding Supporting Actress in a Limited Series or Special:
  *Jane Alexander for *Playing for Time*
Outstanding Supporting Actor for a Limited Series or Special:
  *David Warner for *Masada*

  *denotes winner

THE TROPHY CASE

The following performers have won two or more Emmies (1948–1981):

Performer	#Wins
Edward Asner	7
Mary Tyler Moore	6
Dinah Shore	6
Lucille Ball	5
Don Knotts	5
Carroll O'Connor	5
Don Adams	4
Fred Astaire	4
Art Carney	4
Peter Falk	4
Valerie Harper	4
Hal Holbrook	4
Cloris Leachman	4
Dick Van Dyke	4
Patty Duke Astin	3
Barbara Bain	3
Jack Benny	3
Carol Burnett	3
Sid Caesar	3
Perry Como	3
Tim Conway	3
Ellen Corby	3
Bill Cosby	3
Nanette Fabray	3
Jack Klugman	3
Michael Learned	3
Nancy Marchand	3
Michael Moriarty	3
Laurence Olivier	3
Phil Silvers	3
Jean Stapleton	3
Peter Ustinov	3

Jane Wyatt	3
Loretta Young	3
Robert Young	3
Jack Albertson	2
Alan Alda	2
Judith Anderson	2
Julie Andrews	2
Shirley Booth	2
Raymond Burr	2
Imogene Coca	2
Ann B. Davis	2
Lee Grant	2
Julie Harris	2
Glenda Jackson	2
Werner Klemperer	2
Ted Knight	2
Harvey Korman	2
Kristy McNichol	2
E. G. Marshall	2
Rita Moreno	2
Carl Reiner	2
Rob Reiner	2
Barbara Stanwyck	2
Cicely Tyson	2
Betty White	2

ANSWER SECTION

Answers for photo quiz

1. Michael Landon, Karen Grassle, Melissa Sue Anderson, Melissa Gilbert, Lindsay Greenbush; *Little House on the Prairie*

2. Lucille Ball, Vivian Vance, Desi Arnaz, William Frawley; *I Love Lucy – California, Here We Come!*

3. Martin Milner; *The Life of Riley, The Stu Erwin Show, Route 66, Adam 12, The Swiss Family Robinson*

4. Robert Stack; editor with Howard Publications

5. Burt Reynolds; blacksmith *(Gunsmoke)*

6. Karl Malden; Darleen Carr

7. Michael Landon; 1959

8. Marlo Thomas; *The Joey Bishop Show*

9. Cindy Williams; Eddie Mekka

10. Wayne Rogers, McLean Stevenson, Loretta Swit, Alan Alda; M*A*S*H

11. Penny Marshall; sister-in-law

12. Mary Tyler Moore; *Mary*

13. Sherman Hemsley, Zara Cully, Isabel Sanford; *The Jeffersons*

14. Suzanne Pleshette; educator *(The Bob Newhart Show)*

15. Hal Linden; *The Life and Times of Captain Barney Miller*

16. Jimmie Walker; *Good Times*; James Evans, Jr.

17. Bottom row: Peter Lupus, Greg Morris, Peter Graves. Top Row: Barbara Bain, Martin Landau; *Mission: Impossible*

18. Ted Knight, Ed Asner, Gavin McLeod, Betty White; *The Mary Tyler Moore Show*

19. Telly Savalas, *Acapulco*

20. Ed Asner; Priscilla Morill *(The Mary Tyler Moore Show)*

21. Jack Klugman; *Harris Against the World*

22. Earl Hamner (creator of *The Waltons*) and Richard Thomas (former star of *The Waltons*)

23. Paul Michael Glaser and David Soul; *Starsky and Hutch*

24. Sally Struthers, Carroll O'Connor, Jean Stapleton (holding the baby), Rob Reiner; *All in the Family*; Joey

25. Richard Thomas; *1,2,3 Go*

26. Lucille Ball; William Holden

27. Faye Emerson; Fayzie

233

28. Loretta Young; NBC
29. Jane Wyman; owner of vineyards (*Falcon Crest*)
30. Donna Reed; Donna Stone
31. Dinah Shore; Ticker Freeman
32. Carol Burnett; *The Entertainers*
33. Richard Dawson; *Hogan's Heroes*
34. Sid Caesar; Hickenlooper
35. Bob Keeshan (Captain Kangaroo); Clarabelle
36. Jack Lord; Hawaiian State Police
37. Carroll O'Connor; Prendergast Tool and Die Company
38. Merv Griffin; Freddy Martin
39. Anthony Geary and Genie Ann Francis; *General Hospital*
40. Perry Como; Ted Weems
41. Adam West; *Robert Taylor's Detectives*
42. Robert Young and Jane Wyatt; *Father Knows Best; Star Trek* (played Leonard Nimoy's mother)
43. Mike Connors; *Tightrope, Mannix, Today's FBI*
44. *Ball Four;* Jim Bouton (second from left)
45. Victoria Wyndham; *Another World*
46. John Beradino and Lucille Wall; *General Hospital*
47. *The Brady Bunch;* designer-architect
48. George Reeves and Phyllis Coates; *Superman*
49. Tony Randall; *One Man's Family, Mr. Peepers, The Odd Couple, The Tony Randall Show, Love, Sidney*
50. Susan Lucci; *All My Children*
51. Frances Reid and Susan Seaforth Hayes; *Days of Our Lives*
52. Elizabeth Hubbard; *The Doctors*
53. Al Freeman, Jr. and Michael Storm; *One Life to Live*
54. Standing from left: Malcolm Groome, Irene Kristen, Michael Hawkins, Kate Mulgrew. Seated: Helen Gallagher and Bernard Barrow; *Ryan's Hope*
55. Marcia McCabe; Sherry Mathis, Rod Arrants; *Search for Tomorrow*
56. Frank Runyeon and Rita Walter; *As the World Turns*
57. Lou Criscuolo and Pat Conwell; *The Edge of Night*
58. Cindy Pickett, Don Stewart, Lezlie Dalton; *The Guiding Light*
59. Chandler Harben, Carla Borelli, Jerry Lanning; *Texas*
60. Lilibet Stern and Doug Davidson; *The Young and the Restless;* ABC
61. Freddie Prinze and Tony Orlando; *Tony Orlando and Dawn;* Telma Hopkins and Joyce Vincent Wilson

62. Milton Berle; NBC

63. Morley Safer, Mike Wallace; *Sixty Minutes*

64. Redd Foxx; La Wanda Page; Aunt Esther *(Sanford and Son* and *The Sanford Arms)*

65. Tony Franciosa; *Valentine's Day*

66. Julie London; head nurse at Rampart Hospital

67. Robert Conrad; nightclub singer

68. William Shatner; Captain James T. Kirk

69. Peter Falk; Bing Crosby

70. William Conrad; Matt Dillon

71. Farrah Fawcett; Cheryl Ladd as her sister Kris Monroe

72. Hope Lange; Jenny Preston

73. Elaine Stritch; *My Sister Eileen* and *The Growing Paynes*

74. Robby Benson (guest star) and Bonnie Franklin; *One Day at a Time*

75. Harry Bellaver and John McIntire; *Naked City*

76. Agnes Moorehead, ABC *(Bewitched)*

77. Elisabeth Fraser and Phil Silvers; Colonel Hall played by Paul Ford

78. Shirley Booth; *A Touch of Grace*

79. Cher and Sonny; Chastity

80. Miss Piggy; *The Muppet Show*; Kermit the Frog; Jim Henson

81. Ed Sullivan; Martin and Lewis

82. Jane Rose and Cloris Leachman; *Phyllis*

83. Valerie Harper; window dresser *(The Mary Tyler Moore Show* and *Rhoda)*

84. Bill Macy, Beatrice Arthur, Conrad Bain, Rue McClanahan; *Maude*

85. Harry Belafonte; *Sugar Hill Times*

86. Lloyd Bridges; Adam Shepherd

87. Paula Prentiss and Richard Benjamin; *He and She*; *Quark*

88. Barbara Bel Geddes; Eleanor Southworth Ewing on *Dallas*

89. James Arness; *How the West was Won*; Zeb Macahan

90. Leonard Nimoy; Mr. Spock on *Star Trek* and Paris on *Mission: Impossible*

Answers – KEEP IT IN THE FAMILY

1 – N	6 – L	11 – S	16 – I
2 – T	7 – R	12 – D	17 – O
3 – J	8 – B	13 – C	18 – F
4 – Q	9 – E	14 – G	19 – M
5 – A	10 – P	15 – K	20 – H

Answers – MALE CALL (1)

1 – I, Mr. Adams and Eve
2 – L, I Love Lucy
3 – K, Wagon Train
4 – R, The Big Valley
5 – M, Hogan's Heroes
6 – P, Get Smart
7 – N, Mr. and Mrs. North
8 – Q, Gilligan's Island
9 – O, The Jimmy Stewart Show
10 – F, Mr. Ed
11 – C, Johnny Staccato
12 – S, McHale's Navy
13 – E, Mr. Roberts
14 – D, My Little Margie
15 – H, Nanny and the Professor
16 – J, Big Town
17 – T, Big Town
18 – A, The Mary Tyler Moore Show
19 – G, Judd, For the Defense
20 – B, My Three Sons

Answers – MALE CALL (2)

1 – J, Twelve O'Clock High
2 – M, Acapulco
3 – G, Adventures in Paradise
4 – O, Car 54, Where Are You?
5 – N, Life With Father
6 – Q, Dan August
7 – P, Adam 12
8 – A, Green Acres
9 – L, Mr. Peepers
10 – R, The Addams Family
11 – T, Gunsmoke
12 – S, The Green Hornet
13 – E, The Adventures of Ozzie and
       Harriet
14 – C, The Odd Couple
15 – K, Mission: Impossible
16 – I, My Three Sons
17 – D, Marcus Welby, M.D.
18 – H, Wagon Train
19 – F, Maude
20 – B, Gunsmoke

Answers – MALE CALL (3)

1 – E, Hogan's Heroes
2 – K, The Odd Couple
3 – O, Laverne & Shirley
4 – T, Hawaiian Eye
5 – F, 77 Sunset Strip
6 – A, Riverboat
7 – L, Hill Street Blues
8 – P, The Detectives
9 – G, The Rifleman
10 – B, The Untouchables
11 – R, The Hardy Boys
12 – H, Serpico
13 – C, The Millionaire
14 – M, Kodiak
15 – J, The Mary Tyler Moore Show
16 – S, Happy Days
17 – Q, The Andy Griffith Show
18 – D, Quincy, M.E.
19 – N, M*A*S*H
20 – I, Three's Company

Answers – MALE CALL (4)

1 – D, Happy Days
2 – J, The Andy Griffith Show
3 – H, Laverne & Shirley
4 – O, M*A*S*H
5 – T, The Rockford Files
6 – E, Little House on the Prairie
7 – I, Owen Marshall, Counselor at
       Law
8 – A, Dallas
9 – N, The Waltons
10 – P, Three's Company
11 – F, Phyllis
12 – Q, The Mary Tyler Moore Show
13 – M, The Brady Bunch
14 – R, Dan August
15 – B, Barney Miller
16 – L, Lassie
17 – G, Soap
18 – S, The New Dick Van Dyke
       Show
19 – K, The Jeffersons
20 – C, Maverick

Answers – MALE CALL (5)

1 – D, Happy Days
2 – I, Harbormaster
3 – M, All in the Family
4 – O, M*A*S*H
5 – S, Chico and the Man

6 – E, Sanford and Son
7 – J, Rich Man, Poor Man
8 – T, The Incredible Hulk
9 – H, Dragnet
10 – P, Barney Miller
11 – A, Bronco
12 – K, Broken Arrow
13 – F, Bonanza
14 – Q, Davy Crockett
15 – B, Adventures of Robin Hood
16 – R, The Dick Van Dyke Show
17 – N, Streets of San Francisco
18 – L, Philip Marlowe
19 – G, Peyton Place
20 – C, Streets of San Francisco

Answers – MALE CALL (6)
1 – M, Bonanza
2 – I, Our Miss Brooks
3 – P, C.P.O. Sharkey
4 – O, Hawaii Five-O
5 – T, The Practice
6 – Q, That Girl
7 – N, Peter Gunn
8 – R, Dick Tracy
9 – S, Doc
10 – B, You'll Never Get Rich
11 – G, Welcome Back, Kotter
12 – E, The Jeffersons
13 – C, Jefferson Drum
14 – A, C.P.O. Sharkey
15 – H, The Jim Nabors Show
16 – F, That Girl
17 – L, The People's Choice
18 – J, Private Secretary
19 – K, Welcome Back, Kotter
20 – D, Bonanza

Answers – A STAR IS BORN
1 – G	6 – O	11 – J	16 – D
2 – N	7 – I	12 – F	17 – M
3 – H	8 – R	13 – C	18 – L
4 – A	9 – B	14 – S	19 – Q
5 – P	10 – T	15 – K	20 – E

Answers – CALL ME MISTER
1 – J	6 – C	11 – I	16 – M
2 – O	7 – Q	12 – S	17 – K
3 – A	8 – T	13 – D	18 – H
4 – G	9 – N	14 – R	19 – F
5 – L	10 – B	15 – P	20 – E

Answers – WHO WAS THAT LADY? (1)
1 – F, Laverne & Shirley
2 – J, Happy Days
3 – N, The Andy Griffith Show
4 – O, Bracken's World
5 – P, The Brady Bunch
6 – K, December Bride
7 – A, I Love Lucy
8 – L, The Flying Nun
9 – T, The Carol Burnett Show
10 – R, The Mary Tyler Moore Show and Rhoda
11 – D, Phyllis
12 – I, Mannix
13 – Q, Our Miss Brooks
14 – B, I Love Lucy
15 – C, The Waltons
16 – S, Chico and the Man
17 – E, Three's Company
18 – M, Barney Miller
19 – G, Laverne & Shirley
20 – H, Family

Answers – WHO WAS THAT LADY? (2)
1 – I, The Nancy Walker Show
2 – T, All's Fair
3 – N, The Donna Reed Show
4 – J, Bridget Loves Bernie
5 – P, Three's Company
6 – R, Alice
7 – L, The Mary Tyler Moore Show
8 – S, Barney Miller
9 – Q, Family
10 – B, Soap
11 – O, Phyllis
12 – E, The Jeffersons
13 – K, Maude
14 – D, Happy Days
15 – M, The Waltons
16 – H, Father Knows Best
17 – C, The Dumplings
18 – A, All In The Family
19 – F, M*A*S*H
20 – G, All In The Family

Answers – WHO WAS THAT LADY? (3)
1 – F, Mission Impossible
2 – J, The Big Valley

3 – N, The George Burns and Gracie
       Allen Show
4 – P, The James Stewart Show
5 – T, The Mary Tyler Moore Show
6 – G, Mr. Adams and Eve
7 – S, Get Smart
8 – A, The Nancy Drew Mysteries
9 – O, The Odd Couple
10 – I, Mr. and Mrs. North
11 – R, Gilligan's Island
12 – B, Laverne & Shirley
13 – L, Mr. Peepers
14 – E, Hawaiian Eye
15 – Q, Nanny and the Professor
16 – C, Happy Days
17 – M, My Little Margie
18 – K, Margie
19 – H, The Roaring Twenties
20 – D, The Odd Couple

Answers – WHO WAS THAT LADY?
(4)

1 – G, Wonder Woman
2 – K, The Tony Randall Show
3 – E, The Tony Randall Show
4 – O, Sanford and Son
5 – T, Police Woman
6 – P, My Friend Flicka
7 – J, Karen
8 – A, Honey West
9 – F, The Honeymooners
10 – M, The Avengers
11 – Q, Make Room for Daddy
12 – S, The Dick Van Dyke Show
13 – B, Pistols and Petticoats
14 – I, Peyton Place
15 – R, Peyton Place
16 – N, The Snoop Sisters
17 – C, C.P.O. Sharkey
18 – L, The Practice
19 – H, That Girl
20 – D, Doc

Answers – WHO WAS THAT LADY?
(5)

1 – J, Doc
2 – Q, I Love Lucy
3 – T, What's Happening
4 – N, Gidget
5 – C, The Ghost and Mrs. Muir
6 – S, The George Gobel Show
7 – R, Peter Gunn

8 – A, Bachelor Father
9 – B, Pete and Gladys
10 – P, Petticoat Junction
11 – D, Welcome Back, Kotter
12 – H, The Jeffersons
13 – O, The Jeffersons
14 – E, The Andy Griffith Show
15 – L, The Andy Griffith Show
16 – M, The Ann Sothern Show
17 – F, My Friend Irma
18 – K, My Favorite Husband
19 – G, The People's Choice
20 – I, Pete Kelly's Blues

Answers – WHO WAS THAT LADY?
(6)

1 – G, Private Secretary
2 – M, Charlie's Angels
3 – P, The Thin Man
4 – O, The Big Valley
5 – T, The Bionic Woman
6 – C, The Bob Cummings Show
7 – R, The Bob Newhart Show
8 – S, Charlie's Angels
9 – Q, Bridget Loves Bernie
10 – A, Three's Company
11 – B, Blansky's Beauties
12 – E, The Nurses
13 – F, Doctor's Hospital
14 – I, Gilligan's Island
15 – H, The Goldbergs
16 – N, Green Acres
17 – J, The Bob Cummings Show
18 – L, Gunsmoke
19 – K, The Governor and J.J.
20 – D, The Bob Newhart Show

Answers – BORN AGAIN

1 – K	6 – A	11 – P	16 – E
2 – O	7 – D	12 – F	17 – H
3 – R	8 – S	13 – Q	18 – J
4 – G	9 – M	14 – C	19 – L
5 – T	10 – B	15 – I	20 – N

Answers – AFFIRMATIVE ACTION
(1)

1 – L, Maude and Good Times
2 – R, Barney Miller
3 – O, Baby, I'm Back
4 – T, What's Happening
5 – J, Julia
6 – A, Welcome Back, Kotter
7 – S, The Jeffersons

8 – Q, *Room 222*
9 – M, *Sanford and Son*
10 – B, *Soap and Benson*
11 – G, *Chico and the Man*
12 – C, *Good Times*
13 – P, *That's My Mama*
14 – E, *Barefoot in the Park*
15 – K, *N.Y.P.D.*
16 – F, *I Spy*
17 – I, *Get Christie Love*
18 – H, *Diff'rent Strokes*
19 – D, *Mannix*
20 – N, *McCloud*

Answers – AFFIRMATIVE ACTION (2)

1 – M, *The Jeffersons*
2 – P, *What's Happening*
3 – R, *Sanford and Son*
4 – K, *Chico and the Man*
5 – T, *Barefoot in the Park*
6 – B, *Beulah*
7 – A, *What's Happening*
8 – S, *Beulah*
9 – E, *Amos and Andy*
10 – O, *Julia*
11 – C, *Good Times*
12 – Q, *That's My Mama*
13 – J, *East Side/West Side*
14 – G, *Busting Loose*
15 – H, *Star Trek*
16 – F, *The Young Rebels*
17 – D, *Starsky and Hutch*
18 – I, *Mission: Impossible*
19 – L, *The Silent Force*
20 – N, *The Rookies*

Answers – CONNECTIONS (1)

1. They portrayed detectives.
2. They portrayed Sid Caesar's wives.
3. They portrayed lawyers.
4. They portrayed maids.
5. Singers on *The Arthur Godfrey Show*.
6. Moderators on *Masquerade Party*.
7. They portrayed police officers.
8. They portrayed teachers.
9. Singers on *The Lawrence Welk Show*.
10. Peg Riley in *The Life of Riley*.
11. Trixie Norton in *The Honeymooners*.
12. Hosts on *The Tonight Show*.
13. They portrayed secretaries.
14. Alice Kramden in *The Honeymooners*.
15. Housekeepers on the *Maude* show.
16. They all portrayed *Martin Kane, Private Eye*.
17. They portrayed nurses.
18. They were unseen voices.
19. They portrayed doctors.
20. Singers on *Your Hit Parade*.

Answers – CONNECTIONS (2)

1. They all played skippers of boats.
2. They all played spies.
3. The three highest rated movies shown on TV.
4. They were all hosts on *Death Valley Days*.
5. They were panelists on *To Tell the Truth*.
6. Both played *Mike Barnett, Man Against Crime*.
7. They all played nightclub owners.
8. They all played ghosts.
9. They all played grandmothers.
10. They all played Lassie's owners.
11. They all played homosexuals.
12. They all played Ellery Queen.
13. These were all roles played by Richard Crenna.
14. These were the six wives of Henry VIII in the series of that name.
15. They were the stars of *The Rogues*.
16. They both played Robin Hood.
17. Both played owners of "Arnold's" on *Happy Days*.
18. They all played landladies.
19. They were the original stars of *Four Star Playhouse*.
20. They replaced Rosalind Russell and Joel McCrea on *Four Star Playhouse*.

Answers – SECOND BANANAS (1)

1 – P, *I Love Lucy*
2 – T, *Laverne & Shirley*
3 – M, *Hawaiian Eye*
4 – J, *The Jeffersons*
5 – S, *Happy Days*
6 – O, *Welcome Back, Kotter*
7 – Q, *The Tony Randall Show*

8 – R, The Mary Tyler Moore Show
9 – A, Maude
10 – C, The Dick Van Dyke Show
11 – H, Gunsmoke
12 – G, Mannix
13 – F, Star Trek
14 – D, Rhoda
15 – E, The Big Valley
16 – L, The Odd Couple
17 – B, Marcus Welby, M.D.
18 – I, The Rockford Files
19 – K, M*A*S*H
20 – N, Doc

Answers – SECOND BANANAS (2)
1 – M, Laverne & Shirley
2 – Q, Barney Miller
3 – K, I Love Lucy
4 – S, The George Burns and Gracie
        Allen Show
5 – I, The Jeffersons
6 – T, Laverne & Shirley
7 – R, The Mary Tyler Moore Show
8 – N, Three's Company
9 – P, Hawaii Five-O
10 – C, Happy Days
11 – B, The Mary Tyler Moore Show
12 – G, Perry Mason
13 – J, Mr. Peepers
14 – D, Maude
15 – H, Rhoda
16 – E, Phyllis
17 – A, The Jeffersons
18 – F, Mission: Impossible
19 – L, The Dick Van Dyke Show
20 – O, Happy Days

Answers – WHAT'S IN A NAME? (1)

1 – Q	6 – H	11 – P	16 – T
2 – J	7 – B	12 – C	17 – M
3 – O	8 – S	13 – F	18 – E
4 – L	9 – N	14 – I	19 – K
5 – R	10 – D	15 – A	20 – G

Answers – WHAT'S IN A NAME? (2)

1 – G	6 – P	11 – M	16 – L
2 – O	7 – T	12 – A	17 – E
3 – N	8 – Q	13 – I	18 – H
4 – K	9 – R	14 – D	19 – J
5 – S	10 – F	15 – B	20 – C

Answers – EVERYTHING IS RELATIVE (1)
1 – L, husband, wife – Life With
        Father
2 – T, father, daughter – Little
        House on the Prairie
3 – O, mother, son – Lotsa Luck
4 – Q, sisters – Rhoda
5 – A, father, son – I Love Lucy
6 – R, mother, son – I Remember
        Mama
7 – M, father, daughter – Eight Is
        Enough
8 – S, son, father – The Marge and
        Gower Champion Show
9 – B, mother, daughter – Phyllis
10 – E, brothers – Maverick
11 – P, daughter, mother – Maude
12 – C, nephew, aunt – The Andy
        Griffin Show
13 – I, father, son – Mickey
14 – G, mother, daughter – The
        Mothers-In-Law
15 – J, grandson, grandfather – The
        Munsters
16 – D, mother, son – My Friend
        Flicka
17 – K, sisters – My Sister Eileen
18 – F, uncle, nephew – My Three
        Sons
19 – H, daughter, father – O.K.
        Crackerby
20 – N, wife, husband – The Odd
        Couple

Answers – EVERYTHING IS RELATIVE (2)
1 – K, father, son – It Takes a Thief
2 – R, mother, son – The Waltons
3 – T, wife, husband – The Brady
        Bunch
4 – N, father, daughter – Father
        Knows Best
5 – I, daughter, father – That Girl
6 – S, son, father – The Andy
        Griffith Show
7 – A, uncle, nephew – Happy Days
8 – Q, daughter, father – My Little
        Margie
9 – B, son, mother – Good Times
10 – E, mother, daughter – Rhoda

11 – C, niece, aunt – *The Mary Tyler Moore Show*
12 – P, husband, wife – *The Honeymooners*
13 – D, son, father – *Jamie*
14 – J, husband, wife – *The Jeffersons*
15 – F, cousins – *All in the Family*
16 – H, father, son – *The Jimmy Stewart Show*
17 – L, grandson, grandfather – *Lassie*
18 – G, daughter, father – *Laverne & Shirley*
19 – M, son, father – *Leave It to Beaver*
20 – O, son, mother – *Soap*

Answers – LOVE AND MARRIAGE
(1)

1. Peter Lawford and Phyllis Kirk, *The Thin Man*
2. James Arness and Amanda Blake, *Gunsmoke*
3. Ted Bessell and Marlo Thomas, *That Girl*
4. Leon Ames and Lurene Tuttle, *Life with Father*
5. George Reeves and Phyllis Coates, *Superman*
6. Robert Young and Jane Wyatt, *Father Knows Best*
7. Ted Knight and Georgia Engel, *The Mary Tyler Moore Show*
8. Sherman Hemsley and Isabel Sanford, *The Jeffersons*
9. J. Pat O'Malley and Hermione Baddeley, *Maude*
10. Jack Klugman and Brett Somers, *The Odd Couple*
11. Richard Crenna and Bernadette Peters, *All's Fair*
12. Mike Evans and Berlinda Tolbert, *The Jeffersons*
13. Rob Reiner and Sally Struthers, *All in the Family*
14. Robert Mandan and Katherine Helmond, *Soap*
15. Andy Griffith and Aneta Corsaut, *The Andy Griffith Show*
16. James Broderick and Sada Thompson, *Family*

17. Ron Howard and Lynda Goodfriend, *Happy Days*
18. William Frawley and Vivian Vance, *I Love Lucy*
19. Art Carney and Joyce Randolph (or Jane Kean), *The Honeymooners*
20. Conrad Bain and Rue McClanahan, *Maude*

Answers – LOVE AND MARRIAGE
(2)

1. Henry Winkler and Roz Kelly, *Happy Days*
2. David Birney and Meredith Baxter, *Bridget Loves Bernie*
3. Norman Fell and Audra Lindley, *Three's Company* and *The Ropers*
4. Franklin Cover and Roxie Roker, *The Jeffersons*
5. David Groh and Valerie Harper, *Rhoda*
6. Howard Duff and Ida Lupino, *Mr. Adams and Eve*
7. Bob Newhart and Suzanne Pleshette, *The Bob Newhart Show*
8. Phil Foster and Betty Garrett, *Laverne & Shirley*
9. Don DeFore and Whitney Blake, *Hazel*
10. Gavin McLeod and Joyce Bulifant, *The Mary Tyler Moore Show*
11. Jackie Gleason and Audrey Meadows (or Sheila MacRae), *The Honeymooners*
12. Carroll O'Connor and Jean Stapleton, *All in the Family*
13. Richard Mulligan and Cathryn Damon, *Soap*
14. Carl Betz and Donna Reed, *The Donna Reed Show*
15. Danny Thomas and Jean Hagen, *Make Room for Daddy*
16. Desi Arnaz and Lucille Ball, *I Love Lucy*
17. Ralph Waite and Michael Learned, *The Waltons*
18. David Doyle and Audra Lindley, *Bridget Loves Bernie*
19. Tom Bosley and Marion Ross, *Happy Days*
20. Bill Macy and Beatrice Arthur, *Maude*

241

Answers – BOB, BOB, BOBBING ALONG . . .

1. Bob Newhart, *The Bob Newhart Show*
2. Robert Goulet, *Blue Light*
3. Robert Blake, *Baretta*
4. Robert Stack, *The Untouchables*
5. Robert Urich, *Bob & Carol & Ted & Alice*
6. Robert Cummings, *Love that Bob*
7. Robert Cummings, *The Bob Cummings Show*
8. Robert Young, *Marcus Welby, M.D.*
9. Robert Young, *Father Knows Best*
10. Robert Forster, *Banyon*
11. Bob Crane, *Hogan's Heroes*
12. Bob Crane, *The Bob Crane Show*
13. Rob Reiner, *All in the Family*
14. Robert Vaughn, *The Man from U.N.C.L.E.*
15. Robert Clary, *Hogan's Heroes*
16. Robert Morse, *That's Life*
17. Robert Fuller, *Emergency*
18. Robert Wagner, *Switch*
19. Robert Wagner, *Hart to Hart*
20. Robert Wagner, *It Takes a Thief*

Answers – REINCARNATION

1. Jeff Richards and Chuck Connors
2. James Arness and Peter Graves
3. Brandon DeWilde
4. Jackie Cooper
5. Jackie Coogan
6. Charles Farrell
7. Rose Marie
8. Shirley Temple
9. Ronald Reagan
10. Robert Stack
11. Milton Berle
12. Ed Sullivan
13. Dorothy Malone
14. Ricardo Montalban
15. Buster Crabbe
16. Dick Van Dyke and Jerry Van Dyke
17. Elizabeth Montgomery
18. Lucille Ball
19. Johnny Weissmuller
20. Shirley Booth

Answers – STREET WISE

1 – K	11 – P
2 – Q	12 – B
3 – N	13 – F
4 – T	14 – C
5 – H	15 – J
6 – M	16 – L
7 – R	17 – O
8 – E	18 – G
9 – A	19 – I
10 – S	20 – D

Answers – IDENTITY CRISIS (1)

1. Roger Moore – *Maverick, The Saint, The Persuaders*
2. Peter Lawford – *Dear Phoebe, The Doris Day Show, The Thin Man*
3. Jackie Cooper – *Hennesey, Mobile One, The People's Choice*
4. Robert Conrad – *Baa Baa Black Sheep, Hawaiian Eye, The D.A., Assignment Vienna, The Wild, Wild West*
5. Robert Lansing – *87th Precinct, Twelve O'Clock High, Young Dr. Malone*
6. Brian Keith – *Archer, The Crusaders, Family Affair, The Little People*
7. Robert Wagner – *It Takes A Thief, Switch, Hart to Hart*
8. Robert Vaughn – *The Lieutenant, The Man From U.N.C.L.E., The Protectors*
9. Andy Griffith – *Adams of Eagle Lake, The Andy Griffith Show, Headmaster, The New Andy Griffith Show*
10. David Birney – *The Adams Chronicle, Bridget Loves Bernie, Love Is A Many Splendored Thing, Serpico*
11. Ron Howard – *The Andy Griffith Show, Happy Days, The Smith Family*
12. Tom Bosley – *Happy Days, The Debbie Reynolds Show, The Sandy Duncan Show, Testimony of Two Men, The Dean Martin Show*
13. David Doyle – *Bridget Loves Bernie, Charlie's Angels, The New Dick Van Dyke Show, Ozzie's Girls*
14. Don Knotts – *The Andy Griffith Show, The Steve Allen Show*

15. Jack Lord – *Stoney Burke, Hawaii Five-O*
16. Jack Kelly – *Get Christie Love! Maverick, Kings Row*
17. James Garner – *Maverick, Rockford Files*
18. Buddy Ebsen – *Barnaby Jones, The Beverly Hillbillies, Davy Crockett, Northwest Passage*
19. Robert Fuller – *Emergency, Laramie, Wagon Train*
20. Danny Thomas – *Make Room For Daddy, The Practice*

Answers – IDENTITY CRISIS (2)
1. Audra Lindley – *Bridget Loves Bernie, Doc, From These Roots, Three's Company, The Ropers*
2. Meredith Baxter Birney – *Bridget Loves Bernie, Family*
3. Nancy Walker – *The Mary Tyler Moore Show, Rhoda, The Nancy Walker Show, Blansky's Beauties, McMillan and Wife, Family Affair*
4. Mary Tyler Moore – *Richard Diamond, The Dick Van Dyke Show, The Mary Tyler Moore Show*
5. Elena Verdugo – *Many Happy Returns, Meet Millie, Marcus Welby, M.D.*
6. Elinor Donahue – *Many Happy Returns, Father Knows Best, Mulligan's Stew, The Andy Griffith Show, The Odd Couple*
7. Rosemary DeCamp – *Love that Bob, Life of Riley, Partridge Family, Petticoat Junction, That Girl*
8. June Lockhart – *Lost in Space, Lassie, Petticoat Junction*
9. Bea Benadaret – *Petticoat Junction, The Burns and Allen Show, Peter Loves Mary*
10. Rose Marie – *The Doris Day show, The Dick Van Dyke Show, Honeymoon Suite*
11. Betty White – *The Mary Tyler Moore Show, The Betty White Show, A Date with the Angels, Life with Elizabeth*
12. Stephanie Powers – *The Girl from U.N.C.L.E., Father and Feather Gang, Hart to Hart*
13. Carol Burnett – *The Carol Burnett Show*
14. Cloris Leachman – *Bob & Ray, Charlie Wild/Private Detective, Lassie, The Mary Tyler Moore Show (and Phyllis)*
15. Georgia Engel – *The Betty White Show, The Mary Tyler Moore Show*
16. Sandy Duncan – *Funny Face (and The Sandy Duncan Show), Roots*
17. Marian Mercer – *The Sandy Duncan Show, A Touch of Grace*
18. Kathleen Freeman – *Lotsa Luck, Topper, Funny Face, Hogan's Heroes*
19. Ann B. Davis – *The Bob Cummings Show, The Brady Bunch, The John Forsythe Show*
20. Kate Jackson – *The Rookies, Charlie's Angels, Dark Shadows*

Answers – WHERE IN THE WORLD? (1)

1 – K	6 – T	11 – F	16 – P
2 – N	7 – A	12 – C	17 – E
3 – Q	8 – B	13 – G	18 – O
4 – H	9 – R	14 – I	19 – M
5 – S	10 – D	15 – J	20 – L

Answers – WHERE IN THE WORLD? (2)

1 – L	6 – R	11 – N	16 – G
2 – P	7 – S	12 – B	17 – I
3 – J	8 – O	13 – H	18 – K
4 – T	9 – Q	14 – C	19 – M
5 – A	10 – E	15 – F	20 – D

Answers – WHERE IN THE WORLD? (3)

1 – H	6 – Q	11 – R	16 – L
2 – K	7 – M	12 – P	17 – A
3 – J	8 – T	13 – B	18 – G
4 – S	9 – C	14 – F	19 – E
5 – N	10 – O	15 – I	20 – D

Answers – WHERE IN THE WORLD? (4)

1 – D	6 – Q	11 – P	16 – L
2 – J	7 – N	12 – A	17 – E
3 – K	8 – R	13 – S	18 – B
4 – G	9 – C	14 – T	19 – H
5 – I	10 – O	15 – M	20 – F

Answers – FAIR GAME (1)

1 – H	6 – Q	11 – D	16 – S
2 – M	7 – O	12 – I	17 – E
3 – L	8 – C	13 – A	18 – K
4 – T	9 – P	14 – G	19 – N
5 – R	10 – F	15 – B	20 – J

Answers – FAIR GAME (2)

1 – K	6 – A	11 – P	16 – L
2 – O	7 – S	12 – D	17 – C
3 – T	8 – M	13 – G	18 – J
4 – I	9 – B	14 – F	19 – E
5 – Q	10 – R	15 – H	20 – N

Answers – ALTER EGOS

1 – E	6 – L	11 – H	16 – O
2 – K	7 – A	12 – N	17 – D
3 – J	8 – G	13 – C	18 – Q
4 – F	9 – M	14 – B	19 – T
5 – S	10 – R	15 – I	20 – P

Answers – SIDESADDLE

1 – F, Gunsmoke
2 – L, F Troop
3 – Q, The Big Valley
4 – S, The High Chaparral
5 – A, Annie Oakley
6 – G, The Big Valley
7 – M, Black Saddle
8 – T, Sky King
9 – B, Zorro
10 – H, Maverick
11 – N, Cimarron City
12 – C, Johnny Ringo
13 – I, Hotel de Paree
14 – O, Shane
15 – D, Empire
16 – J, Little House on the Prairie
17 – P, My Friend Flicka
18 – R, Fury
19 – E, Here Come the Brides
20 – K, Bonanza

Answers – TALL IN THE SADDLE (1)

1 – I, Rawhide
2 – N, Gunslinger
3 – T, Gunsmoke
4 – K, Have Gun, Will Travel
5 – Q, The Rounders
6 – O, The Rifleman
7 – L, Bonanza
8 – R, The Big Valley
9 – B, Adventures of Jim Bowie
10 – D, Barbary Coast
11 – S, Bat Masterson
12 – G, Brave Eagle
13 – P, Broken Arrow
14 – A, The Rough Riders
15 – J, Adventures of Rin Tin Tin
16 – E, Bronco
17 – M, The Californians
18 – F, Cheyenne
19 – H, Cimarron City
20 – C, The Road West

Answers – TALL IN THE SADDLE (2)

1 – T, Gunsmoke
2 – J, Bonanza
3 – P, Branded
4 – R, Cimarron City
5 – N, The Deputy
6 – M, Gunsmoke
7 – K, Hopalong Cassidy
8 – D, How the West Was Won
9 – A, Daniel Boone
10 – S, Colt .45
11 – O, The Iron Horse
12 – B, Destry
13 – Q, Jefferson Drum
14 – C, The High Chaparral
15 – G, Johnny Ringo
16 – E, The Life and Legend of Wyatt Earp
17 – L, The Life and Times of Grizzly Adams
18 – I, Laredo
19 – F, The Lawman
20 – H, Wagon Train

Answers – TALL IN THE SADDLE (3)

1 – P, Texas John Slaughter
2 – L, Zorro
3 – N, Yancy Derringer
4 – T, The Wild, Wild West
5 – R, Wild Bill Hickock
6 – J, Wanted; Dead or Alive
7 – A, Wagon Train
8 – O, The Virginian
9 – C, The Travels of Jaimie McPheeters
10 – B, The Texan
11 – F, The Tall Man
12 – S, Tales of the Texas Rangers
13 – D, The Tales of Wells Fargo

14 – Q, Steve Donovan/Western Marshall
15 – I, Shotgun Slade
16 – K, U.S. Marshal
17 – E, Shane
18 – G, The Restless Gun
19 – H, Red Ryder
20 – M, Redigo

Answers – TALL IN THE SADDLE (4)
1 – M, The Loner
2 – N, Hondo
3 – T, High Chaparral
4 – J, Here Come the Brides
5 – Q, The Lone Ranger
6 – R, The Cisco Kid
7 – P, Dusty's Trail
8 – C, The Dakotas
9 – A, The Legend of Jesse James
10 – O, Adventures of Kit Carson
11 – F, Lancer
12 – S, Texas John Slaughter
13 – D, The Legend of Custer
14 – G, The Virginian
15 – I, The Virginian
16 – H, The Rifleman
17 – K, Wagon Train
18 – L, The Best of the West
19 – E, The Cowboys
20 – B, Laramie

Answers – THE ANIMAL KINGDOM
1 – L, stuffed cat
2 – N, mule
3 – P, parrot
4 – M, cockatoo
5 – S, chimpanzee
6 – Q, pig
7 – O, bear
8 – R, dinosaur
9 – A, moose
10 – H, chimpanzee
11 – E, dragon
12 – D, elephant
13 – F, duck
14 – C, monkey
15 – G, frog
16 – K, lioness
17 – T, seal
18 – J, lion
19 – B, rooster
20 – I, mouse

Answers – CHILD'S PLAY

1 – J	6 – T	11 – R	16 – C
2 – S	7 – M	12 – F	17 – L
3 – N	8 – B	13 – I	18 – E
4 – G	9 – Q	14 – H	19 – O
5 – A	10 – D	15 – K	20 – P

Answers – SO YOU WANT TO LEAD A BAND . . .

1 – E	6 – A	11 – Q	16 – J
2 – K	7 – M	12 – B	17 – S
3 – R	8 – T	13 – P	18 – O
4 – F	9 – G	14 – H	19 – I
5 – L	10 – N	15 – C	20 – D

Answers – HORSING AROUND
1 – M, Rawhide
2 – T, Bonanza
3 – S, The Big Valley
4 – G, Gunsmoke
5 – J, Bonanza
6 – R, The Cisco Kid
7 – Q, Mr. Ed
8 – C, Red Ryder
9 – A, Bonanza
10 – E, The Cisco Kid
11 – P, Have Gun, Will Travel
12 – B, The Lone Ranger
13 – F, The Rifleman
14 – K, Sgt. Preston of the Yukon
15 – H, The Restless Gun
16 – N, Broken Arrow
17 – I, The Lone Ranger
18 – D, My Friend Flicka
19 – L, The Adventures of Black Beauty
20 – O, The Adventures of Champion

Answers – WHEN IRISH EYES ARE SMILING . . .
1 – G, Private Secretary
2 – R, The Life of Riley
3 – M, Car 54, Where Are You?
4 – J, Kate McShane
5 – T, Gilligan's Island
6 – P, Kings Row
7 – A, Wagon Train
8 – E, Slattery's People
9 – S, Hawaii Five–O
10 – B, Harrigan and Son
11 – Q, Gunsmoke
12 – D, Marcus Welby, M.D.

13 – C, Alice
14 – I, M*A*S*H
15 – K, My Three Sons
16 – F, Laverne & Shirley
17 – H, The Honeymooners
18 – L, McHale's Navy
19 – N, The Brady Bunch
20 – O, M*A*S*H

Answers – THEY'RE PLAYING
THEIR SONGS (1)

1 – J	6 – N	11 – R	16 – L
2 – T	7 – B	12 – D	17 – G
3 – P	8 – S	13 – O	18 – I
4 – A	9 – C	14 – H	19 – M
5 – Q	10 – F	15 – E	20 – K

Answers – THEY'RE PLAYING
THEIR SONGS (2)

1 – H	6 – S	11 – D	16 – F
2 – P	7 – B	12 – I	17 – N
3 – T	8 – R	13 – E	18 – J
4 – M	9 – C	14 – G	19 – L
5 – A	10 – Q	15 – K	20 – O

Answers – BEDSIDE MANORS

1 – J	6 – T	11 – E	16 – M
2 – N	7 – L	12 – C	17 – F
3 – R	8 – Q	13 – D	18 – H
4 – P	9 – B	14 – G	19 – I
5 – A	10 – S	15 – K	20 – O

Answers – READING, 'RITING,
'RITHMETIC

1 – G	6 – M	11 – Q	16 – D
2 – L or P	7 – S	12 – T	17 – E
3 – J	8 – B	13 – L or P	18 – H
4 – A	9 – N	14 – R	19 – C
5 – K	10 – O	15 – I	20 – F

Answers – MIXED DOUBLES

1 – I, He and She
2 – K, Bridget Loves Bernie
3 – J, The Odd Couple
4 – N, Emergency
5 – O, The Xavier Cugat Show
6 – Q, Topper and Love That Jill
7 – P, The Halls of Ivy
8 – R, Heaven for Betsy
9 – S, The Paul Lynde Show
10 – G, Mission: Impossible and
     Space: 1999
11 – M, Mr. Adams and Eve

12 – L, The Detectives
13 – A, The Marriage
14 – C, Ben Casey
15 – E, The Stu Erwin Show
16 – H, Blondie
17 – F, The King Family Show
18 – T, Your Hit Parade
19 – D, Tex and Jinx
20 – B, The Spike Jones Show

Answers – A CHORUS LINE

1 – M	6 – T	11 – C	16 – K
2 – S	7 – B	12 – O	17 – G
3 – J	8 – R	13 – H	18 – L
4 – Q	9 – D	14 – F	19 – N
5 – A	10 – P	15 – I	20 – E

WITH ENEMIES LIKE THESE . . .

1 – M	6 – A	11 – O	16 – L
2 – S	7 – Q	12 – C	17 – F
3 – K	8 – B	13 – G	18 – N
4 – P	9 – D	14 – I	19 – J
5 – T	10 – R	15 – E	20 – H

Answers – SMALL FRY (1)

1 – L	6 – J	11 – B	16 – I
2 – R	7 – S	12 – C	17 – N
3 – T	8 – A	13 – G	18 – F
4 – O	9 – E	14 – D	19 – H
5 – M	10 – Q	15 – P	20 – K

Answers – SMALL FRY (2)

1 – R	6 – T	11 – S	16 – J
2 – N	7 – Q	12 – G	17 – L
3 – P	8 – A	13 – O	18 – I
4 – M	9 – E	14 – D	19 – H
5 – K	10 – B	15 – C	20 – F

Answers – FRONT MONEY

1 – I	6 – B	11 – O	16 – K
2 – M	7 – D	12 – E	17 – J
3 – A	8 – S	13 – R	18 – H
4 – P	9 – C	14 – F	19 – N
5 – T	10 – G	15 – Q	20 – L

Answers – SOBRIQUETS

1 – F, Steve Forrest, S.W.A.T.
2 – H, Sally Field, Gidget
3 – S, Richard Long, Nanny and the
     Professor
4 – J, Billy Gray, Father Knows
     Best

5 – T, Dan Haggerty, *The Life and Times of Grizzly Adams*
6 – B, Alan Alda, *M*A*S*H*
7 – K, Kristy McNichol, *Family*
8 – L, Larry Hagman, *Dallas*
9 – I, Demond Wilson, *Sanford and Son*
10 – C, Jerry Mather, *Leave it to Beaver*
11 – N, Marjorie Reynolds, *The Life of Riley*
12 – G, Elinor Donahue, *Father Knows Best*
13 – E, Darryl Anderson, *Lou Grant*
14 – R, Alan Hale, Jr., *Gilligan's Island*
15 – A, Donald Keeler, *Lassie*
16 – P, Wayne Rogers, *M*A*S*H*
17 – D, Stephanie Powers, *The Feather and Father Gang*
18 – M, Lauren Chapin, *Father Knows Best*
19 – Q, Fred Grandy, *The Love Boat*
20 – O, Rob Reiner, *All in the Family*

Answers – SPORTIN' LIFE

1 – O, *The White Shadow*
2 – R, *Waverly Wonders*
3 – T, *I Spy*
4 – I, *The Debbie Reynolds Show*
5 – K, *Ball Four*
6 – G, *That's My Boy*
7 – H, *The Duke*
8 – P, *I Spy*
9 – E, *Breaking Away*
10 – Q, *Straightaway*
11 – F, *Ripcord*
12 – N, *Big Eddie*
13 – J, *Stoney Burke*
14 – D, *The Immortal*
15 – C, *Lucas Tanner*
16 – B, *Bad News Bears*
17 – A, *The Odd Couple*
18 – L, *Taxi*
19 – S, *The Aquanauts (Malibu Run)*
20 – M, *Soap*

Answers – LATHER UP (1)

1 – J, *Days of Our Lives*
2 – T, *Another World*
3 – N, *The Doctors*
4 – R, *One Man's Family*
5 – P, *Edge of Night*
6 – A, *Another World*
7 – B, *Somerset*
8 – S, *As the World Turns*
9 – C, *As the World Turns*
10 – M, *Edge of Night*
11 – Q, *The Nurses*
12 – D, *The Guiding Light*
13 – F, *General Hospital*
14 – H, *Search for Tomorrow*
15 – K, *Another World*
16 – E, *Edge of Night*
17 – I, *Dark Shadows*
18 – O, *The Secret Storm*
19 – G, *Search for Tomorrow*
20 – L, *The Doctors*

Answers – LATHER UP (2)

1 – K, *Days of Our Lives*
2 – N, *One Life to Live*
3 – O, *Road to Reality*
4 – Q, *Love is a Many Splendored Thing*
5 – R, *The Secret Storm*
6 – L, *Another World*
7 – C, *One Man's Family*
8 – P, *Days of Our Lives*
9 – D, *Days of Our Lives*
10 – A, *The Doctors*
11 – B, *Edge of Night*
12 – T, *Another World*
13 – S, *Another World*
14 – F, *Another World*
15 – E, *General Hospital*
16 – G, *Search for Tomorrow*
17 – H, *General Hospital*
18 – J, *Another World*
19 – I, *Guiding Light*
20 – M, *Ryan's Hope*

Answers – HOME SWEET HOME

1. Where the Heart Is
2. The Nurses
3. The Guiding Light
4. Days of Our Lives
5. Another World
6. All My Children
7. The Doctors
8. One Life to Live
9. Search for Tomorrow

10. One Man's Family
11. Dark Shadows
12. The Young and the Restless
13. Young Dr. Malone
14. Edge of Night
15. The Secret Storm
16. Love of Life
17. As the World Turns
18. Ryan's Hope
19. Peyton Place
20. Love Is a Many Splendored Thing

Answers – DON'T I KNOW YOU?
1. Another World
2. Days of Our Lives
3. One Life to Live
4. Peyton Place
5. The Secret Storm
6. Search for Tomorrow
7. As the World Turns
8. The Doctors
9. One Man's Family
10. Edge of Night
11. The Greatest Gift
12. Young Dr. Malone
13. The Young and the Restless
14. Dark Shadows
15. Love Is a Many Splendored Thing
16. Soap
17. Dallas
18. Love of Life
19. General Hospital
20. The Guiding Light

Answers – IFS, ANDS, AND MUTTS (1)

1 – L	6 – A	11 – E	16 – N
2 – R	7 – S	12 – I	17 – G
3 – T	8 – C	13 – D	18 – M
4 – J	9 – Q	14 – K	19 – F
5 – P	10 – B	15 – H	20 – O

Answers – IFS, ANDS, AND MUTTS (2)

1 – P	6 – N	11 – Q	16 – K
2 – T	7 – A	12 – C	17 – E
3 – M	8 – D	13 – H	18 – I
4 – S	9 – R	14 – F	19 – O
5 – L	10 – B	15 – J	20 – G

Answers – SCHIZOPHRENIA
1 – F, Lindsay Wagner, The Bionic Woman
2 – D, Lee Majors, The Six Million Dollar Man
3 – M, Bill Bixby, The Incredible Hulk
4 – J, Nicholas Hammand, The Amazing Spider-Man
5 – N, George Reeves, Superman
6 – K, Burt Ward, Batman
7 – R, Adam West, Batman
8 – C, Lynda Carter, Wonder Woman
9 – P, Guy Williams, Zorro
10 – Q, David McCallum, The Invisible Man
11 – L, Debra Winger, Wonder Woman
12 – O, Yvonne Craig, Batman
13 – S, Stephen Strimpell, Mr. Terrific
14 – T, William Daniels, Captain Nice
15 – A, Clayton Moore or John Hart, The Lone Ranger
16 – B, Van Williams, The Green Hornet
17 – H, Patrick Duffy, The Man from Atlantis
18 – I, Stephanie Powers, The Girl from U.N.C.L.E.
19 – G, Jack Cassidy, He and She
20 – E, Roger Moore, The Saint

Answers – VOX POPULI
1 – H, The Adventures of Oky Doky
2 – O, The Alvin Show
3 – I, The Bugs Bunny Show
4 – N, The Bullwinkle Show
5 – Q, Calvin and the Colonel
6 – C, Charlie's Angels
7 – L, Bracken's World
8 – D, The People's Choice
9 – P, Rocky King, Inside Detective
10 – F, Topcat
11 – S, Underdog
12 – B, Rhoda
13 – K, The Millionaire
14 – G, Richard Diamond
15 – A, The Jetsons
16 – E, Where's Huddles?
17 – J, The Flintstones

18 – M, *The Invisible Man* (the actor's identity was never revealed)
19 – T, *The Bullwinkle Show*
20 – R, *My Mother, the Car* (voice for the car)

Answers – VERBATIM (1)
1. Jackie Gleason, *The Honeymooners*
2. Joe E. Ross, *Car 54, Where Are You?*
3. Polly Holliday, *Alice* and *Flo.*
4. William Bendix, *The Life of Riley*
5. Ted Mack, *The Original Amateur Hour*
6. Laurie Anders, *The Ken Murray Show*
7. John Cleese, *Monty Python's Flying Circus*
8. Lawrence Welk, *The Lawrence Welk Show*
9. Ed Sullivan, *Toast of the Town*
10. Jimmy Durante, *The Jimmy Durante Show*
11. Jackie Gleason, *The Jackie Gleason Show*
12. Red Buttons, *The Red Buttons Show*
13. Kay Kyser, *The Kollege of Musical Knowledge*
14. Robin Williams, *Mork and Mindy*
15. Valerie Harper, *Rhoda*
16. Tony Randall, *The Odd Couple*
17. Dinah Shore, *The Dinah Shore Chevy Show*
18. Gabriel Kaplan, *Welcome Back, Kotter*
19. Don Adams, *Get Smart!*
20. John Hamilton, *Superman*

Answers – VERBATIM (2)
1. Jack Webb, *Dragnet*
2. George Gobel, *The George Gobel Show*
3. Jackie Gleason, *The Jackie Gleason Show*
4. Roy Rogers, *The Roy Rogers Show*
5. John Daly, *What's My Line?*
6. Ed McMahon, *The Johnny Carson Show*
7. Redd Foxx, *Sanford and Son*
8. Beatrice Arthur, *Maude*
9. Lorenzo Music, *Rhoda*

10. Jimmie Walker, *Good Times*
11. Everybody, *Happy Days*
12. Carroll O'Connor, *All in the Family*
13. Gale Storm and Charles Farrell, *My Little Margie*
14. Walter Cronkite, *The CBS Evening News*
15. Freddy Prinze, *Chico and the Man*
16. Jim Nabors, *The Andy Griffith Show*
17. Katherine Murray, *The Arthur Murray Dance Party*
18. Gilda Radner, *NBC's Saturday Night*
19. Gertrude Berg, *The Goldbergs*
20. Bob Denver, *The Many Loves of Dobie Gillis*

Answers – MOUTHPIECES
1 – P	6 – R	11 – O	16 – G
2 – S	7 – N	12 – F	17 – K
3 – M	8 – B	13 – H	18 – E
4 – T	9 – Q	14 – D	19 – I
5 – A	10 – C	15 – J	20 – L

Answers – THE PEN IS MIGHTIER . . .
1 – I, *Rich Man, Poor Man*
2 – O, *Peyton Place*
3 – S, *Peanuts*
4 – M, *Shogun*
5 – Q, *The Turn of the Screw*
6 – A, *Macbeth*
7 – B, *Blithe Spirit*
8 – T, *The Bat*
9 – E, *Peter Pan*
10 – C, *Cat on a Hot Tin Roof*
11 – P, *From Here to Eternity*
12 – G, *Nancy Drew* series
13 – D, *Tarzan* series
14 – F, *The Long Hot Summer*
15 – R, *Long John Silver*
16 – N, *Vanity Fair*
17 – K, *The Moneychangers*
18 – J, *The Time of Your Life*
19 – L, *Our Town*
20 – H, *Roots*

Answers – IT'S A LIVING
1 – M, *The Honeymooners*
2 – I, *Casey Jones*

3 – T, *Calucci's Department*
4 – O, *The Super*
5 – L, *Laverne & Shirley*
6 – N, *Movin' On*
7 – R, *The Bob Newhart Show*
8 – B, *The Nancy Walker Show*
9 – S, *Ball Four*
10 – Q, *Malibu Run (The Aquanauts)*
11 – E, *Sanford and Son*
12 – P, *All in the Family*
13 – A, *The Honeymooners*
14 – G, *Alice*
15 – C, *Baretta*
16 – H, *The Ted Knight Show*
17 – J, *The Flying Nun*
18 – K, *Chico and the Man*
19 – F, *Adventures in Paradise*
20 – D, *Happy Days*

Answers – GET THE SCOOP (1)
1 – N, *Kingston: Confidential*
2 – Q, *Hot Off the Wire*
3 – T, *Ichabod and Me*
4 – K, *Honestly, Celeste*
5 – R, *Gibbsville*
6 – A, *Four Just Men*
7 – S, *Foreign Intrigue*
8 – D, *The Files of Jeffery Jones*
9 – B, *Dear Phoebe*
10 – P, *Crime Photographer*
11 – O, *Big Town*
12 – C, *The Andros Targets*
13 – J, *All's Fair*
14 – E, *Superman*
15 – G, *Big Town*
16 – F, *Wire Service*
17 – L, *Whispering Smith*
18 – H, *The Virginian*
19 – M, *That Girl*
20 – I, *The Roaring Twenties*

Answers – GET THE SCOOP (2)
1 – L, *Dear Phoebe*
2 – P, *Big Town*
3 – O, *The Adventures of Hiram Holliday*
4 – R, *Wire Service*
5 – T, *Crime Photographer*
6 – N, *The Roaring Twenties*
7 – S, *The Reporter*
8 – Q, *Return to Peyton Place*

9 – C, *Big Town*
10 – F, *The Odd Couple*
11 – D, *New York Confidential*
12 – A, *Superman*
13 – E, *The Mary Tyler Moore Show or Lou Grant*
14 – I, *The Reporter*
15 – G, *The Name of the Game*
16 – J, *Mobile One*
17 – M, *Lou Grant*
18 – H, *Honestly, Celeste*
19 – K, *Ichabod and Me*
20 – B, *Wire Service*

Answers – WOMEN IN WHITE
1 – E, *Ben Casey*
2 – H, *The Nurses*
3 – F, *Marcus Welby, M.D.*
4 – Q, *Dr. Kildare*
5 – T, *The Practice*
6 – S, *Doc*
7 – G, *Julia*
8 – P, *Emergency*
9 – R, *The Brian Keith Show*
10 – D, *The Rookies*
11 – O, *Rafferty*
12 – N, *Temperatures Rising*
13 – A, *Medical Center*
14 – C, *Janet Dean, Registered Nurse*
15 – J, *Hennesey*
16 – L, *The Waltons*
17 – B, *Mr. Peepers*
18 – K, *M*A*S*H*
19 – I, *House Calls*
20 – M, *A.E.S., Hudson Street*

Answers – FLYING HIGH
1 – M	6 – Q	11 – C	16 – H
2 – I	7 – A	12 – F	17 – L
3 – T	8 – E	13 – R	18 – N
4 – P	9 – S	14 – D	19 – G
5 – B	10 – 0	15 – J	20 – K

Answers – PLEASE BE BRIEF (1)
1 – K, *Perry Mason*
2 – O, *The Amazing Mr. Malone*
3 – H, *Arrest and Trial*
4 – R, *The D.A.*
5 – T, *The Defenders*
6 – S, *The Feather and Father Gang*
7 – B, *For the People*

8 – P, Judd, For the Defense
9 – F, Justice
10 – Q, The Law and Mr. Jones
11 – N, Kate McShane
12 – A, The Defenders
13 – C, Adam's Rib
14 – E, Kaz
15 – D, The Lawyers
16 – G, My Mother, the Car
17 – J, Owen Marshall, Counselor at
Law
18 – I, Perry Mason
19 – L, Petrocelli
20 – M, The Lawyers

Answers – PLEASE BE BRIEF (2)
1 – E, Black Saddle
2 – R, The Trials of O'Brien
3 – T, Willy
4 – S, The Young Lawyers
5 – Q, Hazel
6 – P, Hill Street Blues
7 – M, Bachelor Father
8 – J, Lock Up
9 – I, The Rockford Files
10 – L, Markham
11 – F, Run for Your Life
12 – D, Family
13 – H, Green Acres
14 – C, The Tony Randall Show
15 – O, Owen Marshall, Counselor at
Law
16 – B, I Married Joan
17 – N, Judd, for the Defense
18 – K, Adam's Rib
19 – A, Rosetti and Ryan
20 – G, The Paul Lynde Show

**Answers – IS THERE A DOCTOR IN
THE HOUSE? (1)**
1 – K, Kentucky Jones
2 – L, M*A*S*H
3 – J, Ben Casey
4 – T, Quincy, M.E.
5 – S, Doc
6 – O, Doc Corkle
7 – Q, Doc Elliott
8 – P, Dr. Kildare
9 – R, The Interns
10 – C, Doctor's Hospital
11 – N, The Practice

12 – A, The Brian Keith Show
13 – D, The Practice
14 – E, The Interns
15 – B, Ben Casey
16 – M, The New Doctors
17 – I, The New Doctors
18 – H, Doctor's Hospital
19 – F, The New Doctors
20 – G, The Practice

**Answers – IS THERE A DOCTOR IN
THE HOUSE? (2)**
1 – J, Ben Casey
2 – A, Having Babies
3 – L, Peyton Place
4 – B, The Odd Couple
5 – N, Petticoat Junction
6 – P, The Brian Keith Show
7 – C, Temperatures Rising
8 – R, The Interns
9 – D, Medical Center
10 – T, Peyton Place
11 – H, Westside Medical
12 – E, Man and the Challenge
13 – S, The Psychiatrist
14 – F, Man from Atlantis
15 – Q, The Donna Reed Show
16 – O, The Bob Newhart Show
17 – M, City Hospital
18 – G, The Eleventh Hour
19 – K, Hec Ramsey
20 – I, The Waltons

Answers – CLOAKS AND DAGGERS
1 – N, Secret Agent
2 – I, The Avengers
3 – T, Search
4 – P, Mission Impossible
5 – R, The Man Who Never Was
6 – A, The Man From U.N.C.L.E.
7 – S, I Spy
8 – Q, The Hunter
9 – C, The Hunter
10 – E, The Girl From U.N.C.L.E.
11 – D, Get Smart
12 – F, The Man From U.N.C.L.E.
13 – B, I Spy
14 – H, Five Fingers
15 – G, The Double Life of Henry
Phyfe
16 – J, Get Smart

17 – L, *Doorway to Danger*
18 – M, *The Avengers*
19 – K, *Crusader*
20 – O, *Mission Impossible*

Answers – SCHOOL DAYS, SCHOOL DAYS . . .

1 – M, *Our Miss Brooks*
2 – T, *The Paper Chase*
3 – N, *Mr. Peepers*
4 – L, *Lucas Tanner*
5 – S, *Room 222*
6 – R, *Our Miss Brooks*
7 – Q, *All In The Family*
8 – P, *Hank*
9 – C, *Nanny and the Professor*
10 – O, *Room 222*
11 – D, *Mr. Peepers*
12 – A, *The Jimmy Stewart Show*
13 – F, *The Halls of Ivy*
14 – I, *Gidget*
15 – B, *Welcome Back, Kotter*
16 – E, *The Headmaster*
17 – K, *Mr. Novak*
18 – J, *Ozzie's Girls*
19 – H, *Meet Mr. McNulty*
20 – G, *The Jimmy Stewart Show*

Answers – LAW AND ORDER (1)

1 – K, *Rocky King, Inside Detective*
2 – P, *Amy Prentiss*
3 – M, *Archer*
4 – R, *Arrest and Trial*
5 – T, *Banacek*
6 – S, *Baretta*
7 – A, *The Rockford Files*
8 – N, *The Blue Knight*
9 – Q, *Bronk*
10 – D, *Police Woman*
11 – E, *Burke's Law*
12 – B, *Banyon*
13 – G, *Barnaby Jones*
14 – O, *Cade's County*
15 – F, *Cannon*
16 – I, *Car 54, Where Are You?*
17 – L, *Carter Country*
18 – H, *Charlie's Angels*
19 – J, *Chase*
20 – C, *Barney Miller*

Answers – LAW AND ORDER (2)

1 – J, *Car 54, Where Are You?*
2 – S, *Caribe*
3 – N, *Charlie's Angels*
4 – P, *CHiPS*
5 – A, *City of Angels*
6 – T, *Columbo*
7 – B, *Dan August*
8 – R, *The Detectives*
9 – D, *Dragnet*
10 – Q, *The F.B.I.*
11 – O, *Felony Squad*
12 – I, *Get Christie Love*
13 – E, *Dan Raven*
14 – K, *The Green Hornet*
15 – L, *Hawaiian Five-O*
16 – C, *Delvecchio*
17 – M, *Hawaiian Eye*
18 – H, *Harry-O*
19 – G, *Griff*
20 – F, *Faraday and Company*

Answers – LAW AND ORDER (3)

1 – N, *The Line-Up*
2 – Q, *Ironside*
3 – L, *Interpol Calling*
4 – R, *The Investigators*
5 – T, *Kojak*
6 – J, *Honey West*
7 – A, *Holmes and YoYo*
8 – D, *McCloud*
9 – S, *The Andy Griffith Show*
10 – B, *Hawaiian Eye*
11 – P, *Griff*
12 – C, *The Fugitive*
13 – H, *Four Just Men*
14 – E, *The Felony Squad*
15 – F, *Hawaii Five-O*
16 – I, *M-Squad*
17 – M, *Ellery Queen*
18 – G, *The Thin Man*
19 – O, *87th Precinct*
20 – K, *Barney Miller*

Answers – LAW AND ORDER (4)

1 – L, *Ironside*
2 – J, *Holmes and YoYo*
3 – R, *McMillan and Wife*
4 – T, *The Felony Squad*
5 – Q, *Ellery Queen*
6 – O, *The Lineup*

7 – B, *Barney Miller*
8 – A, *Hill Street Blues*
9 – C, *Honey West*
10 – S, *Dragnet*
11 – P, *The Detectives*
12 – F, *Dan August*
13 – I, *Perry Mason*
14 – D, *Coronado 9*
15 – G, *The Cop and the Kid*
16 – E, *Col. March of Scotland Yard*
17 – K, *CHiPS*
18 – M, *Charlie's Angels*
19 – H, *Barney Miller*
20 – N, *The Odd Couple*

Answers – IN A NUTSHELL (1)
1. *Adventures of Ozzie and Harriet*
2. *S.W.A.T.*
3. *My Little Margie*
4. *Karen*
5. *Hawaiian Eye*
6. *All in the Family*
7. *Gunsmoke*
8. *The Fugitive*
9. *The Rogues*
10. *Eight Is Enough*
11. *Dragnet*
12. *What's My Line*
13. *My Friend Flicka*
14. *Lassie*
15. *Little House on the Prairie*
16. *The People's Choice*
17. *Mr. Ed*
18. *The Six Million Dollar Man*
19. *Marcus Welby, M.D.*
20. *Dr. Kildare*

Answers – IN A NUTSHELL (2)
1. *I Love Lucy*
2. *M*A*S*H*
3. *The Lucy Show*
4. *Sanford and Son*
5. *Here's Lucy*
6. *Family*
7. *Phyllis*
8. *Alice*
9. *Three's Company*
10. *Maverick*
11. *The Honeymooners*
12. *The Waltons*
13. *The Rockford Files*

14. *Peter Gunn*
15. *Mannix*
16. *Perry Mason*
17. *The Beverly Hillbillies*
18. *Bewitched*
19. *Green Acres*
20. *McMillan and Wife*

Answers – IN A NUTSHELL (3)
1. *Ben Casey*
2. *What's Happening*
3. *Soap*
4. *The Snoop Sisters*
5. *Room 222*
6. *Happy Days*
7. *Laverne & Shirley*
8. *Private Secretary*
9. *Big Town*
10. *Father Knows Best*
11. *December Bride*
12. *Hawaii Five-O*
13. *Welcome Back, Kotter*
14. *Barney Miller*
15. *Maude*
16. *The Mary Tyler Moore Show*
17. *Police Woman*
18. *The Odd Couple*
19. *Rhoda*
20. *The Andy Griffith Show*

Answers – IN A NUTSHELL (4)
1. *Kojak*
2. *One Day at a Time*
3. *Chico and the Man*
4. *The Jeffersons*
5. *Baretta*
6. *Adam 12*
7. *Car 54, Where Are You?*
8. *The Addams Family*
9. *The Munsters*
10. *The Real McCoys*
11. *Have Gun, Will Travel*
12. *The Life and Legend of Wyatt Earp*
13. *77 Sunset Strip*
14. *Route 66*
15. *The Millionaire*
16. *Dennis the Menace*
17. *The Flintstones*
18. *Hazel*
19. *The Untouchables*
20. *Hogan's Heroes*

Answers – ¿QUIÉNES?

1 – M, The Cisco Kid
2 – Q, Barney Miller
3 – T, On the Road
4 – J, Chico and the Man
5 – A, Marcus Welby, M.D.
6 – S, All in the Family
7 – B, Dan August
8 – P, Fantasy Island
9 – D, The Bill Dana Show
10 – C, Rawhide
11 – O, Welcome Back, Kotter
12 – E, Zorro
13 – R, CHiPS
14 – H, I Love Lucy
15 – I, Zorro
16 – K, The Cisco Kid
17 – F, A.E.S. Hudson Street
18 – L, C.P.O. Sharkey
19 – G, The Man and the City
20 – N, Doc

Answers – IT'S GREEK TO ME (1)

1. Sid Caesar
2. Lucille Ball
3. Jack Benny
4. Imogene Coca
5. Ed Wynn
6. James Arness
7. Gale Storm
8. Peter Graves
9. Doris Day
10. Phil Silvers
11. Nanette Fabray
12. Milton Berle
13. Carol Burnett
14. Jim Nabors
15. Valerie Harper
16. Bob Crane
17. Cloris Leachman
18. Dean Martin
19. Mary Tyler Moore
20. Ed Sullivan

Answers – IT'S GREEK TO ME (2)

1. Danny Thomas
2. Dinah Shore
3. Perry Como
4. Liza Minnelli
5. Harvey Korman
6. Jean Stapleton
7. Carroll O'Connor
8. Raymond Burr
9. Desi Arnaz
10. Betty White
11. Allen Ludden
12. Amanda Blake
13. Jackie Gleason
14. Audrey Meadows
15. Art Carney
16. Julie Andrews
17. Peter Falk
18. Cher
19. Telly Savalas
20. Beatrice Arthur

Answers – IT'S GREEK TO ME (3)

1. Robert Conrad
2. Chuck Connors
3. Anne Meara
4. Zohra Lampert
5. George Peppard
6. Ann Sheridan
7. Joan Bennett
8. Jack Klugman
9. Tony Randall
10. Sam Jaffe
11. Loretta Swit
12. Spring Byington
13. Sebastian Cabot
14. Raymond Massey
15. Kate Jackson
16. Suzanne Somers
17. Jessica Walter
18. Buddy Ebsen
19. Roscoe Karns
20. Hal Linden

Answers – IT'S GREEK TO ME (4)

1. James Arness
2. Robert Young
3. Donna Reed
4. Vicki Lawrence
5. Ernie Kovacs
6. Pat Boone
7. Billy Graham
8. Ron Howard
9. Shari Lewis
10. Ann Sothern
11. Marlo Thomas
12. Loretta Young
13. Richard Thomas

14. Lorne Green
15. Michael Learned
16. Ward Bond
17. Barbara Stanwyck
18. Redd Foxx
19. Rob Reiner
20. Cindy Williams

Answers – BIG SCREEN, LITTLE SCREEN

1 – K, The Farmer's Daughter
2 – L, Dr. Kildare
3 – E, Destry (Rides Again)
4 – H, Gidget
5 – A, Casablanca
6 – T, The Cisco Kid
7 – Q, Peyton Place
8 – D, Bus Stop
9 – C, Kings Row
10 – S, The Ghost and Mrs. Muir
11 – F, From Here to Eternity
12 – R, Ellery Queen
13 – G, Adam's Rib
14 – J, The Thin Man
15 – P, Dr. Gillespie
16 – O, Nancy Drew
17 – I, Executive Suite
18 – M, Lassie
19 – N, Alice (Doesn't Live Here Anymore)
20 – B, The Saint

Answers – REGARDS TO BROADWAY

1 – K, The Skin of Our Teeth
2 – P, Our Town
3 – G, The Philadelphia Story
4 – S, Idiot's Delight/Harry's Girls
5 – M, Cat on a Hot Tin Roof
6 – A, No Time for Sergeants
7 – T, The Women
8 – R, The Caine Mutiny Court Martial Trial
9 – B, Mister Roberts
10 – C, Stage Door
11 – Q, The Royal Family
12 – F, Barefoot in the Park
13 – O, Anna and the King of Siam
14 – D, The Magnificent Yankee
15 – H, Anything Goes
16 – J, Life with Father
17 – E, My Sister Eileen

18 – L, Blithe Spirit
19 – I, Macbeth
20 – N, Claudia

Answers – WHEN IN ROME . . .

1 – J, Petrocelli
2 – N, Baretta
3 – Q, Columbo
4 – T, The Montefuscos
5 – A, All in the Family
6 – O, Laverne & Shirley
7 – L, Happy Days
8 – B, One Day at a Time
9 – E, Welcome Back, Kotter
10 – S, Bert D'Angelo/Superstar
11 – C, Blansky's Beauties
12 – G, Calucci's Department
13 – D, Joe and Valerie
14 – R, Bronk
15 – I, Delvecchio
16 – F, Gomer Pyle, U.S.M.C.
17 – H, Hot'l Baltimore
18 – K, The Super
19 – M, Johnny Staccato
20 – P, Karen

Answers – MISSING LINKS (1)

1. The Mothers-In-Law; Lawless Years
2. Mr. and Mrs. North; Northwest Passage
3. Chico and the Man; Man from Atlantis
4. All in the Family; Family Affair
5. Accidental Family; Family Holvak
6. Slatter's People; People Are Funny
7. The Super; Super Circus
8. Take It from Me; Me and the Chimp
9. Bachelor Father; Father Knows Best
10. Movin' On; On the Rocks
11. Gentle Ben; Ben Casey
12. Honey West; West Point
13. December Bride; Bride and Groom
14. The Awakening Land; Land of the Lost
15. The $1.98 Beauty Show; Showoffs
16. Run, Buddy, Run; Run for Your Life
17. Most Wanted; Wanted: Dead or Alive
18. The Flying Doctor; Doctor Kildare
19. Mobile One; One Day at a Time
20. To Rome with Love; Love on a Rooftop